The Coming

of the Greeks

ROBERT
DREWS

THE

COMING

OF THE

GREEKS

*Indo-European Conquests
in the Aegean
and the Near East*

PRINCETON
UNIVERSITY
PRESS
Princeton, New Jersey

Copyright © 1988
by Princeton University Press
PUBLISHED BY PRINCETON UNIVERSITY PRESS,
41 William Street, Princeton, New Jersey 08540
In the United Kingdom: Princeton University Press,
Chichester, West Sussex

Publication of this book has been aided by
the Whitney Darrow Fund of Princeton University Press

This book has been composed in Garamond

Princeton University Press books are printed on acid-free paper
and meet the guidelines for permanence and durability of the
Committee on Production Guidelines for Book Longevity of the
Council on Library Resources

Printed in the United States of America by Princeton Academic Press

Second printing, 1989

10 9 8 7 6

Library of Congress Cataloging-in-Publication Data
Drews, Robert
    The coming of the Greeks.
    Bibliography: p.
    Includes index.
      1. Greeks—Origin.   2. Bronze age—Greece.
3. Indo-Europeans—Origin.   4. Bronze age—Near East.
I. Title.
DF220.D73   1988   938   88–15104

ISBN 0-691-03592-X

ISBN 0-691-02951-2 (pbk.)

CONTENTS

LIST OF FIGURES   vii

ACKNOWLEDGMENTS   ix

INTRODUCTION   xi

ABBREVIATIONS   xvii

Chapter One: Origins of the Question   3

Chapter Two: Some Minority Views on the Coming of the Greeks   16

Chapter Three: Linguistic and Archaeological Considerations   25

Chapter Four: Considerations from Near Eastern History   46

Chapter Five: The New Warfare   74
    Horses   74
    The War Chariot and Chariot Warfare   84
    Chronology   93
    Provenance of the Chariot and of Chariot Warfare   107

Chapter Six: The Evolution of Opinion on PIE Speakers and the Horse   121

Chapter Seven: PIE Speakers and the Beginnings of Chariot Warfare   136

Chapter Eight: The Coming of the Greeks   158

CONCLUSION   197

APPENDIXES   203

Contents

Appendix One: The End of the Bronze Age
in Greece   203
Appendix Two: The Umman Manda and the
PIE Speakers   226

BIBLIOGRAPHY   231
INDEX   251

LIST OF FIGURES

1 Map of the Near East (physical features after Burchard Brentjes, *Drei Jahrtausende Armenien* [Vienna:
Verlag Anton Schroll, 1976], p. 19.

2 Copper model of two-wheeled cart, from Tell
Agrab (Iraq Museum 31389). Drawing by J. Morel;
from Littauer and Crouwel, *Wheeled Vehicles*, fig. 7.

3 Detail of "Ur Standard" (British Museum
121201). Drawing by J. Morel; from Littauer and
Crouwel, *Wheeled Vehicles*, fig. 3.

4 Chariot from tomb at Egyptian Thebes (Florence,
Museo Archeologico 2678). Drawing by J. Morel;
from Littauer and Crouwel, *Wheeled Vehicles*, fig. 42.

5 Detail from stone relief of Ramesses III, Medinet
Habu. Drawing by J. Morel; from Littauer and
Crouwel, *Wheeled Vehicles*, fig. 44.

6 Detail from cylinder seal impression, Kültepe.
Drawing by J. Morel; from Littauer and Crouwel,
Wheeled Vehicles, fig. 28.

7 Detail from cylinder seal impression (Metropolitan
Museum of Art acc. no. 66.245.17b). Drawing
by J. Morel; from Littauer and Crouwel, *Wheeled
Vehicles*, fig. 29.

List of Figures

8   Detail of gold ring from Mycenae, Shaft Grave IV
(Athens, Nat. Mus. 240). Drawing by J. Morel;
from Crouwel, *Chariots*, pl. 10.

ACKNOWLEDGMENTS

I wish to express my gratitude to Vanderbilt University for giving me the opportunity to spend much of 1986 in research on the present topic, and to the American School of Classical Studies in Athens for its hospitality and assistance in September of that year. For technical help I thank Bill Longwell, resourceful director of Vanderbilt's microcomputer lab, and Sharon Hardy. Other individuals to whom I am indebted include my colleague Alice Harris, who gave me timely tips on some linguistic matters, and Emmett Bennett, at the University of Wisconsin, who explained for me what could and could not be inferred from the *agrimi* tablets at Knossos. On a wide range of topics I profited from the expertise of James Muhly and William Wyatt, to both of whom I am thoroughly grateful for saving me from error and for encouraging me along the right paths. For errors that remain I am of course entirely responsible.

For permission to publish seven line drawings by Jaap Morel, I thank the Allard Pierson Museum and the publishing house of E. J. Brill, and I am indebted personally to Mr. Morel and Dr. Mary Littauer and J. H. Crouwel. To Eve Pearson I am grateful for her superb work, prompt and meticulous, in editing the manuscript. Finally, I thank Princeton University Press and especially Ms. Joanna Hitchcock for transforming a manuscript into a book.

INTRODUCTION

One of the chief attractions of the early Indo-Europeans, including the Greeks of the Bronze Age, is their magnificent obscurity. So much about them is unknown, so little is certain, that one is encouraged to give the imagination free rein. Not surprisingly, scholarship on the early Indo-Europeans is unusually venturesome. In this field, radical theses cannot be dismissed without a hearing.

The Bronze Age Greeks must be the center of any discussion of the early Indo-Europeans. This is so because more is known about the Greeks than about any other Indo-European people of the second millennium B.C. That is a sobering thought, since the Bronze Age Greeks are themselves hazy enough that specialist opinion about them is sharply divided on most important points. Nonetheless, the evidence of the Linear B tablets, of other archaeological material, and of Homer and the Greek myths does give a modicum of substance to the Bronze Age Greeks. In comparison, the Italic or Celtic Indo-Europeans of the second millennium are hopelessly beyond the historian's power to recreate. The Hittites in Asia Minor are known from a great many tablets, but we know little about them from their art, and nothing at all about them from the tales of their descendants. About the Aryans of India something can be learned from the Rigveda, although it seems that at least five hundred years intervened between the Aryan invasion of India and the crystallization of the Rigveda. More disconcerting is the difficulty that Indian archaeologists have had in locating the Aryans, either temporally or geographically. Thus Indo-Europeanists continue to cast a hopeful eye in the direction of

Bronze Age Greece, on the chance that something there will illuminate the darkness that still surrounds almost everything about the early Indo-Europeans.

Vice versa, those scholars whose main concern is Bronze Age Greece continue to hope that some of the intractable problems about their subject may yet be solved by discoveries about other early Indo-Europeans. Archaeological parallels from outside Greece readily generate excitement, as do the more intelligible conclusions reached by linguists. On balance, however, it seems that the Bronze Age Greeks shed more light on their fellow Indo-Europeans of the second millennium than the other way round.

A third group of scholars, those whose bailiwick is the ancient Near East, tend to consider themselves marginal to the Indo-European question, and it to them. In fact, however, orientalists have provided some of the most valuable evidence thus far discovered on the subject. In return, they seem to have received less help than they have given. In the middle centuries of the second millennium, the Near East was widely and deeply affected by Indo-Europeans, and the nature both of this disturbance and of the slightly earlier Hittite Old Kingdom has apparently been distorted by questionable assumptions about "the Indo-European migrations" and especially about "the coming of the Greeks" to Greece.

In order to discuss this subject efficiently, some terminological clarification is essential. Strictly speaking, there is today no such thing as "an Indo-European," and there never has been. Nor is there or has there ever been an "Indo-European people." Instead, there are and have been communities and individuals who speak one or another of the languages that linguists find it convenient to call "Indo-European." It is generally assumed that these languages are ultimately descended from a single language, for which the term "Proto-Indo-European" is appropriate. More loosely, however, "Proto-Indo-European" may also be used for either the language or *the languages* that were spoken in the homeland from which the various Indo-European languages are supposed to have come. It is unlikely that a single and undifferentiated language prevailed throughout this homeland, but it is quite unclear whether the differentiation was merely a matter of dialects— that is, mutually intelligible forms of the same language—or whether it was a matter of more-or-less distinct languages (a division, for instance, along the so-called *centum* and *satem* lines). At any rate, this essay will use the term "Proto-Indo-European" in the broader sense, standing for the hypothetical language *or languages* spoken in the hypothetical Indo-European homeland, on the eve of the hypothetical Indo-European dispersal. The people who spoke the language(s) of the homeland will here be called Proto-Indo-European speakers, a cumbersome term that may be shortened to the slightly outlandish "PIE speakers." The PIE speakers are the linguistic ancestors of every person able to read this book. Whether any of one's physical ancestors was a PIE speaker is another question altogether.

A century ago, scholars generally employed a rather different set of terms and concepts. Most historians and philologists then believed that language was ideally (although not always in practice) a manifestation of nationality or race. They therefore assumed that there had once been an Indo-European race, and that in some parts of contemporary Eurasia "Indo-Europeans" or "Aryans" were still to be found (although who they were, and how they were to be identified, was controversial). When summarizing early scholarship I have therefore retained the terms—"Indo-Europeans" or "Aryans"—then current.

This essay is an attempt to answer several sets of questions at the same time. These sets seem to be interrelated, perhaps even interlocked, and it is for that reason that a generalist might be able to make a contribution in fields where specialists must have the final word. Few of the specific points made here are original. On almost every topic touched upon in this book, new evidence and new analyses have recently appeared, and I hope that I have given ample credit to those scholars whose work with the primary evidence is responsible for the new interpretations. What is perhaps original in this essay is the general synthesis. That synthesis is admittedly precarious, based as it is on a constellation of tentative positions, and at best it will serve as a rough point of departure for future syntheses. In the meanwhile, it seems to make each of its parts slightly more intelligible and therefore seems worth presenting.

One set of questions has to do with the supposed Indo-European migrations. Where did the PIE speakers come from? Or might the "homeland" of the PIE speakers be as naive a construct as the Garden of Eden? If a dispersal of PIE speakers ever did take place, when did it happen? What was the nature of these movements, and what provoked them? To these large questions many and various answers have been given, and will continue to find adherents, since we are unlikely ever to find a conclusive answer to any one of the questions. But some of the answers are considerably more persuasive than others, especially when the evidence from Greece is seen in a clear light.

About the Bronze Age Greeks in particular, the same questions can be more sharply focused. Was "the coming of the Greeks" a historical event, or is it a modern fiction? If such an event occurred, when did it occur, and how are we to picture it? The controversy over "the coming of the Greeks" has in the past been of interest mostly to Aegean archaeologists, linguists and prehistorians. Indo-Europeanists and orientalists will, I think, find it worth their while to see what the controversy is about, for a great deal of Eurasian history hinges on the conclusion that one comes to on these questions.

Finally, there are a number of questions about the Near East that cannot be separated from those dealing with the Bronze Age Greeks and the dispersal of the PIE speakers. The most important questions here concern the Hittites: who were they, when and whence did they come to central Anatolia, and what sort of state was the Hittite Old Kingdom? Other questions revolve around people who played a lesser role in ancient Near Eastern history. How are the Aryan princes of Mitanni and the

Levant to be explained? What, if any, was the relationship between the Kassite and Hyksos conquests and the supposed *Völkerwanderungen* of Indo-Europeans? Was the horse-drawn chariot introduced into the Near East by PIE speakers, and to what extent was the chariot responsible for the chaos of the second quarter of the second millennium? There is an unfortunate tendency among hellenists to suppose that ignorance about Near Eastern matters is a venial sin, perhaps because orientalists are not always obliged to be well informed about the Greek world. Among specialists on the prehistoric Aegean, this tendency is happily less pronounced, perhaps because it is more dangerous. No explanation for "the coming of the Greeks," or for the Indo-European migrations as a general phenomenon, is likely to be worth very much if it does not accommodate the evidence for the coming of PIE speakers to the only part of the Bronze Age world for which we have historical records.

It is undoubtedly superfluous for me to confess that I am not competent to deal with any one of these broad questions at the depth that it deserves. On those points relevant to the thesis I have tried to inform myself sufficiently to avoid at least the most disabling errors; but as it makes its way from point to point, this essay skirts vast fields of which my knowledge is at best superficial. Something of this is perhaps inevitable whenever one tries to set the Bronze Age Greeks against the backdrop of the general dispersal of the PIE speakers, since that dispersal does not fit comfortably within any of the compartments into which our knowledge of the past has traditionally been divided. In hopes of reducing this compartmentalization, so unfortunate for our topic, I have attempted to make the entire essay intelligible for scholars in each of the several contributing fields. The defect of this kind of presentation is that the discussion of any given point will probably strike the specialist as elementary, but at least an attempt will have been made to reach some common ground. In order to get our bearings, it will be best to begin by looking at the development of scholarly opinion on "the coming of the Greeks," since scholars have traditionally seen that event as central to the wider matter of "the Indo-European migrations."

ABBREVIATIONS

AAA   *Archaiologika Analekta ex Athenon*

AD   *Archaiologikon Deltion*

AJA   *American Journal of Archaeology*

ANET   J. B. Pritchard, ed., *Ancient Near Eastern Texts Relating to the Old Testament*. 3d ed. Princeton: Princeton Univ. Press, 1969.

AR   *Archaeological Reports*

AS   *Anatolian Studies*

BASOR   *Bulletin of the American Schools of Oriental Research*

BICS   *Bulletin of the Institute of Classical Studies of the University of London*

BRL   *Bulletin of the John Rylands Library*

BSA   *Annual of the British School at Athens*

CAH   *I.E.S. Edwards, C. J. Gadd, N.G.L. Hammond, and E. Sollberger, eds. The Cambridge Ancient History*. 3d ed. Cambridge: Cambridge Univ. Press, 1970–

CP   *Classical Philology*

HSCP   *Harvard Studies in Classical Philology*

IF   *Indogermanische Forschungen*

JAOS   *Journal of the American Oriental Society*

JCS   *Journal of Cuneiform Studies*

JEA   *Journal of Egyptian Archaeology*

JHS   *Journal of Hellenic Studies*

JIES   *Journal of Indo-European Studies*

Abbreviations

JNES	*Journal of Near Eastern Studies*
MH	*Museum Helveticum*
PPS	*Proceedings of the Prehistoric Society*
TAPA	*Transactions of the American Philological Association*
ZA	*Zeitschrift für Assyriologie und vorderasiatische Archäologie*

The Coming

of the Greeks

ONE

Origins of the Question

Where did the Greeks come from? The question is natural enough and has been asked and answered as long as the Greek language has been spoken. In Classical times, it was believed by many that the Hellenes had originated with Hellen. That meant that the Greeks had been around longer than anyone else, for Hellen was the firstborn son of Deucalion and Pyrrha, the parents of all mankind. Sole survivors of the Great Flood, the primeval pair made their home in Thessaly, and it was there that Pyrrha gave birth to Hellen. Hellen, in turn, fathered Aeolus, Dorus, and Xuthus, the progenitors of the Aeolic, Doric, and Ionic Greeks.

However flattering and picturesque, the myth was not accepted by critical minds, even in antiquity. At best, to ancient scholars the story symbolized the larger truth that the Greeks had lived in Greece since earliest times. Even that truth was recognized as somewhat more complicated than it first appeared: alongside the Greeks, other peoples had been at home in the lands of the Aegean during the days of the heroes. Of these, the most storied were the Pelasgians, but in addition there had been Dryopes, Minyans, Eteo-Cretans, and others.

Rationalized versions of the ancient myths sufficed in the Renaissance and through the early nineteenth century. Connop Thirlwall's eight-volume *History of Greece* (1835–1838) began with a valiant attempt to sort through the complexities and contradictions of the legendary traditions. A few years later, George Grote argued with considerable subtlety that history

3

can not be distilled from myths, and that the historian can penetrate into the past only so far as the past was literate. For Grote, then, where the Greeks came from, and who the Greeks were, were unanswerable questions, subjects for speculation but not for inquiry.

It was not long before the question was back in the historians' court. This came about because philologists had discovered the Indo-European language family. In 1786 Sir William Jones had observed that Sanskrit, Greek, Latin, and the Celtic and Germanic languages had so many similarities that they must have had a common linguistic ancestor. This insight inspired a few scattered efforts to reconstruct the relationship of the several languages (the term "Indo-European" was apparently first used in 1813), but it was not until Franz Bopp published his *Vergleichende Grammatik* in 1833 that Indo-European philology was put on a firm footing. In addition to analyzing the languages already mentioned, Bopp showed that Avestan, Armenian, and the Slavic languages were also part of the Indo-European family. The philologists' inevitable conclusion was that there had once existed an "original" Indo-European language, from which the historical languages of Europe, Persia, and India were derived, and therefore also an "original" Indo-European people.[1]

There were some clues indicating where the Proto-Indo-European language had been spoken: the Indo-European languages shared words for certain flora and fauna (bears and beech trees are well-known examples). By plotting on a map the natural environment of these diagnostic flora and fauna, philologists established that the Indo-European homeland was a fairly primitive place in the temperate zone. An early supposition, encouraged by the equation of Iran with Aryans and by the belief that Sanskrit was the first language to have separated

1. For a brief but excellent description of the several languages and of their relationship to Proto-Indo-European, see P. Baldi, *An Introduction to the Indo-European Languages* (Carbondale, Ill.: Southern Illinois Univ. Press, 1983).

itself from its Proto-Indo-European parent, was that the Indo-European homeland was in south-central Asia, between the Caspian and the Himalayas. By the end of the nineteenth century, however, a rival school of thought favored northern Europe as the Indo-European *Urheimat*. The principal support for the rival theory seems to have been the belief that there once was an "original Indo-European race" and that the people of this race were tall and white-skinned. Such a race, it was generally assumed, must have been indigenous to northeastern Europe.[2]

The question—"Where did the Greeks come from?"—was obviously much affected by the philologists' discoveries. Quite clearly, whether they came from central Asia or from northern Europe, they came from far away. They had not been aboriginal inhabitants of the Greek mainland after all. Further philological inquiry showed that many of the place names in the Aegean had been given by a non-Greek people, a people whom the Greeks must have conquered or driven out. Thus in the second half of the nineteenth century, historians were obliged to say much more about the origins of the Greeks than George Grote had said.

It is an unfortunate coincidence that studies of the Indo-European language community flourished at a time when nationalism, and a tendency to see history in racial terms, was on the rise in Europe. There was no blinking the fact, in the nine-

2. J. P. Mallory, "A Short History of the Indo-European Problem," *JIES* 1 (1973): 21–65, has traced the evolution of opinion on the Indo-European homeland. A good review of what was then called the "Aryan question" was presented by I. Taylor, *The Origin of the Aryans* (New York: Humboldt Publishing Co., 1890), 1–31. The term "Aryan" as a synonym for "Indo-European" was popularized by Max Müller in the 1850s, when central Asia still seemed the most likely Indo-European cradle ("Aryans," of course, is what both the Persians and the Rigveda warriors called themselves, and it survives in the name "Iran"). Isaac Taylor himself believed that the "Aryans" were originally a northern European race, of unusual talents and energy, and that their language was eventually disseminated among peoples of very different racial stock.

teenth century, that most of the world was dominated by Europeans or people of European descent. The easiest explanation for this was that Europeans, or at least most members of the European family, were genetically superior to peoples of darker complexion. It was thus a welcome discovery that the ancient Greeks and Persians were linguistically—and therefore, one could assume, biologically—"related" to the modern Europeans. The same racial stock, it appeared, had been in control of the world since Cyrus conquered Babylon. This stock was obviously the white race. India, it is true, presented a problem and required a separate explanation. Aryans had invaded India no later than the second millennium B.C., and successfully imposed their language on the aboriginal population, but the Aryan race had evidently become sterile in that southern clime and was eventually submerged by the aboriginal and inferior stock of the subcontinent.

From these assumptions about a masterful Indo-European race there readily flowed an enthusiasm for discovering or inventing the original Indo-European institutions. So, for example, in his *La cité antique* (1864), Numa Fustel de Coulanges argued that private property had characterized "Aryan" society from its very beginning. Other historians commended the Indo-Europeans' innate gift for government and statecraft, and their seemly moderation in matters of religion.

In such a context, the question of Greek origins could be answered in only one way. Since ancient Greek civilization was one of the highest achievements of mankind, one could only conclude that the Greek people must have possessed extraordinary natural capacities. From the Indo-European homeland there had evidently come to Greece a racial stock of unparalleled genius. For an early illustration of this phase of historical interpretation, we may look at what Ernst Curtius said on the subject. Curtius's three-volume *Griechische Geschichte* was published between 1857 and 1867. Quickly becoming the definitive work on Greek history in German universities, it was translated into English and was widely read in England and

America. Curtius discussed the Indo-European family of nations at some length, and then went on to deal specifically with the Greeks. They "were a race of men distinctly marked out by nature, and combined into a united body by common mental and physical gifts. . . . They were freer than other mortal races from all that hinders and oppresses the motion of the mind."[3]

Subsequent definitions of who the Greeks were became even more dogmatic. In K. J. Beloch's *Griechische Geschichte* the opening chapters are devoted to the topography and climate of Greece. They end with the observation that however beneficent and stimulating the land and climate may be, those things are not in themselves enough to produce a great civilization:

> Geographical circumstances are only one factor in the historical process. In vain do the gods lavish their gifts upon the person who knows not how to use them; and just as man is the only species to have raised himself above the level of the beasts, so of all human communities only one has been able to construct a culture in the full sense: we Aryans. It is quite likely that if by chance some other Indo-Germanic people had been brought to Greece, it too would have achieved essentially what the Greeks achieved. But it is entirely certain that however advantageous the land and environment, they would have led to nothing had a people of some other race come into permanent possession of Greece.[4]

3. E. Curtius, *The History of Greece* (New York: Scribner, Armstrong and Co., 1876), 1: 36–37.

4. K. J. Beloch, *Griechische Geschichte*, 2d ed. (Berlin and Leipzig: De Gruyter, 1924), 1: 66: "Aber wir sollen nicht vergessen, dass die geographischen Verhältnisse nur der eine Faktor im historischen Werdeprozess sind. Die Götter verschwenden ihre Gaben vergebens an den, der sie nicht zu brauchen versteht; und wenn von allen Lebewesen allein der Mensch über die Beschränktheit des tierischen Zustandes sich zu erheben vermocht hat, so ist von allen Völkergruppen nur eine imstande gewesen, eine Vollkultur hervorzubringen: wir Arier. Es ist sehr wahrscheinlich, dass, wenn ir

Once it was clear who the Greeks were, and whence they had come, questions arose about the date of their arrival. Curtius said nothing on the topic, in part because he wrote before archaeological work in Greece had begun. Heinrich Schliemann's excavations at Troy, Mycenae, Tiryns, and Orchomenos not only revealed the greatness of the Greeks' Heroic Age but also suggested that the sudden destruction of the three latter sites could have been the result of the last of the Greek migrations, the Dorian. According to the ancient chronographers, that migration had occurred in the twelfth century. The creation of the Heroic Age must therefore have begun some centuries earlier, and was to be attributed to earlier Greek immigrants.[5]

Philology was also of some help in dating the arrival of the Greeks in Greece. In reconstructing the prehistory of the Greek dialects, Paul Kretschmer concluded that there had been three Greek invasions of Greece during the Bronze Age.[6] The last of these, ca. 1200 B.C., was surely the Dorian Invasion. The two earlier invasions brought in the Ionians and "Achaeans" respectively ("Achaean" was supposed to be the linguistic ancestor of both the Aeolic and the Arcado-Cypriote dialects).[7] Since several centuries must have separated each of these invasions, the

---

gendein anderer indogermanischer Stamm vom Schicksal nach Griechenland verschlagen worden wäre, er im wesentlichen dasselbe geleistet haben würde, wie die Hellenen; ganz sicher aber, dass alle Vorteile der Lage ohne Wirkung geblieben sein würden, wenn eine Volk anderen Stammes in den dauernden Besitz Griechenlands gekommen wäre."

5. Not all scholars of Schliemann's generation accepted a twelfth-century date for the Dorian migration. The legend of the Return of the Heraclidae warranted the thesis that the Dorians had been in the Peloponnese during the heyday of Mycenae, and some archaeologists and historians proposed that the Dorian migration had occurred ca. 1500 B.C.

6. P. Kretschmer, "Zur Geschichte der griechischen Dialekte," *Glotta* 1 (1909): 1–59.

7. The name and definition of "Achaean" had been put forward by O. Hoffmann, *De mixtis graecae linguae dialectis* (Göttingen: Vandenhoeck, 1882).

first of them must have occurred very early, perhaps as early as 2000 B.C.

The breakup of the Indo-European family was, of course, put long before the arrival of the Greeks in Greece. Both Beloch and Eduard Meyer concluded that the dispersal of the Indo-European race, and the beginning of the individual Indo-European nations, took place ca. 2500 B.C. Meyer rested his conclusion on three considerations: (1) the first wave of Greeks seems to have arrived in Greece no later than ca. 2000 B.C.; (2) since Sanskrit and Greek were already differentiated by 2000 B.C., each must by that time have been going its own way for at least half a millennium; (3) Indo-European cognates indicate that at the time of the dispersal the Indo-Europeans had an Early Copper Age culture.[8]

Circuitously, when dating the arrival of the first Greeks in Greece, Meyer advanced as an argument the likelihood that the Indo-European community broke up ca. 2500 B.C.[9] But there were other arguments. Meyer noted, as did other historians, that the Greeks (unlike the Israelites) had no legends about their entry into the land in which they lived. The lack of such saga indicated that their migration from the Eurasian steppe had occurred long before the Heroic Age, about which the Greeks had so many legends. Beloch added the argument, eccentric at the time, that the differentiation of Greek into its various dialects—a differentiation that obviously was complete by the end of the Bronze Age—must have occurred in Greece itself, and would have required many centuries. Both Beloch and Meyer regarded 2000 B.C. as the latest possible date for the Greeks' arrival in Greece.[10]

8. E. Meyer, *Geschichte des Altertums*, 3d ed. (Stuttgart and Berlin: Cotta, 1913), 1, 2: 856–57.

9. Ibid., 806–808.

10. Beloch, *Griechische Geschichte*, 1: 71 ("nicht unter das Ende des III. Jahrtausends"); Meyer, *Geschichte des Altertums*, 1: 808. Not surprisingly, Georg Busolt did not deal at all with either the Indo-European question or with the coming of the Greeks to Greece.

At this point it may be helpful to see how historians *pictured* the event we have been discussing. A particularly vivid picture can be seen in James Breasted's *Ancient Times*. "The great white race" began its historic breakup in the middle of the third millenium: "Divided into numerous tribes, they wandered at will, seeking pasture for their flocks. . . . They were the most gifted and the most highly imaginative people of the ancient world. . . . In the West these wanderers from the northern grasslands had already crossed the Danube and were far down in the Balkan peninsula by 2000 B.C. Some of them had doubtless already entered Italy by this time."[11] What Breasted imagined was a vast Völkerwanderung, analogous to the Germanic peoples' invasion of the Roman Empire. "Driving their herds before them, with their families in rough carts drawn by horses, the rude Greek tribesmen must have looked out upon the fair pastures of Thessaly, the snowy summit of Mount Olympus, and the blue waters of the Aegean not long after 2000 B.C."[12]

Beloch, too, explained the "Ausbreitung der Indogermanen" as the westward and southward expansion of a pastoral population: the Aryans, a prolific but decent and responsible people, pushed on from one river frontier to the next, searching out new pastures for their herds as the Aryan population continued to expand.[13] Similarly, in the mind of Eduard Meyer the dispersal of the Indo-European language family was visualized as "grossen Völkerbewegungen."[14] This picture of the

11. J. Breasted, *Ancient Times: A History of the Early World* (Boston: Ginn and Co., 1916), 174–75.

12. Ibid., 253.

13. Beloch, *Griechische Geschichte*, 1: 68–69: "Natürlich kann die Einwanderung nicht in einem Zuge erfolgt sein." Since the expansion of the Indo-Europeans continued until the end of classical antiquity, and stretched from India to the Atlantic Ocean, it was an entirely gradual affair, occasioned by the need to find "neue Weidegründe" for the growing number of Aryan herds and flocks.

14. Meyer, *Geschichte des Altertums*, 1: 805.

"Indo-European invasions" is still widely accepted today. In the first volume of the *Cambridge History of Iran*, published in 1985, I. M. Diakonoff imagines that when the Indo-Iranians came to India and Iran "the main tribal mass, at first all of it, later the majority, moved along on foot with its cattle, probably accompanied by heavy carts. Pastoral tribes . . . in time exhaust the steppe within the region they inhabit and are thus continually compelled to resettle in new places."[15] Moving on from one temporary settlement to another, Diakonoff concludes, the Indo-Iranian pastoralists gradually worked their way toward their eventual homelands, keeping to routes that provided "passage and food for cattle and human masses moving on foot."

A massive folk migration, such as those described above, would of course leave an archaeological trail. In particular, archaeologists at the beginning of our century supposed that a procession of populations across the continents was reflected in the vagaries of pottery styles. An archaeologically secured date for the arrival of the Greek nation in Greece was furnished by English and American excavators in the 1920s: after a close study and classification of pottery, they concluded that the first Greeks (whether these were Ionians or "Achaeans" was not clear) had come to Greece ca. 1900 B.C. Since this date has until recently enjoyed almost canonical status, it will be worthwhile to see how it was established. We might begin with Sir Arthur Evans, who subdivided the spectacular prehistory of Crete into a neolithic period and three periods of Bronze Age history: Early, Middle, and Late Minoan, which roughly corresponded to Egypt's Old, Middle, and New Kingdoms. For each of his prehistoric periods, Evans identified characteristic pottery types. A parallel scheme for the Greek mainland was worked out by Alan Wace and Carl Blegen in 1918.[16] Bor-

15. I. M. Diakonoff in *Cambridge History of Iran* (Cambridge: Cambridge Univ. Press, 1985), 2: 49.
16. A. Wace and C. Blegen, "The Pre-Mycenaean Pottery of the Mainland," *BSA* 22 (1916–1918), 175–89.

rowing Evans's Cretan divisions, Wace and Blegen introduced what would become the standard terminology for Bronze Age Greece: the Early, Middle, and Late Helladic periods. Wace and Blegen based their scheme squarely on an analysis of changes in—and evolution of—mainland pottery through the prehistoric millennia. Such an analysis was feasible because excavations that the youthful Blegen had carried out at small sites near Corinth (Korakou and Zygouries) had yielded a fairly complete pottery sequence.

As the diagnostic pottery for their Middle Helladic period, Wace and Blegen settled upon "Minyan Ware." This is a gray, wheelmade pottery that feels pleasantly soapy rather than abrasive, and contrasts markedly with the handmade and coarser pottery of earlier levels. It had first been encountered by Schliemann at Orchomenos. Although some of his contemporaries referred to it prosaically as "Orchomenos Ware," the name that prevailed was Schliemann's more romantic Minyan Ware, which recalled the glorious but tenuous Minyans of Greek mythology. The ware was subsequently found at many sites in Boeotia, Attica, the Peloponnese, and elsewhere. Because of its ubiquity, and because at several sites it appeared above a destruction level, Wace and Blegen found it a convenient feature for distinguishing Middle from Early Helladic levels. An absolute date for this break was eventually furnished by Troy. In the continuing excavations at Troy, it became clear that Minyan Ware began with Troy VI. The wonderfully complete stratigraphy at Troy established the date of this archaeological horizon as ca. 1900 B.C.

In their 1918 article, Blegen and Wace did not yet associate Minyan Ware with "the coming of the Greeks." They did observe, however, that the sudden appearance of Minyan Ware at the beginning of the Middle Helladic period was one of only two interruptions in the otherwise unbroken evolution of pottery on the Greek mainland from neolithic times to the Mycenaean Age. The only other interruption, they found, was the advent of Minoan and Minoanizing pottery at the beginning of the period they called Late Helladic. Wace and Blegen concluded that "Minyan Ware indicates the introduction of a new cultural strain,"[17] but they did not yet identify this new strain with the Greeks. However, since there were only two interruptions in the Bronze Age pottery sequence, and since the second of these had to do with Minoans, the only alternative was to tie the Greeks' arrival in Greece to the appearance of Minyan Ware.

That conclusion Blegen presented in a second influential article, this one written in collaboration with a philologist, J. B. Haley and published in 1928.[18] Basing his part of the article on work done at the turn of the century by Paul Kretschmer and August Fick,[19] Haley listed the non-Greek place names of Greece, most of them being in east central Greece, the Peloponnese, Crete and the Aegean islands. He also showed that a surprising number of these place names (many of them ending in *-nthos*, *-ssos*, or *-ndos*) duplicated names in western Asia Minor, some rather far inland.

In his half of the article, Blegen proceded to match Haley's findings with the archaeological record of these areas, looking for a period during which a rough homogeneity in pottery and other artifacts obtained from western Asia Minor through Crete and the southeastern areas of the Greek mainland. The Early Bronze Age, Blegen concluded, was such a period, and pottery indicated that at the beginning of the Early Bronze Age the people who lived in southwestern Anatolia expanded into Crete and across the Aegean to the Greek mainland. Throughout the third millennium B.C., therefore, there was a common language and a common culture in Crete and the Greek main-

17. Ibid., 189.

18. J. B. Haley and C. Blegen, "The Coming of the Greeks," *AJA* 32 (1928): 141–54.

19. P. Kretschmer, *Einleitung in die Geschichte der griechischen Sprache* (Göttingen: Vandenhoeck & Ruprecht, 1896); A. Fick, *Vorgriechische Ortsnamen als Quelle für die Vorgeschichte Griechenlands* (Göttingen: Vandenhoeck & Ruprecht, 1905).

land (as well as southwestern Asia Minor). At the beginning of the Middle Bronze Age, on the other hand, the Greek mainland diverged radically from Crete and the other areas, with Gray Minyan Ware blanketing southern Greece, while on Crete the older pottery traditions continued to develop. Blegen also observed that many of the sites identified with the pre-Greek place names were destroyed at the end of the Early Bronze Age. The import of all this was clear: a non-Greek people, whose language included many names with suffixes in *-nthos*, *-ssos*, and *-ndos*, occupied much of the Greek mainland, the Cyclades, Crete, and southwestern Asia Minor through the Early Bronze Age; ca. 1900 B.C. a new people arrived in the Greek mainland, and this new people must have been the first wave of the Greek nation.

It is important to note that Blegen saw his proposed date as nicely congruent with other evidence for Indo-European migrations and "the coming of the Greeks."[20] Further support for the new date was provided by what seemed to have been an Indo-European migration to the other side of the Aegean. In 1915 Bedrich Hrozny had announced his decipherment of the language conventionally called "Hittite," and startled philologists and historians alike with his identification of Hittite as an Indo-European language. Although Hrozny's somewhat extravagant claims met with disbelief, Ferdinand Sommer's more conservative presentation of the case in 1920 eventually carried

---

20. Cf. his remarks at "The Coming of the Greeks," pp. 153–54: "At any rate we can hardly go far astray if we take, in round figures, the year 1900 B.C. as marking the passing of Early Helladic civilization on the mainland and its supersession by the earliest form of Hellenic culture. The results of our enquiry have, therefore, led us to push backward some three hundred years the date of the arrival of the first Hellenic stock, which Professor Buck, on the linguistic evidence, would place at least as early as 1600 B.C. The still earlier date, *ca.* 1900 B.C., corresponds far better with a clearly indicated cultural break. . . . We find ourselves, therefore, in essential agreement with E. Meyer and Beloch, who on other grounds have placed the first entry of people of Indo-European stock into Greece at the end of the third millennium B.C."

conviction.[21] That the great kingdom of the Hittites was an Indo-European state was remarkable, and so was its chronology. Babylonian records indicated that Hammurabi's dynasty had been terminated, and Babylon sacked, by Mursilis the Hittite. The date of the sack was calculated to have been shortly before 1900 B.C., and one could therefore suppose that the Hittites had established themselves in Asia Minor some time during the twentieth century B.C. Thus Blegen's date for the arrival of the Greeks in Greece was seen as fitting closely with the coming of other Indo-Europeans to a land immediately to the east. Also helpful for Blegen's thesis was the possibility that a third Indo-European nation may have poured across the Alps into Italy early in the second millennium (the Proto-Italic speakers were occasionally identified with the Lake Dwellers, an archaeological population of Switzerland and the Italian piedmont). Finally, Blegen did not have to contend with the fact that the Aryans' arrival in India was a relatively late event in Indian prehistory. The Indus valley civilization was virtually unknown until the 1920s, when excavation at Harappa and Mohenjo-daro began. Thus the old assumption, that the Aryan conquest of India took place in remotest antiquity (and that the Rigveda was composed ca. 1500 B.C.) still prevailed when Blegen and Haley wrote their article.

Everything fit together quite well, and there seemed to be good and ample evidence from several quarters that Indo-European peoples were arriving at their historical destinations at the turn of the second millennium B.C. As we shall see in the next chapter, Blegen's date for "the coming of the Greeks" eventually lost its hold on specialists in Aegean prehistory. But on the wider topic of the date and nature of "the Indo-European Völkerwanderungen," it is still influential.

21. Sommer, *Hethitisches*, 2 vols. (*Boghazköi Studien*, 4 and 7) (Leipzig: Hinrichs, 1920 and 1922), argued only that in grammar and morphology Hittite was Indo-European. He conceded that there were few Indo-European cognates in the Hittite vocabulary (Hrozny had proposed many such cognates).

TWO

Some Minority Views on the Coming of the Greeks

Today the debate about "the coming of the Greeks" has become quite lively. The conventional date, as we have seen, has been the interface between Early and Middle Helladic, ca. 1900 B.C., and some surveys still present this date without qualification or defense. But specialists have for some time been canvassing other possibilities. The several dates currently proposed for this event are, of course, all archaeologically based. The disruptions or "breaks" in the material record are here all-important, since the arrival of the Greeks is assumed to correspond to one of these breaks. All along, those few scholars who did not agree that the arrival of the Greeks occurred at the break between Early and Middle Helladic (ca. 1900 B.C.) traditionally located it at the break between Middle and Late Helladic (ca. 1600 B.C.), or between Late Helladic IIIB and IIIC (ca. 1200 B.C.). And recently, a fourth possibility has found a few strong advocates: the break between Early Helladic II and III (ca. 2100 B.C.). Let us briefly look at the evidence on which each of these variant proposals is based.

The latest date—ca. 1200 B.C.—is now championed by only a small minority of scholars, all of whom dispute Michael Ventris's and John Chadwick's demonstration that the language of the Linear B tablets is Greek.[1] The grounds for this

1. For a full argument in favor of the late date, see F. Hampl, "Die Chronologie der Einwanderung der griechischen Stämme und das Problem der Nationalität der Träger der mykenischen Kultur," MH 17 (1960): 57–86, and E. Grumach, "The Coming of the Greeks," BRL 51 (1968–1969): 73–103 and 399–430.

dating are primarily archaeological: the destruction levels found at so very many sites at the end of the LH IIIB period, and the overwhelming fact that Bronze Age Greece was completely different from historical Greece. But for most scholars a date ca. 1200 B.C. for "the coming of the Greeks" has disqualifying liabilities. Even before Ventris's decipherment this view had its difficulties, since (as mentioned earlier) Greek legend knows nothing of the Greeks' migration into Greece. Legend did recall a Dorian migration from Doris to the Peloponnese after the Trojan War, and a migration of Aeolians and Ionians to the coast of Asia Minor at about the same time, but the legends quite consistently recalled that during the Heroic Age, Greeks were already living in Greece. Although it is unwise to construct history on the basis of a legend, it is far more perilous to posit a momentous event of which subsequent generations remembered nothing at all (especially when oral tradition seems to have commemorated other, and lesser, events of the same time). In addition, as a later chapter will show in some detail, there is virtually no archaeological evidence for a Volkswanderung into Greece at the beginning of or during the twelfth century. As for the destruction levels, archaeologists and historians have traditionally explained them as the result of the Dorian Invasion or (more recently) of hit-and-run raiders. Thus, the belief that the Greeks first came to Greece ca. 1200 B.C. has no support in either legend or archaeology, and is incompatible with the conclusion of most Linear B scholars that the language of the tablets is Greek. Not surprisingly, the theory has few adherents today, and I shall not deal with it further in this essay. One of the better known books in which it is advocated is Sinclair Hood's *The Home of the Heroes*.[2]

Another and increasingly more popular view is that "the coming of the Greeks" occurred at the break between Early Helladic II and EH III, ca. 2100 B.C. For this relatively recent proposal, Blegen's reconstruction was a prerequisite and a

2. S. Hood, *The Home of the Heroes: The Aegean before the Greeks* (London: Thames and Hudson, 1967).

point of departure. For almost a generation there was a rough consensus among scholars, based on Blegen's studies, that the Greeks had arrived in Greece at the beginning of the Middle Helladic period. Dissension eventually arose among archaeologists. There are only a few mainland Greek sites at which the stratigraphy for the late third and early second millennia is complete; and at what is probably the most important of these few sites, the evidence did not square with the prevailing theory. At this site a destruction level was found not at the interface between Early and Middle Helladic, but between EH II and EH III. Furthermore, an early form of Minyan Ware was here shown to have been in use during EH III, the final phase of the Early Helladic period. Such were the results of the excavations that John Caskey began in 1952 at Lerna, in the Argolid, a town that may well have been the most important Early Helladic center in all of Greece. The findings at Lerna indicated that a moderately sophisticated society, with monumental architecture, had evolved in the Argolid from ca. 3000 to ca. 2100 B.C. At that point, however, Lerna was destroyed, and the subsequent EH III period was comparatively poor and unaccomplished. And in the postdestruction levels at Lerna, Caskey's excavations unearthed what has been called "Proto-Minyan" pottery, gray and wheelmade.[3]

Upon investigation, a handful of other sites in the Argolid, Attica, and even southern Laconia also seemed to have been destroyed ca. 2100 B.C., at the transition from EH II to EH III. And although in general the evidence on the EH III period is scanty, a careful review of what there is showed that in most respects MH was closely tied to EH III.[4] Further, although in-

3. This is almost the earliest wheelmade pottery known from the Greek mainland. At Kritsana, in the Chalcidice, specimens from the late third millenium have also been found. Cf. Caskey, *CAH* I, 2: 775 and 786.
4. For a good review of the nonceramic evidence, see R. J. Howell, "The Origins of the Middle Helladic Culture," in *Bronze Age Migrations in the Aegean: Archaeological and Linguistic Problems in Greek Prehistory*, ed.

direct, support for the new theory was provided by James Mellaart's demonstration that on the other side of the Aegean the Anatolian Early Bronze II period ended in a vast calamity: most of the EB II sites in Anatolia were destroyed ca. 2300 B.C., and only a fraction of them were reoccupied in the EB III period. From ca. 2300 B.C. until the end of the Bronze Age ca. 1200 B.C., the material culture of Anatolia showed an unbroken development and continuity. Mellaart proposed that the Anatolian destruction was the work of Luwians, whom he regarded as a nation closely related to the Hittite nation.[5] If the destruction at EH sites in Greece was not equally spectacular, it was because at most EH II sites there was nothing very spectacular to be destroyed.

But the destruction in Greece at the end of EH II was undoubtedly broad and catastrophic. In the words of M. I. Finley, archaeologists have seldom found an episode of destruction "so massive and abrupt, so widely dispersed, as occurred at this particular time. In Greece, nothing comparable was to happen again until the end of the Bronze Age a thousand years later."[6] The evidence for disruption ca. 2100 B.C., along with the evidence for continuity from the EH III to the MH period, persuaded a number of historians and archaeologists (although not Caskey himself) that the first Greeks entered Greece not at the outset of the Middle Helladic period, but at least two centuries earlier. Finley's analysis is straightforward and clear:

> If, as appears, the Argolid was the centre of destruction by intruders in the late third millennium,

---

R. A. Crossland and A. Birchall (Park Ridge, N.J.: Noyes Press, 1974), 73–99.

5. Mellaart, "The End of the Early Bronze Age in Anatolia and the Aegean," *AJA* 62 (1958): 1–31. In *CAH* I, 2: 406, Mellaart presents in tabular form the extent of the destruction between Anatolian EB II and EB III (which he dates ca. 2300 B.C.): for EB II there are 421 known habitation sites in southern and western Asia Minor, and for EB III there are only 108.

6. M. I. Finley, *Early Greece: The Bronze and Archaic Ages*, 2d ed. (New York: Norton, 1981), 13.

the further implication is that it was from this district that there eventually grew and spread the culture of the Early Helladic III and Middle Helladic periods out of which, in turn, there emerged the Late Helladic (or Mycenaean) civilization. That is a very different picture from the romantic one of the conquest which blanketed the whole, or even most, of Greece in one great swoop. The "coming of the Greeks," in other words, meant the arrival of a new element who combined with their predecessors to create, slowly, a new civilization and to extend it as and where they could.[7]

In Caskey's more conservative (and therefore more ambiguous) reconstruction of events there are two very similar invasions: a first contingent of Indo-European and Greek-like (but not quite Greek) newcomers arrives at the end of EH II, destroys Lerna and much else, and settles down, especially in the Argolid. At ca. 1900 B.C. a second and perhaps larger wave of invaders arrives; these are the first people who can truly be called Greek. They are "kindred" to the earlier invaders, however, and speak what the earlier group would have found an "intelligible language." These invaders therefore spare the EH III towns of their kinsmen, while destroying the settlements whose populations spoke an altogether alien language.[8] This "two-wave" hypothesis, with invasions distributed between the end of EH II and the beginning of MH, has most recently been advanced in a lengthy study by M. B. Sakellariou.[9]

7. Ibid., 19.

8. Caskey, *CAH* II, 1: 136–40. Caskey tentatively identified the invaders at the beginning of EH III as Luwians, an identification that Mellaart also favored in his "The End of the Early Bronze Age." The most glaring contradiction in Caskey's reconstruction is that his EH III people are responsible for the pre-Greek and non-Greek names of places such as Corinth and Tiryns, but yet speak a language intelligible to the Proto-Greeks.

9. M. B. Sakellariou, *Les Proto-grecs* (Athens: Ekdotikè Athenon, 1980).

Yet another suggestion about "the coming of the Greeks" has with varying force been put forward from time to time. In this view, the Greeks (or at least the most important contingent of them) came to Greece relatively late: ca. 1600 B.C., at the interface between the Middle and Late Helladic periods. A rough equivalent of this suggestion was made first by Georges Perrot in 1892 and by J. I. Manatt and Christos Tsountas in 1897,[10] but it was first argued at length and in sophisticated fashion by Martin Nilsson a generation later.[11] More recently, it appeared as a subthesis in L. R. Palmer's controversial *Minoans and Mycenaeans*,[12] and as the main thesis in out-of-the-way articles by William Wyatt and James Muhly.[13] It has also in recent years been advocated by Dutch archaeologist Jan G. P. Best and his collaborators, among whom was the distinguished Israeli general and archaeologist, Yigael Yadin.[14]

10. G. Perrot, "Les fouilles de Schliemann à Mycènes," *Journal des Savants* (1892): 449; Chr. Tsountas and J. I. Manatt, *The Mycenaean Age* (London, 1897), 71, 248, and 345.

11. In his *Minoan-Mycenaean Religion and its Survival in Greek Religion* (Lund: Gleerup, 1927) and again in *Homer and Mycenae* (London: Methuen, 1933).

12. L. R. Palmer, *Minoans and Mycenaeans* (London: Faber and Faber, 1961).

13. W. F. Wyatt, Jr., "The Indo-Europeanization of Greece," in *Indo-European and Indo-Europeans. Papers Presented at the Third Indo-European Conference at the University of Pennsylvania*, ed. G. Cardona, H. M. Hoenigswald, and A. Senn (Philadelphia: Univ. of Pennsylvania Press, 1970), 89–111. James Muhly's article, "On the Shaft Graves at Mycenae," appeared in *Studies in Honor of Tom B. Jones* (*Alter Orient und Altes Testament*, Bd. 203), ed. M. A. Powell and R. H. Sack (Neukirchen-Vluyn: Neukirchener Verlag, 1979), 311–23. Muhly had earlier given his support to the thesis in *AJA* 79 (1975): 289–91, in reviewing *Acta of the Second International Colloquium on Aegean Prehistory: The First Arrival of Indo-European Elements in Greece* (Athens: Ministry of Culture and Science, 1972).

14. In bibliographies, *The Arrival of the Greeks* (Amsterdam: Hakkert, 1973), might appear to be a book coauthored by Jan Best and Yigael Yadin. It is in fact a twenty-one-page essay ("An Outline") by Best, followed by a twenty-page article by Yadin ("And Dan, Why Did He Remain in Ships?") originally published in 1968 in the *Australian Journal of Biblical*

The Coming of the Greeks

The dating of the arrival of the Greeks ca. 1600 B.C. has been supported by a variety of arguments. Among them must be mentioned the dubious doctrine that the *megaron* first appeared in the Late Helladic period. A somewhat sounder argument was Nilsson's emphasis on the prevalence of amber at LH sites of the sixteenth and fifteenth centuries and its complete absence at earlier sites: since the amber found in Greece came from the Baltic, Nilsson proposed that a people with northern connections must have arrived in Greece at the beginning of the LH period. Another of Nilsson's arguments centered on the horse: the horse, Nilsson believed, was brought to the Mediterranean by Indo-Europeans, and so far as he knew, the horse first appeared in Greece in the sixteenth century B.C. Other and more recent arguments have focused on supposed changes in dress and in burial practices at the beginning of the LH period, on the chariot, on the evidence of destruction levels, and on the evidence of language.

The most obvious reason, however, for dating "the coming of the Greeks" to ca. 1600 B.C. has always been the shaft graves of Mycenae. Because of their importance to this argument, a reminder about the shaft graves is in order here. The sensational *corredo* that Schliemann discovered is well known: the many gold ornaments, cups, diadems, and death masks; the bronze daggers with inlays of silver and niello; the haul of other weapons and grave goods. There is general agreement today (because of correspondences, in the later tombs, with Late Minoan Ia decorative motifs) that these six shaft graves, now referred to as Grave Circle A, date from the sixteenth and the very early fifteenth century B.C. Most of the twenty-four burials of Grave Circle B—which was found in 1951 and was not quite so astounding as Grave Circle A—are also from the sixteenth century, although the earliest (which are cist graves

---

Archaeology. R. A. van Royen and B. H. Isaac, *The Arrival of the Greeks: The Evidence from the Settlements* (Amsterdam: Grüner, 1979), is a tightly focused seventy-six-page monograph. Neither of these two publications was widely reviewed.

rather than true shaft graves, and which contained no grave goods other than pottery) are Middle Helladic and seem to date from shortly before 1600 B.C.[15]

The wealthy and warlike lords who were buried in the shaft graves of both circles have usually been identified as Greeks. Schliemann regarded the occupants of his circle as Agamemnon and his friends, hastily though sumptuously buried by Aegistheus. Evans, it is true, decided that the people buried in Circle A were Minoans, since many of the grave gifts were either manufactured or inspired by Cretan craftsmen. Since Evans's time, however, it has become quite clear that Mycenae was ruled by Greeks during its heyday. Because there is no evidence that the Shaft Grave Dynasty ended by violence (and in fact the later lords of Mycenae treated Grave Circle A as hallowed ground), it is reasonable to conclude that the people buried in the shaft graves were indeed Greeks.

What suggests that they might have been newcomers to Greece, freshly arrived from the land of the PIE speakers, is the fact that the deposits found in the shaft graves seem to be without precedent at Mycenae or anywhere else in Greece. The more archaeologists have learned about the Middle Helladic period, the more convinced some observers have become that no evolution or gradual progress led up to the bellicose opulence of the Shaft Grave Dynasty.[16] They argue instead, as

15. O.T.P.K. Dickinson, *The Origins of Mycenaean Civilisation* (*Studies in Mediterranean Archaeology*, 49) (Göteborg: Paul Aströms Förlag, 1977), provides a good commentary on the two grave circles and their contents. At pages 50–51 Dickinson suggests that together the two circles span a period of no more than "four or at most five generations, which need not represent much more than a century in a period when average life-expectancy was so short."

16. Cf. Muhly, "On the Shaft Graves," 316: "The one dramatic transition in prehistoric Greece came towards the end of M.H.III, in the latter part of the seventeenth century B.C., and is represented by the Shaft Graves at Mycenae. Nothing yet known from the impoverished Middle Helladic period prepares one for the wealth and splendor of Shaft Grave Mycenae."

Muhly has most recently done,[17] that the best analogies for the grave goods of Circles A and B are to be found in the kurgans of southern Russia (in the great kurgan at Maikop, for example, not far north of the Caucasus, a late third-millennium "treasure" that anticipates some of the characteristics of the Mycenaean material). The abrupt appearance in Greece of all this splendor of the shaft graves has long seemed to many scholars inexplicable without the concession that at least *some* Greeks came from a distant place to the Argolid ca. 1600 B.C. Within the framework of Kretschmer's view that the Greeks came to Greece in several dialect-waves, the invaders of ca. 1600 B.C. were most often identified with the second or "Achaean" wave of Greek immigrants (the Ionians, on this same view, were held to have been the first wave of Greeks to enter Greece, arriving three centuries before the Achaeans).

A few scholars, however, have seen the shaft graves as evidence that simply "the Greeks"—either the first of them, or by far the most important contingent of them—came to Greece ca. 1600 B.C. The view that "the coming of the Greeks" occurred at this time, and that the grave circles at Mycenae are the material record of that event, involves more than the question of chronology. If one dates the arrival of the Greeks in Greece to the beginning of the LH period, one tends to picture the first Greeks as warriors rather than as herdsmen. And instead of a massive Volkswanderung, what comes to mind is a conquest of the indigenous population by a relatively small number of intruders.

17. Ibid., 316–22.

THREE

Linguistic and Archaeological Considerations

All three of the preferred dates for "the coming of the Greeks" are archaeologically based, but in weighing them, one must consider more than the archaeological evidence. Studies in linguistics very obviously have a special relevance here, and developments in this field have been somewhat startling. Specialists on the Greek dialects have come to some conclusions that pertain directly to the date at which the Greek language (or, more accurately, the form of Proto-Indo-European— whether dialect or language—out of which the Greek language would develop) arrived in the Aegean. And from Indo-European linguistics has come a novel suggestion about the place from which the first PIE speakers may have come to Greece. It will be useful here to review rather broadly the current theses about the Indo-European homeland and Völkerwanderungen, and to see how they arose.

A few devout scholars in the early days of Indo-European philology believed that "the Indo-Europeans" came ultimately from Mesopotamia (since that is where the Tower of Babylon was built and where the Confusion of Tongues occurred) and more directly from eastern Anatolia, since the Table of Nations seemed to identify Asia Minor with the progeny of Japheth. That, however, was a minority view. As we have seen, from the time that Franz Bopp published his influential comparative grammar in 1833 until late in the nineteenth century, most philologists located the Indo-European homeland in the general vicinity of what is today Afghanistan, and what was once

Bactria. And by the beginning of the twentieth century, as we have also seen, the racial argument had promoted more northerly and westerly lands for the location of the Indo-European cradle. Early enthusiasts for an Indo-European race placed it in the Pripet Marshes of eastern Poland and western Russia,[1] but that region was little recommended by its later history and accomplishments. More popular was Paul Kretschmer's identification of the cradle with Thuringia, or central Germany, and the identification of the original Indo-Europeans with an archaeological population known as the Schnurkeramik people. Others placed the Indo-European homeland in Scandinavia, or along the Baltic, or the North Sea.

This "northern European" hypothesis was slightly undermined by V. Gordon Childe's *The Aryans*.[2] Childe surveyed much of Eurasia in search of the most probable Indo-European cradle and concluded with a *non liquet*: archaeological and philological considerations, he thought, both pointed to southern Russia (specifically, to the steppes that run from above the Black Sea to the Lower Volga and the Caspian), but a homeland in Scandinavia could not be ruled out. Perhaps a more damaging blow to the "northern European" hypothesis was struck, ironically, by a German scholar during the heyday of Nazi racial doctrines. In the middle of the 1930s, Gertrud Hermes published studies on the history of the "tamed" horse,[3] and eventually these studies (which we shall look at in some detail

---

1. The racial or the "anthropological" argument was pioneered by Th. Poesche, *Die Arier: Ein Beitrag zur historischen Anthropolologie* (Jena: H. Costenoble, 1878). Poesche was convinced that the original Indo-Europeans were an exceptionally white race, and he surveyed the world to find a place where albinism, or depigmentation, is pronounced. This place he found in the Pripet Marshes, or the Rokitno swamp, between the Pripet, the Dnieper, and the Beresina rivers.

2. V. G. Childe, *The Aryans* (New York: Knopf, 1926).

3. G. Hermes, "Das gezähmte Pferd im neolithischen und frühbronzezeitlichen Europa?" *Anthropos* 30 (1935): 803–23; "Das gezähmte Pferd im alten Orient," *Anthropos* 31 (1936): 364–94, and "Der Zug des gezähmten Pferdes durch Europa," *Anthropos* 32 (1937): 105–46.

in Chapter Six) persuaded most Indo-Europeanists that the homeland of the Indo-Europeans could not have been in northern Europe. Hermes essentially showed the incompatibility of two theses that in her day were generally accepted: the Indo-European homeland was in northern Europe, and the Indo-Europeans pioneered the use of the horse-drawn chariot. The "tamed" horse, Hermes demonstrated quite conclusively, was not known in northern Europe before ca. 1500 B.C. Her articles encouraged Indo-Europeanists to look for the Indo-European Urheimat in places where the "tamed" horse was attested at an early date, and in the last forty years the favorite candidates have been the steppe above the Black Sea or, alternatively, Hungary and the rest of the Carpathian Basin.[4]

The credentials of the Carpathian Basin, or more broadly of the entire expanse of central Europe covered by the Early Danubian (or Bandkeramik) Culture, were urged by Giacomo Devoto in 1962, and a more southerly variation of the same case has recently been defended by I. M. Diakonoff. The Pontic steppe, however, seems to have a slight edge among Indo-Europeanists as the most likely site for the Proto-Indo-European community. The arguments marshaled by Childe have in recent decades been augmented and effectively advocated by Marija Gimbutas, a specialist (as was Childe) in the archaeology of prehistoric Europe and the Eurasian steppe.[5] A popular synthesis of the two options is that the land of the PIE speakers was a vast place, stretching from the Urals to central Europe, and so included both the Carpathian Basin and the Pontic steppe. This theory was favored by Anton Scherer[6] and was

4. The beginnings of this controversy are chronicled in A. Scherer, ed., *Die Urheimat der Indogermanen* (*Wege der Forschung* 166) (Darmstadt: Wissenschaftliche Buchgesellschaft, 1968).

5. G. Devoto, *Origini Indoeuropee* (Florence: Sansoni, 1962); on Gimbutas and Diakonoff, see below.

6. A. Scherer, "Das Problem der indogermanischen Urheimat," *Archiv für Kulturgeschichte* 33 (1950): 3–16.

given its archaeological articulation by Pedro Bosch-Gimpera.[7] According to Bosch-Gimpera's reconstruction, the *centum* branch of the Indo-European family came into being in central Europe, and the *satem* branch above the Black Sea and the Caucasus range.

During the last fifty years, the dates of the "breakup" of the Proto-Indo-European community, and of "folk migrations" of the PIE speakers, have either held their place or slipped backwards in archaeological and linguistic scholarship. An initial impetus for earlier dates seems to have come from the classification of Hittite as an Indo-European language. So little did Hittite share with Sanskrit, or with Greek, that one was forced to assume that the Proto-Indo-European community must have begun splintering a very long time before the Hittites invaded Asia Minor. The discovery of the Indus valley civilization, and its publication in the 1930s, did not much discourage an early date for the Indo-European dispersal: that civilization, like pre-Kassite Mesopotamia, was then dated several centuries earlier than it is today (after the Second World War, the date for the destruction or abandonment of the Indus valley sites was lowered considerably, but by the time of the revision, the early dating of the Indo-European dispersal was well entrenched; the Aryan conquest of India, therefore, has in recent decades been seen as a bird out of season, later than the main migrations by centuries or even millennia). More recently, archaeological arguments have encouraged earlier dates for the Indo-European invasions. The earlier dating of Minyan Ware, of Corded Ware in central Europe, and of Gray Ware in northern Iran persuaded Homer Thomas that the conventional dates for the main Indo-European movements were four or five centuries too low.[8] On the basis of new carbon-14 dates (and calibration of

7. P. Bosch-Gimpera, *Les Indo-européens: problèmes archéologiques* (Paris: Payot, 1961).

8. H. Thomas, "New Evidence for Dating the Indo-European Dispersal in Europe," in *Indo-European and Indo-Europeans*, ed. G. Cardona et al., 199–215.

the old dates), Gimbutas has in the last twenty years raised her chronology by almost a millennium.

Not surprisingly, Indo-Europeanists must now choose between several chronologies for the Indo-European Völkerwanderungen. In the reconstruction offered by Bosch-Gimpera, the Proto-Indo-European community existed from the fifth millennium onward, but about 2000 B.C., disturbances in the Eurasian steppe dislodged portions of both the satem and the centum provinces, sending PIE speakers southward. The chronology constructed by Homer Thomas, almost entirely on the basis of pottery, is somewhat earlier, and dates the main dispersal to the middle of the third millennium. The same conclusion, supported by both archaeological and linguistic arguments, had been presented by Devoto: the Proto-Indo-European community began to break up before 2500 B.C., with some PIE speakers (whose language would develop into something other than Greek) reaching Thessaly during the neolithic period. Devoto concluded that a second wave of PIE speakers brought Minyan Ware and Proto-Greek into Greece ca. 1900 B.C., and that the Aegean was thus Indo-Europeanized by degrees.

Among Indo-Europeanists, however, the most influential chronology for the folk migrations appears to be the very high chronology that serves as a scaffold for Gimbutas's "Kurgan hypothesis."[9] According to Gimbutas, Indo-European pastoralists from the Kurgan Culture of the Pontic steppe migrated into Europe in three massive waves: the first ca. 4400 B.C., the

9. The thesis has been regularly recast (the successive revisions pushing the dates upward), but remains fundamentally what it was. For relatively recent and succinct statements of her position, see Gimbutas, "Proto-Indo-European Culture: The Kurgan Culture during the Fifth, Fourth and Third Millennia B.C.," in *Indo-European and Indo-Europeans*, ed. G. Cardona et al., 815–36; "The First Wave of Eurasian Steppe Pastoralists into Copper Age Europe," *JIES* 5 (1977): 277–338; "The Three Waves of the Kurgan People into Old Europe, 4500–2500 B.C.," *Arch. suisses d'anthropol. gen.* 43 (1979 [1981]): 113–37.

second ca. 3400 B.C. (a linguist has recently assigned the Hittite invasion of Anatolia to this "Indo-European II" wave),[10] and the last ca. 2800 B.C. (it was in this third wave that the Proto-Greeks arrived in Greece). The Aryan invasions of India and Persia, on this theory, occurred much later than the migrations to Europe and were of a different kind.

Although Gimbutas's "Kurgan hypothesis" enjoys high standing among Indo-Europeanists, it is becoming increasingly suspect in archaeological circles. Stuart Piggott finds the thesis "not susceptible of demonstration by direct archaeological evidence, but at best by second-order inferences or sheer assumptions"; he also complains that "where direct archaeological evidence is used to support the 'Kurgan' thesis, it is too often treated in an uncritical, if not tendentious manner."[11] Piggott's special concern was Gimbutas's claim that wheeled vehicles originated in the Eurasian steppe ca. 4500 B.C., and that the innovation was introduced into Europe by invaders who came from the steppe above the Black Sea and the Caucasus (this claim is one of the principal underpinnings of the "Kurgan hypothesis"). Piggott's conclusion is that the diffusion of the wheeled vehicle throughout much of Europe occurred at the end of the fourth or the beginning of the third millennium. In addition, Piggott argues that the diffusion was not the result of invasions from the east: the wheeled vehicle was not invented until late in the fourth millennium, and its spread into much of Eurasia was the result of a "technological explosion," or the rapid adoption of a "rather specialized technological contraption." Another very recent but narrower archaeological study of wheeled vehicles in the Pontic steppe supports Piggott's reservations about the "Kurgan Peoples" as disseminators of wheeled transport. Alexander Häusler con-

10. F. Adrados, "The Archaic Structure of Hittite: The Crux of the Problem," *JIES* 10 (1982): 1–35.

11. S. Piggott, *The Earliest Wheeled Transport: From the Atlantic Coast to the Caspian Sea* (Ithaca, N.Y.: Cornell Univ. Press, 1983), 61.

cludes that neither the wagon in the early third millennium nor the chariot in the early second was pioneered on the Pontic steppe. Häusler's review of the evidence, in fact, argues that the wagon was in use in the Balkans before it was adopted by the peoples above the Black Sea.[12] Finally, David Anthony has now submitted a comprehensive criticism of the "Kurgan hypothesis" from an archaeological and anthropological perspective.[13]

A somewhat eccentric response to the various chronologies that have been proposed for the PIE speakers' migrations, and to the archaeological arguments that undergird these chronologies, was registered by Colin Renfrew, who suggested (although tentatively) that the entire notion of an "Indo-European homeland" was unwarranted: archaeological evidence, he argued, does not indicate that massive migrations *ever* inundated Europe, and perhaps the various Indo-European languages that we find there in the historical period were descended from indigenous Indo-European languages of the neolithic period.[14] Renfrew's suggestion is in some ways a less radical version of Herbert Kühn's thesis that the period of Proto-Indo-European unity must have been the Ice Age, and

12. A. Häusler, "Neue Belege zur Geschichte von Rad und Wagen im nordpontischen Raum," *Ethnogr.-Archäolog. Zeitschrift* 25 (1984): 629–92. On page 675, Häusler comments that the chronological priority of the Balkans over the Pontic steppe in the adoption of wheeled vehicles "ist ein entscheidendes Argument gegen das von Gimbutas vertretene militante Geschichtsbild der alles überrollenden östlichen Erobererscharen."

13. D. W. Anthony, "The 'Kurgan Culture,' Indo-European Origins, and the Domestication of the Horse: A Reconsideration," *Current Anthropology* 27 (1986): 291–304.

14. C. Renfrew, "Problems in the General Correlation of Archaeological and Linguistic Strata in Prehistoric Greece: the Model of Authochthonous Origin," in *Bronze Age Migrations*, ed. Crossland and Birchall, 263–75. A longtime critic of diffusionist theories, Renfrew based his argument entirely on the negative evidence of archaeology. For a linguist's response, see Crossland's comments on Renfrew's paper, ibid., 276–79.

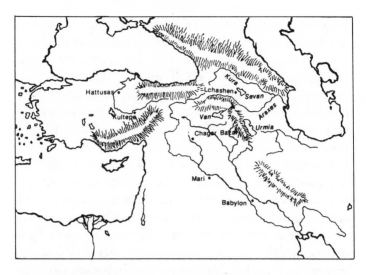

1   Map of the Near East (physical features after Burchard Brentjes, *Drei Jahrtausende Armenien*).

specifically the Aurignacian period.[15] Altogether, scholarly opinion both on the Indo-European homeland and on the time and the nature of the Indo-European movements is in some disarray.

A new direction, however, may have been given to Indo-European studies by a massive study published in 1985. Two Soviet linguists—T. V. Gamkrelidze and V. V. Ivanov—have presented an uneven but plausible case for identifying the land of the PIE speakers with the area just south of the Caucasus: the lands roughly corresponding to what was once Armenia, and to what is now northeastern Turkey, the northwestern tip of Iran, and the Soviet republics of Armenia, Azerbaijan, and Georgia (see map, Fig. 1). Gamkrelidze and Ivanov outlined their rather remarkable thesis in two articles in *Vestnik drevnej*

15. H. Kühn, "Herkunft und Heimat der Indogermanen," *Proceedings of the First International Congress of Prehistoric and Protohistoric Sciences* (London: Oxford Univ. Press, 1932), 237–42.

istorii and have now presented it in full in two large volumes (together running to more than thirteen hundred pages).[16]

It is very clear that Gamkrelidze and Ivanov are at their weakest in dealing with matters of chronology, history, and archaeology. They speak confidently but vaguely about the fourth and fifth millennia B.C. Perhaps because they did not wish to deny entirely Gimbutas's "Kurgan hypothesis" they proposed that Armenia was the Proto-Indo-European homeland *before* some PIE speakers moved north across the Caucasus and settled in the Pontic steppe. According to Gamkrelidze and Ivanov, it was only the "European" branch of the Indo-European family (this branch included Celtic, Italic, Germanic, Baltic, and Slavic) that lived in the Pontic steppe in the third millennium. In the fifth and fourth millennia (before the "European" branch split off from its Hittite-Indo-Iranian-Greek-Armenian fellows), the undivided PIE speakers lived in

16. T. V. Gamkrelidze and V. V. Ivanov, *Indoevropejskij jazyk i indoevropejcy* (*The Indo-European Language and the Indo-Europeans*), 2 vols. (Tbilisi: Tbilisi University, 1985). I am deeply indebted to my colleague, Professor Alice Harris, for calling my attention to this important study and for showing me the galley proofs of John Greppin's *TLS* review. An English translation of the two-volume Russian edition is now being prepared. In the meanwhile, for those of us who are unable to read Russian, the *Journal of Indo-European Studies* devoted the spring and summer issues of its 1985 volume to the thesis, offering not only an English translation of the *Vestnik drevnej istorii* articles, but also vigorous assaults by I. M. Diakonoff and Marija Gimbutas. From *JIES* 13 (1985) I shall make reference to Gamkrelidze and Ivanov, "The Ancient Near East and the Indo-European Question: Temporal and Territorial Characteristics of Proto-Indo-European based on Linguistic and Historico-Cultural Data," 3–48; Gamkrelidze and Ivanov, "The Migrations of Tribes Speaking Indo-European Dialects from their Original Homeland in the Near East to their Historical Habitations in Eurasia," 49–91; I. M. D'iakanov, "On the Original Home of the Speakers of Indo-European," 92–174; Gamkrelidze and Ivanov, "The Problem of the Original Homeland of the Speakers of Indo-European Languages in Response to I. M. Diakonoff's Article," 175–84; M. Gimbutas, "Primary and Secondary Homeland of the Indo-Europeans: Comments on the Gamkrelidze-Ivanov Articles," 185–202.

Armenia. Most of the historical and chronological arguments seem fragile at best, and of those that I am able to judge, some are evidently wrong.[17]

On the other hand, on the questions of how the Indo-European languages are related to each other, and how the Indo-European family is related to other language families, Gamkrelidze and Ivanov may have made a substantial contribution. In its broad lines, their thesis may very well prove attractive to linguists. Not only does it offer a detailed explanation for the influence of Proto-Indo-European upon the southern Caucasian languages (the Kartvelian family), but it also accounts, in a systematic way, for the substantial number of Semitic loanwords in Proto-Indo-European (the English words "horn," "goat," and "wine," for example, are of Semitic origin). In the opinion of one Indo-Europeanist who has reviewed their work, the hypotheses of Gamkrelidze and Ivanov are "the most com-

---

17. Occasionally it is a matter of bad information. For example, at "Migrations," p. 53, Gamkrelidze and Ivanov still tie "the coming of the Greeks" to the appearance of Minyan Ware, and then worsen matters by deriving Minyan Ware from Asia Minor (here following James Mellaart into the ditch). The argument culminates ("Migrations," 54) with the following: "The hypothesis that the Greeks came to mainland Greece from the east across Asia Minor also puts the question of the Greek 'colonies' in Asia Minor, and especially the problem of Miletus, in a new light. In the light of the eastern hypothesis, these 'colonies' may be regarded as very early Greek settlements established along the path of migration of the Greek tribes to their historical habitat on the Aegean Islands and mainland Greece." This proposal that the Ionian cities were settled ca. 2000 B.C. (a wild guess, inspired by the fact of a Late Bronze Age horse burial in Miletus) flies in the face of literary, archaeological, and linguistic evidence on the origins of the Ionian settlements. Unfortunately, it is not unusual for Gamkrelidze and Ivanov to leap from a small and simple fact to a far-reaching and outrageous conclusion. Of a host of instances one may cite the statement ("Problem," 179) that we have "data which prove the presence of ethnic Indo-Europeans in the ancient Near East earlier than the Indo-Aryans, for example, the remains of domesticated horses in Central and East Anatolia (Demirci-Hüyük, Yarikaya, Norsuntepe), dating from the end of IVth millennium B.C."

plex, far-reaching and fully supported of this century and the discussion of them will go on well into the future."[18] At the least, the new thesis will need to be taken into consideration when archaeologists and historians attempt to reconstruct the movements of PIE speakers into the lands where Indo-European languages were spoken in historical times. According to Gamkrelidze and Ivanov, the Greeks came to Greece not from the north but from the east.

On the question of chronology, Indo-European linguistics has less to offer. In the days of Beloch, Breasted, and Meyer, as indicated in Chapter One, the dispersal of "the Indo-European nations" was placed around the middle of the third millennium. In part, a date ca. 2500 B.C. was based on the belief that in its material culture the Indo-European community had not risen above a "Copper Age" level: the initial assumption was that Proto-Indo-European *ayos* was the word for copper, and that no other metal was known to the original Indo-Europeans. That assumption, however, has long since been replaced by the more cautious identification of Proto-Indo-European *ayos with either copper or bronze.[19] In general, the "metals" argument no longer necessarily points to a very early date for the dispersal of the PIE speakers. Even if one interprets *ayos as "copper," one can date the dispersal to the end of the third millennium. For it now appears, as Crossland has observed, that even at the end of the third millennium all of the various areas that have traditionally been proposed as the Indo-European homeland were "at a neolithic or chalcolithic cultural

18. From J. Greppin's review of the two-volume work, in *TLS* (March 14, 1986, p. 278).

19. H. Hirt, *Die Indogermanen. Ihre Verbreitung, ihre Urheimat und ihre Kultur* (Strasburg: Trübner, 1905), 1: 358–59, conceded that the word could have stood for either copper or bronze, but he proposed that because copper was in use earlier than bronze, the Proto-Indo-Europeans' *ayos* probably denoted copper. On the ambiguity of the word, see the entry *aes* in A. Ernout and A. Meillet, *Dictionnaire étymologique de la langue latine* (Paris: Klincksieck, 1939).

level."[20] The same seems to be true for the most recently proposed homeland in Armenia. In the steppes that run along the Kura and the Aras (Araxes) rivers, and around Lakes Sevan, Urmia, and Van, a homogeneous chalcolithic culture from the third millennium has recently come to light.[21] The alternative possibility—that *ayos denoted bronze—would place the splintering of the Proto-Indo-European community in the second millennium, since bronze did not come into common use in any of the putative Urheimat locations until ca. 2000 B.C.

The view that the Proto-Indo-European community broke up no later than ca. 2500 B.C. depends in part on some venerable assumptions about the rate and mechanics of linguistic change. Observing that ca. 1000 B.C. Sanskrit and Greek (as attested in the Vedas and in the Homeric epics) had diverged quite far from each other, nineteenth-century scholars assumed that the dispersal of the Indo-European race must have occurred a very long time before 1000 B.C. It was supposed that each Greek dialect represented one temporal stage in the evolution of the Greek language; since several centuries must have been required for each stage, the earliest Greek dialect (Arcadian, Aeolic, "Achaean," and Ionic were all possibilities) could

---

20. R. A. Crossland, *CAH* I, 2: 828.

21. Archaeological work in this area has barely begun, but what is known suggests a chalcolithic culture lasting at least until the end of the third millennium and perhaps well into the second. James Mellaart notes little more than the obscurity of the area in the third millennium (*CAH* I, 2: 367–69; on page 690 of the same volume, Mellaart indicates that even less is known of eastern Anatolia in the first half of the second millennium). After Mellaart's chapters went to press (his bibliographies include nothing written after 1962), a survey of the relevant material was presented by T. N. Chubinishvili, *Ancient Culture of the Twin Rivers Kura and Araxes* (Tbilisi: Sabchota sakartvelo, 1965; in Georgian, with Russian summary). More accessible for English-speaking scholars is S. Piggott's excellent but very brief summary of this material in "The Earliest Wheeled Vehicles and the Caucasian Evidence," *PPS* 34 (1968): 274ff. For a fuller survey, see C. Burney and D. M. Lang, *The Peoples of the Hills: Ancient Ararat and Caucasus* (London: Weidenfeld and Nicolson, 1971), 14–85.

hardly have come into existence any later than ca. 2000 B.C. The divergence of this original Greek from an original Sanskrit was accordingly placed well back in the third millennium.

Today many linguists are quite aware that linguistic change has not always proceeded at a glacial pace. In preliterate societies, language may change rather rapidly: literature has a conservative influence upon both vocabulary and grammar, and a people without literature might be relatively uninhibited in its linguistic innovation.[22] Arabic, for example, has changed less in thirteen hundred years than some nonliterary languages have changed in the last two centuries. It is quite certain that the rate of linguistic change for Greek was far more rapid before Homer's time than after. The same may have been true for Sanskrit before and after the Vedas were composed.

A specific linguistic argument takes us much further. This argument, most clearly seen and presented by William Wyatt,[23] has been hammered out by specialists on the Greek dialects. Indicating as it does that "the coming of the Greeks"

22. In his retrospect on the several linguistics papers delivered at the First International Colloquium on Aegean Prehistory, held at Sheffield on March 24–26 of 1970, Crossland noted that "a key question in work on all these problems is that of the rate at which linguistic change takes place" (*Bronze Age Migrations*, 330). Crossland goes on to comment that "most studies of language-differentiation within historical periods have been concerned with languages whose rate of change may well have been abnormal, because they were used in the administration of empires or large states, like Latin, or as traditional literary or religious media." The languages of prehistoric societies, Crossland suggests, may have changed much more rapidly than "literary, liturgical and administrative languages" (p. 331).

23. W. F. Wyatt, Jr., "Greek Dialectology and Greek Prehistory," *Acta of the Second International Colloquium on Aegean Prehistory*, 18–22. Wyatt presented the argument here in clear and simple terms (his audience at the colloquium was largely made up of archaeologists), and it is unfortunate that the volume in which it was published has barely been noticed (see Muhly's review of it in *AJA* 79 [1975]: 289–91). Wyatt dealt with some aspects of the same argument, but not with chronological matters, in a detailed and technical study, "The Prehistory of the Greek Dialects," *TAPA* 101 (1970): 557–632.

occurred toward the beginning of the Late Helladic period,[24] it also suggests that the splintering of the Proto-Indo-European community may have been an event of the second millennium rather than of the third (to say nothing of the fourth- and fifth-millennium dates posited in Gimbutas's thesis). Taking temporary leave of the larger problem, let us focus on the more specific question: when did "the Greeks" arrive in Greece?

As noted above, the Greek dialects of historical times were once thought to have arrived in Greece in waves. According to this reconstruction, successive waves of Greeks came from their northern homeland to the Aegean, each bearing with it that form of Greek that was current in the homeland at the time of the wave's departure. Although the theory that three prehistoric dialects corresponded to three waves of invaders held the field for half a century after it was systematically set out by Kretschmer, today it has been abandoned by most specialists. The theory began to unravel in 1954 when Walter Porzig, using a new approach called *Sprachgeographie*, showed that Ionic was not the most ancient Greek dialect, but that it came into being quite late: Arcado-Cypriote and Ionic were both descended from a common "East Greek" dialect of the prehistoric period.[25] Porzig's insight came at an opportune moment. Although Porzig had written his article in 1945, long before the decipherment of the Linear B tablets, the decipherment nicely confirmed and extended his thesis.

The next step was taken by Ernst Risch, who in 1955 abandoned the wave theory altogether.[26] Basing his arguments in

24. Wyatt, "Greek Dialectology," 18, summarizes thus: "the evidence of the Greek dialects and their distribution points to a rather late date, say around 1400, for the introduction of Greek speech to the Peloponnesus." Wyatt concluded that the Greeks were in Thessaly before they appeared in the Peloponnese, but that "we have no linguistic evidence for Greek speech in any part of Greece prior to 1600 B.C."

25. W. Porzig, "Sprachgeographische Untersuchungen zu den griechischen Dialekten," *IF* 61 (1954): 147–69.

26. E. Risch, "Die Gliederung der griechischen Dialekte in neuer

part on Ventris's decipherment of the tablets, Risch proposed that in the Late Helladic period there were only two Greek dialects in Greece. In the Mycenaean south—central Greece, the Peloponnese, and Crete—there was South Greek (Risch's South Greek was the same as Porzig's East Greek; because it was spoken in the southern part of LH Greece, South Greek seems the more appropriate name). The Bronze Age Greeks living north and west of Boeotia spoke a more conservative North Greek dialect. After the Bronze Age ended, Risch showed, Ionic emerged when South Greek speakers came under the influence of North Greek speakers (South Greek survived in a purer form in Arcado-Cypriote). Aeolic, on the same argument, arose from reversed circumstances: some time after 1200 B.C. (the date of the last Linear B tablets), a North Greek substrate was overlaid by a South Greek superstrate (Doric and Northwest Greek preserved more faithfully the North Greek dialect of the Bronze Age). Thus all the dialects of historical times came about through the differentiation and recombination of two prehistoric dialects. And where had these two dialects—North and South Greek—come from? They had, according to Risch, emerged from Common Greek, or Proto-Greek. Their differences were not the result of the passage of time, but of geography. The Greek dialects had arisen *in Greece*. From an original Proto-Greek, the several dialects developed as the language spread over a geographical area too large and politically divided to be linguistically unified.

The explanation of the Greek dialects as geographical deviations from Proto-Greek is now accepted by most students of the Greek dialects (some linguists further afield, however, have thus far ignored it).[27] Among specialists there is now a rough

---

Sicht," *MH* 12 (1955): 61–75. Risch had first advocated the geographical approach to dialect-analysis in "Altgriechische Dialektgeographie?" *MH* 6 (1949): 19–28.

27. The insiders' view has been forcefully stated by Wyatt in "The Prehistory of the Greek Dialects," 558: "We must assume that whatever dialectal variations were to be found within it arose within it, that is, in

consensus that Aeolic developed in eastern Thessaly, which was—as John Chadwick proposed in an important article in 1956—a "buffer zone" between North and South Greek.[28] And most important for our present purposes, it is now generally agreed that this differentiation into dialects had not progressed very far by the end of the Bronze Age, when the Linear B tablets were baked during the burning of the palaces. Specifically, it is now clear that the Ionic dialect did not exist in 1200 B.C.[29] It also appears (although on this point there is more debate)[30] that ca. 1200 B.C. Aeolic and Doric were not yet—or not much—differentiated.[31] Finally, there is considerable agreement that ca. 1200 B.C. North and South Greek were linguistically not very far apart: speakers of North and South Greek were more readily intelligible to each other in the

Greece, and were not imported into Greece by speakers of a later form of Proto-Indo-European. We must be very clear about this and not imagine, as older generations of scholars were sometimes tempted to do, a series of Indo-European incursions into Greece: the Greek dialects arose on the soil of Greece." It is not surprising that linguists who have not specialized in the Greek dialects are not well informed about recent directions in that branch of the discipline. Gamkrelidze and Ivanov, for example, still assume ("Ancient Near East," 7–8) that "by the middle of the second millennium B.C., the Arcadian, Ionian and Aeolian dialects already existed as distinct entities." They also suppose ("Migrations," 81 n. 16) that by the end of the third millennium "Proto-Greek . . . must have been differentiated into its basic dialect groups somewhere in Asia Minor before the Greeks migrated to mainland Greece."

28. J. Chadwick, "The Greek Dialects and Greek Pre-History," *Greece and Rome* n.s. 3 (1956): 38–50.

29. Cf. ibid., 44: "round about 1000 B.C. a dialect of the Arcadian type came for a period under Doric influence; but this soon ceased, and the dialect continued its development separately. . . . The Ionic invasion of Greece is a fiction."

30. The argument on behalf of the thesis has been made most fully by J. L. García-Ramón, *Les Origines postmycéniennes du groupe dialectal éolien* (Salamanca: Universidad de Salamanca, 1975).

31. Risch, "Die Gliederung," 71, concluded that not a single one of the differentia between those two dialects can with certainty be dated before ca. 1200 B.C.

twelfth century B.C. than were Dorians and Ionians in the seventh century B.C.[32] Altogether, the new linguistic argument indicates that "the historical Greek dialects are so akin that no more than a few centuries are allowed for their differentiation."[33] It is, in short, quite incredible that the process of differentiation into dialects—a process that operated to great effect in the four centuries between the end of the Bronze Age and the composition of the Homeric epics—could have begun a thousand years before 1200 B.C. One is therefore not surprised to find that among students of the Greek dialects there is—as Wyatt noted in his short and trenchant article on the subject—a tendency to favor 1600 B.C. as the date for the Indo-Europeanization of Greece.[34]

If linguistic arguments weigh heavily against the early dates for "the coming of the Greeks," what is the archaeological support for an early date? Minyan pottery, the original support for the thesis that the Greeks arrived in Greece ca. 1900 B.C., at the beginning of the Middle Helladic period, is no longer perceived as a break in the ceramic evolution on the mainland. Instead, it is now generally acknowledged to have been a development from, and a proliferation of, the gray ware that Caskey found in EH III levels at Lerna, and that has turned up in

32. J. Chadwick, "Aegean History 1500–1200 BC," *Studii Classice* 11 (1969): 7ff.; A. Bartoněk, "The Place of the Dorians in the Late Helladic World," in *Bronze Age Migrations*, ed. Crossland and Birchall, 308–10.

33. Sp. Marinatos, "The First Mycenaeans in Greece," in *Bronze Age Migrations*, ed. Crossland and Birchall, 109. Marinatos was not entirely in sympathy with the new arguments and rather curiously cautioned that "only when linguistic arguments do not contradict the archaeological evidence may they be adduced as a welcome help towards the solution of the problem."

34. Wyatt, "The Indo-Europeanization of Greece," 95–96. His statement that "linguists" tend to favor the lower date, however, needs some qualification: although the tendency can be observed among specialists in Greek linguistics, most comparatists of the Indo-European languages do not seem to share in it.

the same levels elsewhere in the northern Peloponnese and on the island of Euboea. Jeremy Rutter goes so far as to say that the EH III gray ware "is universally recognized to be the direct ancestor of MH Gray Minyan."[35] That is not literally the case, since some scholars still adhere to Blegen's assumption that Minyan Ware was suddenly brought into Greece ca. 1900 B.C. by the first Greeks; but there is no doubt that the old view is on the way out. It now appears that late in the third millennium, potters learned how to make pottery that resembled silver vessels. The gray color and the highly burnished exterior of the pots were important in producing this effect (the same technique in imitation of gold resulted in "Yellow Minyan"), and within a rather narrow range of shapes the new style achieved a sudden popularity in the northern Peloponnese and in Euboea. Rutter finds it likely that "production was in the hands of a relatively small group of specialized potters, resident at a number of sites, who had a monopoly on such technological innovations as the fast wheel and the ability to achieve the controlled reducing conditions necessary to fire this ceramic."[36] Early in the second millennium, production of the new pottery spread rapidly into Attica, Boeotia, southern Thessaly, and other places. Thus Minyan Ware no longer testifies to a Greek Volkswanderung into Greece ca. 1900 B.C.

With the argument from pottery discounted, the case for dating "the coming of the Greeks" ca. 1900 B.C. must fall back on the fact that five mainland sites show a destruction level at that date.[37] That is one more than can be counted at 1600 B.C., but one less than is attested for 2100 B.C. Since the total number of sites with legible stratigraphy is not more than ten at any of the three interfaces, we may safely assume that quite a lot of destruction occurred on all three occasions. The

35. J. B. Rutter, "Fine Gray-Burnished Pottery of the Early Helladic III Period: The Ancestry of Gray Minyan," *Hesperia* 52 (1983): 349.

36. Ibid., 351.

37. The five are Argos and Berbati in the Argolid, Eleusis and Haghios Stephanos in Attica, and Eutresis in Boeotia. See van Royen and Isaac, *Arrival*, Table 2, at p. 57.

statistical argument can in fact be said to favor the latest of the three dates, since all four of the sites with legible stratigraphy at the juncture of MH and LH I show a destruction level at that point.[38]

When the material culture of a place is not much different after a destruction than it was before, the destruction is more reasonably attributed to a local conflict or disaster than to an invasion from afar. On this criterion, there is almost nothing to suggest that ca. 1900 B.C. the Greeks entered Greece from a distant Indo-European homeland. Along with Minyan Ware, other features of Middle Helladic material life seem to continue EH III traditions. The EH III settlements were without exception also occupied in the MH period. The architecture of the two periods is very similar, as are the artifacts of metal, stone and bone. Finally, the burial customs of the MH period seem to continue those of the EH III period. In brief, it is difficult to find anything "alien" in the material record of Middle Helladic Greece.[39]

The cultural innovations at the beginning of EH III, on the other hand, are significant; and coming on the heels of destruction, they make it not unlikely that the Argolid was invaded ca. 2100 B.C. Contrary to Caskey's initial expectations, however, the invasion of 2100 B.C. has not yet manifested any links to lands that could conceivably be designated as the Indo-European homeland. Since scholars had so long assumed that when one finds Minyan Ware one has found Greeks, Caskey reasonably concluded that the presence of Proto-Minyan Ware meant that Proto-Greeks were present in Lerna during the EH III period. It now seems that Proto-Minyan Ware was an invention of Early Helladic potters, specifically of potters in central Greece.[40] There may well have been an invasion of the Argolid

38. The point is made by van Royen and Isaac, ibid., 45.

39. Cf. Howell, "The Origins of Middle Helladic Culture," 73–79.

40. Rutter, "Fine Gray-Burnished Pottery," presents the argument in detail. He concludes (p. 349) that the EH III Gray Ware originated as "a formal and technological synthesis of Anatolianizing and central Greek elements which occurred in central Greece" during the EH II period.

ca. 2100 B.C, but if there was, the invasion would have originated not in some distant Indo-European Urheimat, but in nearby Boeotia.[41]

Taken together, the archaeological evidence in no way supports a thesis that the Greeks arrived in Greece ca. 2100 or ca. 1900 B.C. The vogue that the EH III date has recently enjoyed is simply a result of the fact that the grounds for the old consensus—that the arrival of the Greeks occurred ca. 1900 B.C.—have been undermined. The argument on behalf of either date ultimately depends on an erroneous observation and a dubious presupposition. The observation, made by Wace and Blegen and recently shown to be incorrect, is that Minyan Ware was an invaders' ware that broke in upon the otherwise steady evolution of mainland pottery. The dubious presupposition is that any significant movement of people will be detectible in the pottery record. This assumption, which was scarcely questioned in Blegen's day, is no longer unchallenged. Certain migrations, about whose reality the literary records leave no doubt, seem to have introduced nothing that can be detected by achaeologists. Thus the Ostrogothic and Hunnic invasions of the Roman Empire, or the slightly later Slavic migrations into Greece and other parts of the Balkan peninsula, left virtually no material documentation. Even more dramatic is the complete absence throughout the Peloponnese of any intrusive pottery style or decoration corresponding to the Dorian Invasion (although this analogy will obviously have no force for those scholars who, precisely because it is not ceramically attested, deny that there was a Dorian Invasion).[42]

Historians therefore have good reason today to be wary of the assumption, promoted in some of the early archaeological

41. Cf. ibid., 349–50: "The source of such an immigrant population, it is now becoming clear, must have been central Greece in general and probably Boiotia in particular."

42. Since they concerned themselves only with pre-Mycenaean pottery, Blegen and Wace did not deal with the presence or absence of a Dorian pottery in the material record of the twelfth century B.C.

literature, that every ethnic group must be identifiable by its own peculiar pottery. If such a requirement is waived, the possibility that "the coming of the Greeks" occurred ca. 1600 B.C., at the beginning of the Late Helladic period, becomes far more serious. The principal argument against the later date has been that no pottery that could conceivably be regarded as specifically Greek was introduced into Greece at that time[43] (the Minoanizing pottery of the shaft graves is another matter, to which we shall return).

In conclusion, the arguments for dating "the coming of the Greeks" either to 2100 B.C. or to 1900 B.C. are deeply flawed. The archaeological evidence does not indicate an immigration into the Greek mainland at the beginning of the EH III period, and linguistic considerations virtually exclude the possibility that the Greeks could have come to Greece at so early a date.[44] A date at the beginning of the MH period, while not quite so vulnerable to the linguistic arguments, has now lost entirely the archaeological basis on which alone it depends. The third possibility—that the Greeks arrived in Greece ca. 1600 B.C., at the beginning of the Late Helladic period—becomes attractive by default, and we shall come back to it after examining in some detail related matters in the Near East.

43. For example, in his otherwise excellent book, *Mycenaean Greece* (London: Routledge and Kegan Paul, 1976), J. T. Hooker devotes only half a page to the possibility that the Greeks arrived in Greece ca. 1600 B.C., and states (p. 16) that "it can be discounted on purely archaeological grounds . . . because no archaeological break is discernible at the end of Middle Helladic: at least, no break so serious or so widespread as to give any indication of the arrival of a new people. The facts were set out by Mylonas . . . and they constitute an insuperable obstacle to the class of theory under discussion here."

44. They do not, however, exclude the possibility of someone *proposing* a date ca. 2100 B.C., or indeed much earlier. See, for example, Gimbutas, "Primary and Secondary Homeland of the Indo-Europeans," 200: "The very latest arrival for Indo-Europeans in Greece can be set in Early Helladic II times, sometime between 2900 and 2600 B.C."

FOUR

Considerations from Near Eastern History

The question we have been worrying about thus far is "When did the Greeks arrive in Greece?" No less important than the date, however, is the nature of "the coming of the Greeks." Meyer, Beloch, and Breasted imagined it as a massive movement of pastoralists, and in many quarters that is how it is imagined today: a large, disadvantaged (and probably dispossessed) nation on the move, coming from the pasture lands of the Eurasian steppe, descends into the Balkan peninsula and makes the place Greek. A smallish company, numbering only a few thousand, would have been overwhelmed or turned back; thus, it is necessary to imagine a migratory nation large and cohesive enough to prevail. In this picture, a human tide inundates the land: whether or not the indigenous population is spared, the arrival of the Greeks represents an ethnic transformation of the Greek mainland. Now, it is possible that such a picture is valid, but it is also possible that the hellenization of Greece happened in a very different way. These other possibilities are suggested by a review of the history of the known world in the late third and early second millennia.

During the period from 2500 to 1500 B.C., literary sources from the Near East describe a great deal of destruction, death, and upheaval, but few instances of a massive and destructive migration by a primitive or pastoral people. An example of an overwhelming folk migration would be the Magyar descent into what is now Hungary, and what was then Great Moravia, at the end of the ninth century. Of this kind of thing the literary sources for our period know nothing. Archaeological evidence has been interpreted to indicate a recurring pattern of such migrations, but this may be in part because the early archaeological literature assumed that every new pottery style testified to the arrival of a new ethnic group.

Although the copious records of the late third and early second millennia describe no massive and sudden migration of a primitive nation, they do speak of gradual infiltrations by nomadic or barbarian peoples. It was in this way that the "Amorites" (*amurru*, lit. "westerners") arrived in Mesopotamia from the twentieth to the seventeenth centuries. Although occasionally the immigration of "westerners" from the Levant became such a nuisance that an imperial king might set up a wall to prevent their entrance, most of the time Amorite immigration was accepted as part of the natural order of things. After a particular group of Amorites had attached itself to a city's periphery, its members would typically find menial employment (often being hired by the city's king as soldiers) in their new home. The more ambitious would learn Akkadian, rise in status, and eventually one might succeed in making himself king and establishing a dynasty. Thus, for example, we find that Hammurabi's "westerner" dynasty in Babylon was Akkadianized at least in its official language, but retained Amorite personal names.

A similar infiltration occurred with the westward and southward drift of people from what cuneiform sources called "the land of Hurri" (somewhere in southern Armenia or northeastern Mesopotamia)[1] during the late third and early second mil-

---

1. R. T. O'Callaghan, *Aram Naharaim. A Contribution to the History of Upper Mesopotamia in the Second Millennium B.C.* (Rome: Pontificium Institutum Biblicum, 1948), 80, concluded that at least for part of the second millennium, Hurri was one of the several synonyms (Hanigalbat and Naharin being others) for Mitanni. However, "the land of Hurri," seems to exhibit a certain southward drift in the sources, and it may be that in the late third millennium the land of Hurri was somewhat to the north of the later Mitanni.

lennia. The "Hurrian" language was neither Semitic nor Indo-European, nor does it seem to have been related to Kassite or Hattic. In the middle of the second millennium, Hurrian was the principal language in the Great Kingdom of Mitanni, which stretched across the Mesopotamian plain between Nineveh and Carchemish; and in the first millennium, an offshoot of Hurrian was the language of Urartu, the mountainous country around and south of Lake Van and Lake Urmia. Wherever their homeland may have been, Hurrian speakers had already begun drifting toward the centers of civilization by the Akkadian period: at Chagar Bazar, on the Habur River, tablets from that period include Hurrian names.[2] In the Ur III period (2113–2006 B.C.), Hurrians began what Ignace Gelb described as "their peaceful infiltration of Babylonia."[3] Soon after 2000 B.C., people with Hurrian names turn up in the Kültepe tablets in Cappadocia, and by the time of Hammurabi, people whose names were Hurrian (and who presumably spoke Hurrian as well as the language of their new home) were numerous in most of the cities of northern Mesopotamia and eastern Syria. It is, then, no surprise that by the middle of the second millennium the Hurrian language was dominant in Mitanni.

This movement of Hurrian speakers, strung out over five or six centuries, was obviously no "invasion" or Volkswanderung in the usual sense of that word. Like the amurru who made their way into Mesopotamia, the "Hurrians" who at this time moved into central Asia Minor or into the northern arc of the Fertile Crescent were part of no national movement. As individuals or as small communities, they were drawn toward a higher civilization than they had at home (although at the same time, of course, bringing change to their adopted cities, in the form of a new language, new gods, and new traditions).

It is possible that still another infiltration, this time involv-

2. C. J. Gadd, "Tablets from Chagar Bazar and Tall Brak, 1937–38," *Iraq* 7 (1940): 27–28.

3. I. F. Gelb, *Hurrians and Subarians* (Chicago: Univ. of Chicago Press, 1944), 89.

ing people whose language was related to the Indo-European family, affected the central and north central region of Asia Minor (known during the Bronze Age as "Hatti") during the third millennium. The evidence for this we shall need to look at in some detail, since questionable assumptions about a "Hittite invasion" of central Anatolia have long muddied the scholarly waters. It has often been supposed that a Hittite nation, the first to splinter off from the Indo-European community, made its way southward and "invaded" Asia Minor some time late in the third millennium or early in the second. In his valuable work, *The Hittites*, Oliver Gurney wrote without qualification that "the Indo-European Hittite language was superimposed on the non-Indo-European Hattian by an invading people," and suggested that this invasion had already occurred by the time of Naram-Sin (ca. 2250 B.C.).[4] Other authorities place the purported invasion ca. 2000 B.C., or even later.[5] Let

4. O. Gurney, *The Hittites* (Harmondsworth: Penguin, 1961), 18; at page 69 Gurney suggests that according to the linguistic evidence "a group of Indo-European immigrants became dominant over an aboriginal race of 'Hattians.' "

5. H. A. Hoffner, "The Hittites and Hurrians," in *Peoples of Old Testament Times*, ed. D. J. Wiseman (Oxford: Clarendon, 1973), states that "the immigrant Indo-Europeans . . . arrived about 2000 B.C. on the central plateau of Asia Minor" (p. 197). H. Otten, "Das Hethiterreich," in *Kulturgeschichte des Alten Orients*, ed. H. Schmökel (Stuttgart: Kröner, 1961), concludes that the invasion had taken place by the eighteenth century B.C., but notes that it is uncertain whether the *Wanderweg* of these first Indo-Europeans had been by way of the Dardanelles or the Caspian Gates (p. 333). Mellaart, *CAH* I, 2: 703, will have none of this: "The general opinion that Hittites, Luwians, Palaeans all migrated simultaneously into Anatolia at the end of the Early Bronze Age, c. 1900 B.C., a theory not disputed until 1958, is flatly contradicted by archaeological evidence." Mellaart, as we have seen in the preceding chapter, placed a Luwian invasion of Anatolia ca. 2300 B.C., and he argued that the Luwians came to Anatolia from Thrace; as for the Hittites, Mellaart concluded (on archaeological grounds) that they came to central Anatolia from the east, and that they arrived between 2000 and 1950 B.C. Mellaart's theory is in turn (and in the same *CAH* volume) roughly handled by Crossland, who argues (*CAH*

us examine the evidence for this "Hittite invasion" and for the existence of a Hittite nation.

In the second millennium, three closely related languages—Luwian, Palaic, and the so-called Hittite language—were spoken in central and western Asia Minor. These languages, of which "Hittite" is far and away the best documented (although it was perhaps not the most widespread), appear to have evolved from a single "Proto-Anatolian" language. Proto-Anatolian was in turn either a daughter or a sister language of Proto-Indo-European, but it has little of the family resemblance that one finds in most of the Indo-European languages. Alongside some early enthusiasm for Hittite as an Indo-European language was a skepticism that Hittite was Indo-European at all. Not only did very little Hittite vocabulary derive from Indo-European roots, but even in morphology and grammar Hittite lacked some features that were common to all or most of the Indo-European languages. In Hittite there was no comparative degree of the adjective, and no feminine gender.[6] Even stranger, by Indo-European standards, is the Hittite verb. It lacked the aorist and perfect tenses, and the optative and subjunctive moods. Whereas the Indo-European verb system seems to have begun in complexity and to have evolved toward simplicity, the verb in Hittite was as simple as in modern French.

For Indo-Europeanists, all of this presented a dilemma. Unless some relationship between Hittite and the Indo-European languages was admitted, one could hardly explain why Hittite resembled these languages in a number of important ways. On the other hand, if one chose to include Hittite in the Indo-

---

1, 2: 841–45) that Luwian and Hittite were so similar that they could not possibly have entered Asia Minor from opposite ends, four hundred years apart.

6. J. Puhvel, "Dialectal Aspects of the Anatolian Branch of Indo-European," in *Ancient Indo-European Dialects*, ed. H. Birnbaum and J. Puhvel (Berkeley: Univ. of California Press, 1966), 237. On the entire question, see Baldi, *An Introduction to the Indo-European Languages*, 151–64.

European family, one was forced to pare drastically the common denominators of that family, and to revise even the basic
definitions of what the hypothetical Proto-Indo-European had
been. An expedient course was to keep the name "Indo-European" for the languages conventionally included under that ru-
bric, and to suppose that Hittite (or, on our present understanding, Proto-Anatolian) had at a very early date separated
itself from the community out of which—many centuries
later—the truly Indo-European languages would come. As a
convenient name for the parent stem from which Hittite and
the Indo-European languages would have successively
emerged, E. H. Sturtevant proposed "Indo-Hittite."[7]

An alternative to the Indo-Hittite hypothesis is to suppose
that the creators of Proto-Anatolian left the PIE speakers' fold
no earlier than did the creators of the mainline Indo-European
languages, but that for some reason Proto-Anatolian innovated
much more rapidly and thoroughly than did its siblings. Until
very recently this reconstruction has had more support than has
Sturtevant's among Indo-Europeanists.[8] There is little doubt
that Proto-Anatolian was a rampant innovator. Much more of
the Hittite vocabulary is borrowed than inherited, and the
simplicity of the Hittite verb is most reasonably attributed to
the loss of moods and tenses in Hittite (the other Indo-European languages being in this respect far more conservative).

Quite obviously, however, the likelihood that Proto-Ana-

7. E. H. Sturtevant, "The Relationship of Hittite to Indo-European," *TAPA* 60 (1929): 25–37; see also Sturtevant's 1938 lecture, eventually published as "The Indo-Hittite Hypothesis" in *Language* 38 (1962):
105–10.

8. In the last few years, perhaps, the trend has been reversed. Adrados, "The Archaic Structure of Hittite," 1, presents his study as a contribution to "the ever more widely accepted thesis of the archaic structure of
Hittite within the context of those IE languages known to us." For a detailed study of the problem, see E. Neu and W. Meid, eds., *Hethitisch und
Indogermanisch: Vergleichende Studien zur historischen Grammatik und zur dialektgeographischen Stellung der indogermanische Sprachgruppe Kleinasiens* (Innsbruck: Innsbruck Institut für Sprachwissenschaft der Universität, 1979).

tolian was a rampant innovator could be a supplement rather than an alternative to the Indo-Hittite hypothesis. That Sanskrit, Greek, and Latin have much more in common with each other than any of the three has with Hittite might in fact be most easily explained by a combination of the two hypotheses: (1) at a very early date, a single linguistic trunk divided into two, one of which was to evolve into Proto-Anatolian, the other into Proto-Indo-European, and (2) the Proto-Anatolian trunk was much more susceptible to innovation than was the Proto-Indo-European trunk or any of its eventual branches.

However Proto-Anatolian came to be what it was, at the end of the third millennium many of the people in Hatti, or central Anatolia, spoke a (or the) Proto-Anatolian language, although they perhaps also spoke something else. The evidence for Proto-Anatolian speakers in Hatti at this time comes in the form of Proto-Anatolian personal names, and a few loan-words, in the tablets of Assyrian merchants resident at Kültepe, a hundred miles south of Boghazköy. In 1900 B.C., however, people whose first language was Proto-Anatolian were a minority in the Kültepe area, where the traditional language of the cult centers was Hattic, a language that (unlike the Proto-Anatolian languages) has no relation to Indo-European.[9] In Hatti,

9. Although no inscriptions in Hattic have been found anywhere (presumably Hattic speakers never became literate in their language), the number of Hattic-looking names in the Kültepe tablets is considerable. In a close study of the personal names and the place names in the tablets, E. Bilgiç ("Die Ortsnamen der 'kappadokischen' Urkunden im Rahmen der alten Sprachen Anatoliens," *Archiv für Orientforschung* 15 [1945–1951]: 1–37) found that most of the names appeared to be either Hattic or characteristic of the pre-Luwian language of southern and southwest Asia Minor, and that a minority were Hittite or Hurrian. In one and the same family, however, names belonging to several of the language communities were attested, and often a single personal name or place name combined elements from two languages. As for the principal language of ancient Kültepe, Bilgiç, declared (p. 17) a *non liquet*: "Welche Sprache in dieser gemischten Bevölkerung zur Zeit der Handelskolonie gesprochen wurde, lässt sich dem unzureichenden Material nicht entnehmen."

some men with Proto-Anatolian names seem to have risen to high position, and even to the kingship of one city or another.[10] Most, however, were to be found at the lower levels of society. Whether princes or paupers, individuals with Proto-Anatolian names were by 1900 B.C. fully integrated in the life of the central Anatolian cities. It thus may be that well before 1900 B.C. a fair number of Proto-Anatolian speakers (numerous enough to make Proto-Anatolian a commonly heard language at Kültepe and elsewhere) had migrated to Hatti. Whence they may have come is not known. It is possible that in the third millennium Proto-Anatolian was spoken over most of the Anatolian plateau; if so, it may have been introduced into Hatti from the west or even the south. Wherever it may have proceeded from, there is no reason to suppose that this migration would have differed from that of Hurrians or Amorites in the third and early second millennia. In each case we would be dealing with small groups who leave a more primitive and less urbanized life and take up residence in or on the fringes of cities or towns. Kültepe (ancient Kanesh?), like most Near Eastern cities of the time, was a multilingual community, and nationalism was of little concern.

That a Proto-Anatolian or Hittite nation invaded central Asia Minor ca. 2000 B.C. seems to be a scholarly construct, encouraged by the belief that the Greek nation invaded Greece at about the same time. Eighty years ago, scholars were already curious about the "racial" affinities of what were then the "mysterious Hittites," and various anthropological arguments were advanced about the physiognomy (especially the prominent nose) and the physical traits of Hittites portrayed by ancient artists. When Hrozny and Sommer showed that the Hittite language had Indo-European affiliations, the immediate and undisputed inference was that the Hittites were invaders, who had come to Asia Minor from afar. Where they had come

10. H. Lewy, *CAH* I, 2: 716, lists the kinglets Peruwa of Kushshar and Warpa and Warshama of Kanesh as "either Hittites or Luwians."

from was less clear, and the answer depended on one's beliefs about the Indo-European homeland. In his 1928 revision of *Geschichte des Alterums*, Meyer declared it virtually certain that they had come across the Caucasus from a homeland in central Asia, and had done so around the middle of the third millennium.[11] On the other hand, Louis Delaporte and Eugene Cavaignac routed them via the Bosporus from a "patrie septentrionale."[12] No evidence—archaeological, linguistic, or documentary—was advanced in behalf of either view, and no historian even suggested that such evidence was necessary. That nothing Indo-European could have been indigenous to Asia Minor was simply assumed by all scholars, whether orientalists, Indo-Europeanists, or historians. If the Hittites were Indo-European, at some time and some place the Hittite nation must have invaded Asia Minor.

The thesis of Gamkrelidze and Ivanov—that Proto-Indo-European developed in Armenia—now suggests a rather different explanation for the appearance of Proto-Anatolian speakers in Hatti. Many centuries before 2000 B.C., what until then had been a single linguistic continuum—possibly stretching from the Caspian to the Aegean—may have broken in two, one of the two portions falling under those linguistic influences that differentiated Proto-Anatolian from the more conservative stream that evolved into Proto-Indo-European.

At any rate, it was from a Proto-Anatolian area of Asia Minor that migrants came to Hatti. This movement was certainly not an invasion. The fact that ca. 1900 B.C. Proto-Anatolian

---

11. Meyer, *Geschichte des Alterums*, 2d ed. Vol. 2, pt. 1, 22–23. Meyer argued that since the Hittites would not have been so foolish as to prefer the Anatolian plateau to the fertile Balkans we can be sure that they came to Anatolia from central Asia ("Dass sie in derselben Weise, wie später die Kimmerier, über den Kaukasus gekommen sind, wird man kaum bezweifelm können, da sie sich sonst gewiss in den reichen Ebenen des Westens angesiedelt haben würden").

12. L. Delaporte, *Les Hittites* (Paris: La Renaissance du Livre, 1936), 54–55; E. Cavaignac, *Les Hittites* (Paris: Maisonneuve, 1950), 15.

speakers were an integral element of Hattic society, while Hattic continued to be the language of the cults, shows clearly enough that the Proto-Anatolian speakers had not entered Hatti in a violent invasion or a massive Volkswanderung. Immigrants there evidently had been, and perhaps even a steady and—to some—unwelcome flow of Proto-Anatolian speakers into Hatti for an extended period in the third millennium. But whatever migration had occurred would have been a movement of individuals, or families, or small groups.[13] No Proto-Anatolian or Hittite *nation* is known to have migrated anywhere.

Such are the relocations of barbarous or primitive peoples attested in documents for the late third and the early second millennium (the seventeenth and sixteenth centuries are something of a dark age, from which few documents survive). This is not the sort of thing that most of us have envisaged for "the coming of the Greeks," and I do not suggest that this is how the Greeks did indeed come to Greece. It was, however, the normal way in which nomadic peoples moved into settled regions in the Early and Middle Bronze Age, and provides us with a useful point of reference.

Another phenomenon attested (although rarely) in our souces is barbarian harassment. The Mesopotamian cities were tempting targets for raiders in the late third and early second millenium. Beginning ca. 2200 B.C., raiders from Gutium (along the Zagros mountains) began to harass the cities in the plain, and continued to do so for over a century. Shortly before 2000 B.C., the less barbarous but equally fearsome Elamites pillaged and destroyed Ur itself, the bulwark of southern Mesopotamia.

Much more frequent than harassment by the godless barbar-

13. On the implications of the occasional evidence for the Hittite language in the Kültepe tablets, cf. Bilgiç, "Ortsnamen," 18: "Diese geringen Spuren des indogermanischen Hethitisch möchten wir im Gegensatz zu anderen nicht als Zeugnisse für einen zur Kolonistenzeit schon bestehenden hethitischen Staat, sondern vielmehr einer beginnenden Infiltration deuten."

ians was the pious harassment by would-be Great Kings. The precedent for imperial rule had been set by Sargon of Akkad and was rarely forgotten. City kings with ambitions to become Great Kings (that is, to make other city kings their subjects) were a feature of the age when Hammurabi was king of Babylon. On the standard chronology, which I shall follow in this essay, Hammurabi reigned from 1792 until 1750 B.C. (in the low chronology, those dates must be lowered by sixty-four years). During his reign, Hammurabi, Rim-Sin of Larsa, Shamshi-Adad of Ashur, and Zimri-Lim of Mari all demonstrated their valor and their piety by "going forth" to commit mayhem. The thinking behind this was that the gods intended one of the Mesopotamian kings to hold hegemony over the others, and competition was keen among the kings to determine who was the divine favorite. Once in motion, the game spilled over into the Levant and Asia Minor, and the phenomenon culminated with the first two imperial Hittite kings, Hattusilis and Mursilis. Hattusilis I crossed the Taurus range into Syria in order to sack Aleppo and Alalakh, and his successor became a legend by traveling almost a thousand miles in 1595 B.C. to sack, ironically, Babylon.

Although it may seem pointless and artificial to define yet another general phenomenon, I believe it is worthwhile to distinguish what might be called a "takeover" both from the barbarian raid and from the pious atrocity that a Great King might commit against a city that did not acknowledge his imperial rule. For purposes of this essay, I shall use the term "takeover" for those occasions when outsiders came neither to plunder nor to extend an imperial network, but rather to establish control over a population. We must imagine (documents furnish no details) that the takeover was usually a violent coup d'état, but that evidently it was aimed specifically at the reigning king and his army and must have spared the general population. The man who took over seems regularly to have presented himself as a champion and a servant of the local gods. What distinguishes our takeover from a common coup d'état or palace revolution is that the takeover is accomplished by a force that is essentially alien to the city or land being taken over. Takeovers of this sort seem to have occurred with unusual frequency toward the middle of the second millennium B.C.

The most familiar (though in some ways also the most obscure) of these takeovers may be the so-called Hyksos conquest of Egypt. The extinction of the Twelfth Dynasty in 1786 B.C. seems to have led to rival claimants for the Egyptian throne, and eventually to a fragmentation of the kingdom. Perhaps as early as ca. 1700 B.C., ambitious Amorite princes from the Levant began to make themselves lords of small portions of Lower Egypt. Their "kingdoms" must have been tiny, since some two hundred men were, or claimed to be, "kings" in the period between 1786 and ca. 1550 B.C. All of these Asiatic princes were called *hyksos* by the Egyptians (the word meant nothing more than "foreign chiefs," but has become a nationality in some histories). Eventually, however, a heterogeneous group of Asiatics established a royal house at Avaris, in the very northeastern corner of the Delta. This regime (Manetho's Fifteenth Dynasty) had at least pretensions of ruling the entire land and did extend its dominion over all of Lower Egypt and into many of the nomes of Upper Egypt. These "Great Hyksos," whose ethnic identity has troubled many investigators (the names appear to be mostly Amorite, but some seem to be Hurrian and a very few may be Aryan), were able to maintain their regime at Avaris for several generations, being finally expelled by Ahmose of Thebes, founder of the Eighteenth Dynasty, in the eleventh year of his reign at Thebes (probably 1541 B.C.).[14] Although the Great Hyksos tried to assimilate themselves to the country they ruled and supposed themselves

14. The chronological table in *CAH* II, 1: 819, indicates a date some twenty years earlier. That the accession of Ahmose should be placed in 1552 B.C., and his expulsion of the Great Hyksos in 1541 B.C., is argued cogently by M. Bietak, "Problems of Middle Bronze Age Chronology: New Evidence from Egypt," *AJA* 88 (1984): 471–85.

to be the legitimate rulers of the land, they were castigated as interlopers by their Theban adversaries.

A more cleanly defined takeover occurred in Babylon soon after the city was raided by Mursilis the Hittite. Two or three years after 1595 B.C., a Kassite took over Babylon (and apparently most of southern Mesopotamia), establishing a dynasty that was to last almost four centuries. Its durability was in large part the result of the fact that the Kassite rulers were quickly Babylonianized, and one assumes that they had taken over southern Mesopotamia with little or no bloodshed. The Kassite language is known only from a few texts, the personal names of the rulers, and a few words that later Babylonian scholars included in their lexical lists. From the scant evidence, Kassite seems to have been unrelated to any known language. Circumstantial evidence, however, suggests that the Kassites were once neighbors of the PIE speakers. Although the Kassites were assiduous in their piety toward the deities of Mesopotamia, they also worshipped several gods dear to the Aryans.[15]

Another takeover, or cluster of takeovers, occurred in the Levant. Throughout this area, from the Upper Euphrates to southern Palestine, intruders from afar seem to have gained control of cities and districts about the middle of the second millennium. Many of the intruders had Hurrian or—more remarkably—Aryan names ("Aryan" is here used in the technical sense of "Indo-Iranian," that is, belonging to the Indo-Iranian branch of the Indo-European family of languages).[16] Unfortu-

15. Some specialists have suspected that Kassite may have been an Indo-European language, but the evidence is apparently very slight. What evidence there is has been assembled by K. Balkan, *Kassitenstudien I: Die Sprache der Kassiten* (Amer. Orient. Ser., no. 37) (New Haven: Amer. Orient. Soc., 1954). For a general assessment, see Margaret S. Drower, *CAH* II, 1: 437–39.

16. For a detailed study of the names, see M. Mayrhofer, *Die Indo-Arier im Alten Vorderasien* (Wiesbaden: Harrassowitz, 1966), and the same author's "Zur kritischen Sichtung vorderasiatisch-arischer Personennamen," *IF* 70 (1965): 146–63. Mayrhofer finally settles on 114 personal names as being "very likely" Aryan.

nately, the takeovers themselves are not documented (presumably they occurred during the *hyksos* occupation of Egypt). But records from the Egyptian New Kingdom reveal the situation in the aftermath of the takeovers. The Amarna letters show that in the early fourteenth century most of the important cities of Palestine and Syria were controlled by men with either Aryan or Hurrian names. At Ugarit the kings have Semitic names, but their military force includes many men of Hurrian descent. Among the Aryan princes of Palestine whose doings are detailed in the Amarna letters, we find an Indaruta as lord of Achshaph: this kinglet "bears the same Indo-Aryan name as his contemporary Indrota or Indrauta of the Rig Veda."[17] Aryan names are also attested for the princes of Megiddo (Biridiya), Ashkelon (Widia), the Hebron area (Shuwardata), Acre (Zatatna and Surata), Damascus (Biryawaza), and other places. The kinglet of Jerusalem has a Hurrian name (Abdu-Heba), as do several of his colleagues.

Obviously, speakers of Aryan and Hurrian had come to the Levant, but it is just as obvious that we are not dealing here with a Volkswanderung or even with an infiltration similar to those described a few pages earlier. Of the general population of the Levant in the fourteenth century B.C., so far as can be gathered from documents such as legal tablets, some 90 percent had Semitic names, and men with Hurrian or Aryan names are seldom to be found outside the palace or the army. The foreign princes belonged to, or relied upon, groups of men called *maryannu* in the Akkadian texts. These maryannu constituted a prestigious military class in both the Levant and Mitanni. (The plural "maryannu" attaches a Hurrian suffix to the singular *marya*, identical to Sanskrit *marya*, which meant "young warrior."[18])

17. For the letter and the commentary, see *ANET*, 484 and n. 3 on the same page (translation and notes by W. F. Albright, G. Mendenhall, and W. Moran).

18. R. T. O'Callaghan, "New Light on the *maryannu* as Chariot-Warriors," *Jahrbuch für kleinasiatische Forschung* 1 (1950): 309ff.

As for the time of these takeovers in the Levant, a *terminus ante quem* is furnished by tablets from Taanach, near Megiddo, that show that in the middle decades of the fifteenth century B.C., kinglets with Aryan names were in control.[19] On the other hand, documents from the eighteenth century B.C. mention no Indo-European names and no maryannu.[20] It would seem that Aryan speakers came to the Levant in the dark period of the late seventeenth and early sixteenth centuries. By the beginning of the fourteenth century, it seems that Aryan was no longer spoken in the Levant, even by the maryannu or the princes with Aryan names, and one may infer that the Aryan names and class designation are a vestige of what had once been a thin but elevated stratum of Aryan speakers.[21]

We also find kings with Aryan names in Mitanni, which by the middle of the second millennium was largely Hurrian speaking. A Hittite text from early in the sixteenth century refers to petty kings with Aryan names in three of the cities of Hurri.[22] In the second half of the century, another Aryan dynasty (featuring names such as Shuttarna, Paratarna, Shaushatar, Artatama, and Tushratta) had established, with the help of its many maryannu, a "great kingship" in what was thenceforth called the kingdom of Mitanni. Although the kings, of course, worshiped the gods of their Hurrian-speaking subjects,

19. W. F. Albright, "Further Observations on the Chronology of Alalakh," *BASOR* 146 (1957): 32 n. 19.

20. M. S. Drower, *CAH* II, 1: 420–21.

21. J. Friedrich, "Arier in Syrien und Mesopotamien," *Reallexikon der Assyriologie*, 1: 148, concluded that the Aryans of the Amarna period were thoroughly assimilated—in culture, religion, and language—to the Semitic majority in the Levant, and that the incursion of Aryans into the Levant must have occurred many generations prior to the Amarna period.

22. For text and translation of the pertinent lines of this Old Kingdom Hittite text, see H. Güterbock, "Die historische Tradition und ihre literarische Gestaltung bei Babyloniern und Hethitern bis 1200, II (Hethiter)," *ZA* 44 (1938): 108–109. On the date, cf. O'Callaghan, *Aram Naharaim*, 62 and 64, and W. F. Albright, "New Light on the History of Western Asia in the Second Millennium BC," *BASOR* 78 (1940): 30.

they also retained the cult of gods who are prominent in the Vedas: Indra, Mithra, Varuna, and the Nasatya twins were invoked by Matiwaza of Mitanni, toward the middle of the fourteenth century, when making a treaty with Suppiluliumas of Hatti. At one time it was supposed that the Aryans of Mitanni spoke Indo-Aryan (as opposed to Irano-Aryan), and that from India they had come westward to Mitanni,[23] but that no longer seems likely. A treatise on the acclimatizing and training of chariot horses, whose author was Kikkuli of Mitanni, contains a number of Aryan glosses. In her definitive edition of this text, Annelies Kammenhuber concluded that the Aryan words came not from the Proto-Sanskrit of India, but from the still undivided Aryan language.[24] Stated another way, Aryan speakers came to Mitanni *before* the Aryan-language community was sundered into its Indian and Iranian components, and so before the Aryan conquest of northwest India.

The imperial kingdom of Mitanni was destroyed by the Assyrian Ashur-uballit I late in the fourteenth century B.C., but when it first appeared is less certain. The list of imperial kings in Mitanni begins with Shuttarna I, and using the standard chronology, one can estimate that Shuttarna came to power in the middle of the sixteenth century.[25] In Mitanni, the Aryan and Hurrian speakers seem to have been thoroughly fused (the

23. Cf., for example, Gurney, *The Hittites*, 105.

24. A. Kammenhuber, *Hippologia Hethitica* (Wiesbaden: Harrassowitz, 1961). Kammenhuber further elaborated the argument in her *Die Arier im vorderen Orient* (Heidelberg: Carl Winter Universitätsverlag, 1968). On page 238 of *Die Arier* she concludes that the Aryan speakers of Mitanni spoke a "noch ungeteiltes Indo-Iranisch = Arisch," but that within that language in the seventeenth or sixteenth century there were already several dialects. That the Mitanni-Aryans's speech belonged "zum Dialekt der später nach Indien eingewanderten Indien" was indicated, for example, by their word for "one" (*aika* in the Kikkuli text; the word for "one" in Sanskrit is *eka*, whereas it is *aeva* in Avestan).

25. In the first half of the sixteenth century three petty kings in cities of Hurri had Indo-Aryan names; see O'Callaghan, *Aram Naharaim*, 62 and 64.

tablets from fifteenth-century Nuzi indicate that there "most of the Indo-Aryans . . . are close relatives of persons with Hurrian names").[26] The Aryan speakers of Mitanni were never more than a minute minority and were soon completely Hurrianized. Even when the Great Kingdom was established, perhaps ca. 1550 B.C., Aryan speakers may have numbered no more than 2 percent or 3 percent of the population of Mitanni, and by the fourteenth century Aryan was no longer a spoken language in Mitanni.[27]

Finally, we must also include in this list of takeovers—all of which occurred in the middle centuries of the second millennium—the Aryan conquest of northwest India. This conquest has been strangely ignored in debates about the time of the Indo-European dispersal, probably because its evidently late date is incompatible with the general opinion that the dispersal occurred no later than the third millennium. For orientalists, there is no avoiding the conclusion that the Aryan takeover of northwest India was related, somehow, to the appearance of Aryans in Mitanni and the Levant. But this takeover, which had probably occurred by ca. 1500 B.C., seems to have resembled the others only in its objectives and not in the way in which it was carried out. Even though its relationship to the end of the Indus Valley civilization remains unclear, the Aryan takeover of northwest India must have been far more violent and destructive than the other takeovers reviewed here, and must have been effected by a force far larger than those that took over states in the Fertile Crescent.[28] The Aryan invaders

26. Ibid., 65.

27. O'Callaghan (ibid., 53) analyzes the prosopography of Nuzi, on the eastern fringe of Mitanni: of 2,989 names mentioned in the Nuzi tablets, some 1,500 are Hurrian, 631 are Akkadian, 53 are Kassite, only 27 are Indo-European, and 23 are Sumerian (the remainder cannot be classified).

28. For the date (rather precariously based on the Mitanni evidence, a variety of conjectures from and about the Rigveda, and Indian archaeology), see W. A. Fairservis, Jr., *The Roots of Ancient India* (New York: Mac-

apparently waged a long war against the *Dasyus*, dark-skinned natives, and after defeating them became a dominant warrior caste. Their language eventually became the language of two-thirds of the subcontinent.

In each of these takeovers a relatively small force, sometimes but not always homogeneous in language and provenance, gains control of an alien city or region. The new rulers are in most cases a dominant minority, constituting only a tiny fraction of the population. This was especially true of the Aryan rulers in Mitanni and the Aryan and Hurrian princes in the Levant; it seems also to be true of the Kassites in Babylon and the *hyksos* in Egypt. The Aryan speakers who took over northwest India may have gone there en masse but were nonetheless a minority in their newly acquired domain.

The establishment of the Hittite Old Kingdom may in some way resemble these takeovers, but in more important ways it does not. Discussion of anything Hittite is bedeviled by our nomenclature, and so we must begin with that. In second-millennium Hatti, the existence of "the Hittites" (in the modern sense of the word) was not recognized. If one looks through the translations of the Boghazköy tablets, the Hittites one finds

---

millan, 1971), 311–12 and 346. M. Wheeler, *The Indus Civilization*, 3d ed. (Cambridge: Cambridge Univ. Press, 1968), 129–34, believed that the Aryans were responsible for destroying the Harappan cities in the Indus Valley, but other opinion holds that the cities were abandoned (because of chronic flooding) before the Aryans arrived in India; see Fairservis, *Roots of Ancient India*, 310. I. M. Diakonoff, in *Cambridge History of Iran*, 2: 42–43, supposes that "the ancestors of the speakers of Indo-Aryan and 'Western' Iranian idioms (Median, Persian and Parthian) must have reached the south-western part of Central Asia and Eastern Iran already . . . by the end of the 3rd or the beginning of the 2nd millennium B.C." But the "evidence" on which Diakonoff relies are theories about population expansion in central-southeastern Europe, where Diakonoff supposes the Indo-European homeland to have been. There is some evidence that the dynasty in control of southwestern Iran, based at Anshan and Susa, was Elamite speaking until the second half of the seventh century B.C., at which time Persian speakers took control: see P. de Miroschedji, "La fin du royaume d'Anšan et de Suse et la naissance de l'Empire perse," *ZA* 75 (1985): 265–306.

there are, quite simply, "the people of Hatti." The scribes of course had names for languages, and so might refer to one text as written *hattili* ("in the language of Hatti," that is, our "Hattic") and to another as written *nesili* (that is, our "Hittite"; the word apparently meant "in the language of Kanesh," perhaps indicating that by the seventeenth century "Hittite" was the language most widely spoken in the streets of Kanesh [Kültepe?]). Similarly, the scribes could write of "the people of Hatti" or of "the people of Arzawa." For the scribe, "Hittites" (that is, "the people of Hatti") included all those who lived in Hatti, regardless of the language they spoke. A person living in second-millennium Hatti did not see the world in ethnic terms and did not perceive himself, or his countrymen, as belonging to this or that nation. As he saw it, although barbarians might have nothing but a national identity, civilized people were identified by their city or by their land, and above all by the gods of the city or the land in which they lived. It is an eloquent fact that our "Hittites" had no name for themselves, and therefore—we may assume—no conception of a "Hittite nation." They saw themselves only as "the people of Hatti."

The concept of nationalism, on the other hand, derives from the tribal world to which the early worshipers of Yahweh belonged. The author of the Table of Nations at Genesis 10 regarded mankind as consisting of several dozen nations, each nation being the lineal descendants of a single ancestor. As he understood it, a man must worship only the god or gods of his ancestors and must not add to his cult the deities of the city or the land in which he happened to live. In this tribal *Weltanschauung*, Canaanites (descended from Canaan) were or ought to be as distinct from Moabites (descended from Moab) or from Israelites (descended from Israel) as one animal species was from another. So too, in the world of the ancient Hebrew writer there were Hittites (*Khittim*), descended from a primal ancestor named Heth. Our word for, and our concept of "Hittites" come from the translation of the Bible authorized by King James I.

When, at the beginning of this century, the great kingdom centered at Boghazköy was discovered, it was called by its proper name—the kingdom of Hatti (this term had been known from Egyptian and Assyrian records and was legible in the Akkadian tablets from Boghazköy). "Hatti," of course, was a geographical term and, at least initially, referred to the region of central Anatolia. Scholars also supposed, however, that they were dealing with a nation, and for the people of this supposed nation they used the name "Hittites," a name already familiar among the Bible-reading public. Historians in the beginning of the twentieth century had a rather different understanding of a nation than had the author of the Table of Nations. For the modern historian, a man's nationality was evident not in his religion, which was a matter of individual choice, but in his physical appearance and in his language (the early worshipers of Yahweh, in contrast, saw nothing diagnostic in physical characteristics or in the language one spoke: they themselves looked like Canaanites and by their own admission spoke "the language of Canaan"). Thus, in modern parlance, "Hittites" was not simply an equivalent for "the people of Hatti." If there had once been Hittites, these Hittites should have had their own physical and linguistic identity. As it happened, philologists chose to use the name "Hittite" for the principal language found in the archives at Boghazköy. Thus the Hittites were the people whose "ancestral" language was the language of these tablets and who presumably were physically distinguished from other national stocks in Anatolia. Too late it was discovered that, at least at the outset, most of the people of Hatti may have spoken a language other than "Hittite." That other language was called, by the tablets themselves, "the language of Hatti," and scholars had little choice but to call it "Hattic." All of this meant that—at least in the early days of the "Hittite" Old Kingdom—many of the people of Hatti may not have been Hittites. Did the Hittite nation grow geometrically during the period of the Old Kingdom? And then, since documents in Hittite are not found from the

Iron Age, did the Hittite nation suddenly die out? Such are the questions that arise if one accepts the reality of the "Hittite nation" conjured up early in this century.

In order to keep our concepts straight, we must begin by recalling that Hittite is one of several second-millennium languages, descended from an earlier, single Proto-Anatolian language, that in one way or another was related to Proto-Indo-European (although with manifold borrowings from other language communities). Specifically, Hittite seems to be derived from that Proto-Anatolian dialect spoken here and there in Hatti in the late third and early second millennium (other and more widespread Proto-Anatolian dialects in other areas, one assumes, eventually gave rise to Luwian and Palaic). The Proto-Anatolian language, for all we know, may have been dominant in most parts of Asia Minor ca. 2000 B.C., but in Hatti itself it was possibly spoken by only a minority, most of whose members very likely could also speak Hattic. At any rate, the presence of Proto-Anatolian speakers in Hatti in the twentieth century B.C. cannot, as we have seen, testify to an "invasion" of Hatti by a Proto-Indo-European nation.

Much less can a "Hittite invasion" be invoked in connection with the creation of what is called the Hittite Old Kingdom, in the second half of the seventeenth century B.C. That event, it is now quite clear, involved no ethnic conflict at all. Not long after 1650 B.C., the king of Kushshara, whose name may have been Labarnas, conceived the much larger ambition of making himself an imperial king. He seized the strong but abandoned fortress of Hattusas and thereupon became known throughout Hatti as "Hattusilis" ("The Man of Hattusas"). It is our good fortune that the annals of Hattusilis I were discovered at Boghazköy in 1957, shedding much light on the dark age of the late seventeenth century B.C.[29] One of the most

29. For the text and a thorough commentary, see P.H.J. Houwink ten Cate, "The History of Warfare according to Hittite Sources: The Annals of Hattusilis I," *Anatolica* 11 (1984): 47–83.

striking features of the document (although it has seldom been remarked) is the absence of any ethnic animosity by the upstart Great King, or any ethnic support for him. Hattusilis's concern in his annals is to tell the world that he not only made all of Hatti subject to himself, but also conducted long-distance raids into Arzawa (somewhere on the coast) and Syria, plundering cities far and wide and impressing upon them the majesty of his name and therefore of the gods whose steward he was. The tradition of imperial kingship begun by Hattusilis I endured (although with several changes of dynasty) until ca. 1190 B.C., when Hattusas was sacked and the reigning king, Suppiluliumas II, was killed.

The great kingdom at Hattusas was Hittite in the sense that the Hittite language was the primary language of the palace and its provincial administrators. This linguistic preference suggests that Hattusilis I and his close associates were Hittite speakers. That, however, was the extent of the Hittite character of the kingdom. The throne names of Hattusilis I and all his successors were not Hittite, but Hattic, and the newly discovered annals of Hattusilis give not the slightest hint that he regarded himself as a Hittite in our sense of the word, or as anything other than the lord of all Hatti. In their inscriptions and annals, the Hittite kings are tireless in proclaiming their piety toward the sun goddess of Arinna, the weather god, and the other traditional deities of Hatti. The Hittite kingdom demonstrates quite clearly that ethnic consciousness was not much of a factor in second-millennium history.

The kingdom of Hattusilis and his successors was not a "national state," such as those familiar in European history, and was not an expression of "the Hittite nation." On the contrary, the closest approximation to a Hittite nation may have arisen as a *result* of Hattusilis's achievement. When the imperial kingship began, some years after 1650 B.C., some of the people in Hatti may still have been speaking Hattic. By the end of the Old Kingdom (ca. 1470 B.C.), Hittite and Luwian seem to have been the only languages spoken in Hatti; and it is certain that by 1190 B.C.—when the Hittite Empire ended—Hattic was only a language of ritual and ancient texts, while Hittite and especially Luwian (on its way to becoming the language—misleadingly called Hieroglyphic Hittite—attested on Iron Age inscriptions) were the languages spoken in the realm. There is no sign of ethnic antagonism between Hittite speakers, Hattic speakers, and Luwian speakers (this is not surprising, since presumably many people were bilingual or even trilingual), and one must imagine that in the first half of the second millennium, the people of Hatti for one reason or another found it expedient to learn a Proto-Anatolian language. If we must use such terms, "Hattians" had evolved into "Hittites" and "Luwians."

Although not propelled to imperial kingship by a nation, Hattusilis required the services of a community of another kind. During the period of the Old Kingdom, the Hittite kings were to some extent dependent upon a body known as the *pankus*, defined in Hittite texts as an assembly of "the fighting men" or of "the fighting men, servants, and grandees." Many historians, on the assumption that a Hittite nation had invaded Hatti shortly before Hattusilis's time, have described the pankus as a quintessentially Indo-European institution—a *Volksversammlung*, and the voice of the Hittite nation.[30] In fact it was none of these things. In most tribal societies, whether ancient or modern, the tribesmen (each of whom is also a warrior) meet in assembly to decide on matters of gravity. If some Proto-Indo-European communities were still at the tribal level, they would very likely have known such a tribal assembly. But since there is no evidence whatever for the existence

30. Gurney, *The Hittites*, 69, describes the pankus as an "assembly of the 'whole body of citizens.' " According to Goetze, in "State and Society of the Hittites," p. 26 in *Neuere Hethiterforschung* (*Historia Einzelschrift* 7), ed. G. Walser (Wiesbaden: Steiner, 1964), the pankus was "a council of the noblemen." This definition, which seems to be close to the mark, is echoed by Otten, "Das Hethiterreich," 365 (Otten refers to it as an *Adelsgemeinschaft*).

of a Hittite tribe or nation, we need not even try to imagine how a Hittite tribal assembly might have worked, or how such an institution could have survived among the Proto-Anatolian speakers of Hatti through the long period during which they were a well-integrated minority in a civilized land. We know of the pankus only from the seventeenth century to the fifteenth, and there is no reason to suppose that it existed before the creation of the imperial kingship at Hattusas.

The most likely explanation of the pankus is that it was a convocation of the Great King's vassals, each of whom had at his command a small troop of soldiers. Although some historians have imagined the army of the Hittite king as a militia of the "Hittite nation," perhaps similar to Alaric's Visigoths, it was in fact drawn from various language groups, and many of the most important units were "mercenary" (we can not even be certain that the majority of the troops serving in this Hittite monarchy spoke Hittite). Thus in the Hittite Law Code there appear "the Manda warriors" and "the Sala warriors" alongside various local units.[31] It is becoming clear that in the second millennium a generic term for "mercenary soldiers" was the word *hapiru* or the Sumerogram SA.GAZ. The hapiru (or SA. GAZ) appear in fourteen documents from the period of the Hittite Empire and have recently turned up in two texts from the Old Kingdom.[32] In these two texts, which Heinrich Otten dates to the seventeenth or sixteenth century, "the troops from Hatti and the SA.GAZ troops" appear almost as a formula, and it appears that the king's relationship to the mercenaries was no different from his relationship to the militias conscripted from the towns of Hatti.[33] Both the SA.GAZ units and the units from

31. See E. Neufeld, *The Hittite Laws* (London: Luzac & Co., 1951), 18 (Section 54 of the code), and commentary on page 168.

32. H. Otten, "Zwei althethitische Belege zu den Hapiru (SA.GAZ)," *ZA* 52 (1957): 216–23.

33. Of the SA.GAZ in the period of the Hittite Old Kingdom, Otten concludes ("Zwei althethitische Belege," 223): "Ihre militärische Dienstleistung ist offenkundig. Deutlich wird jetzt, dass die diesbezüglichen

Hatti were personally bound to the king, and he to them, by formidable oaths. The military oath was taken by all commanders, whether of local levies or of professional troops, and invited upon the oath-breaker (whether king or vassal) a long and horrible catalog of divine punishments. [34]

That the Hittite king and his army were quite divorced from the subjects over whom he ruled has long been apparent. As summarized by Gurney, "the conclusion seems to be clear: the Hittite state was the creation of an exclusive caste superimposed on the indigenous population of the country, which had originally been loosely organized in a number of independent townships." [35] Whatever the nature of his petty kingship at Kushshara may have been, it is evident that the imperial monarchy which Hattusilis established at Hattusas was quite irregular and unprecedented (the assertion that it was typical of primitive Indo-European monarchies is unfounded: quite apart from the fact that Hittite speakers did not constitute a nation, we have no evidence that the PIE speakers lived under monarchies). [36] In the Hittite Old Kingdom no fixed principle of succession applied until late in the sixteenth century B.C., when the criterion of primogeniture was established by Teli-

---

Belege sich auf die Zeit des Alten Reiches, also auf die Periode der Konsolidierung des hethitischen Staates in Anatolien vor 1500 v. Chr (17./16. Jh.) konzentrieren. Neu tritt dabei ihre rechtliche Stellung zum Hofe hervor, indem der König sich eidlich zur Einhaltung von Abmachungen verpflichtet, wobei die Hapiri anderen militärischen Formationen und Chargen offensichtlich gleichgestellt werden. Das zeigt eine soziale Lage dieser Hapiri auf, wie sie bisher den Texten nicht zu entnehmen war."

34. In the form that it has come down to us, the oath dates from the fifteenth century B.C. See N. Oettinger, *Die militärishce Eid der Hethiter* (Wiesbaden: Harrassowitz, 1976).

35. Gurney, *The Hittites*, 68–69. In *CAH* II, 1: 252, Gurney observes that at Hattusas "there was a sharp cleavage between the government and the governed."

36. I skirted this problem in *Basileus. The Evidence for Kingship in Geometric Greece* (New Haven: Yale Univ. Press, 1983), but plan to return to it in a future study.

pinus. Although the king would designate a member of his family (or of the queen's family) as his successor, the death of a king was often an occasion for intrigue and bloodshed. On such occasions, the pankus seems ultimately to have decided the succession. At any rate, the "fighting men" of the pankus seem to have been persons of some standing, on a level with the courtiers and grandees, and there is no possibility whatever that the pankus was an assembly of all adult male Hittite speakers. Weaned as most of us have been on national histories, we have tended to imagine that the Hittite king was dependent upon a "Hittite" court and a "Hittite" army, but such a picture is anachronistic. As Gurney observed, "there is no textual support for the view that this class division had a racial basis."[37] Many Hittite speakers were among the governed, and within the "government" there were several groups whose first language was something other than Hittite.

In summary, although the Hittite Old Kingdom was in no sense a national monarchy, neither did it—like the Kassite kingdom in Babylon or the Aryan kingdom in Mitanni—represent a takeover by an intruder from a foreign land. At the outset, it was undoubtedly perceived by the people of Hatti as a dreadful novelty, to be escaped from at all costs (the annals of Hattusilis I reveal that at one point, except for his citadel at Hattusas, all of Hatti was in revolt against him). But it was created by the king of Kushshara, who was a native of Hatti and a devout worshiper of Hatti's gods. With every victory and every sack of an enemy city, the Great Kings proved to themselves and to their subjects that the gods looked with favor upon the kingdom. And so, eventually it seems to have won a measure of esteem (though hardly of affection) from the people of the land.

The period in which "the coming of the Greeks" must somewhere fall—the end of the third millennium and the first half of the second—is illuminated for us only in the Near East.

---

37. Gurney, *CAH* II, 1: 252.

There we see that for the most part "nations" did not yet play a role in history. Völkerwanderungen are not attested, nor is any massive migration by a primitive people. The barbarians who appear in the documents are sometimes infiltrators who peacefully attach themselves to a city or civilized land. On occasion we meet barbarian raiders. Most importantly, toward the end of our period we find that Aryan speakers played a considerable role in what for the sake of convenience we may call takeovers: the relatively benign takeovers of cities in Mitanni (followed by the creation of a Great Kingship over all of Mitanni) and of small principalities in the Levant, and the much more violent takeover of northwest India. The "Hittite nation" turns out, upon inspection, to be as illusory as the "Hittite invasion" of central Anatolia. Thus the history of the Near East during our critical period offers some useful analogies and caveats. But in addition it offers a well-demarcated period of chaos and turmoil in which perhaps "the coming of the Greeks" will fit.

Quite clearly the second quarter of the second millennium was tumultuous in the Near East. It began with the pretensions of city kings to become imperial kings and degenerated into a dark age blanketing the whole of the Fertile Crescent and Egypt. In Egypt, contemporary records fail in the eighteenth century, well before the arrival of the first *hyksos*, and do not resume until the expulsion of the Great Hyksos after 1550 B.C. Documentation for Mesopotamia is relatively full in the reign of Hammurabi (1792–1750 B.C.), but then dwindles and virtually ends with the reign of Ammisaduqa late in the seventeenth century: Ammisaduqa's successor fell victim to Mursilis's raid, and much later king lists show that thereupon Hammurabi's dynasty was replaced by the Kassites. The Kassite dynasty in Babylon seems to have controlled most if not all of southern Mesopotamia. To the east of Babylonia, the land known as Elam (and called Persis by the Greeks) falls into darkness in the sixteenth century and is not again illuminated until the thirteenth. In the Levant the seventeenth and sixteenth centuries are almost totally obscure. When the darkness lifts, we find imperial kingships in Hatti and in Mitanni, and new-comers (many of them descended from Hurrian or Aryan speakers) in control of various city-states in the Levant. From ca. 1500 B.C. until the end of the Bronze Age three centuries later, the entire Near East enjoyed relative stability, as Great Kingships ensured security for the lands under their control. But the second quarter of the second millennium was a time of unparalleled upheaval.

FIVE

The New Warfare

Horses

What contributed most to the chaos of the period was the advent of a weapon that transformed warfare in the ancient world: the horse-drawn chariot. The bare generalization is almost a truism and would need no substantiation. The entire matter, however, is both more complex and more significant than it might at first glance appear and must be appreciated in some detail.

Although horses have been horses for a million years, for well over 99 percent of that period people did nothing with them except eat them. During the Ice Age, horses were perhaps the favorite game animal for hunters in both Eurasia and northern Africa. After the retreat of the glaciers, other equids flourished in the warmer regions: three species of zebra in southern and central Africa; the ass (*Equus asinus*) in northern Africa and southern Europe; and in southwestern Asia, from India to Anatolia and Palestine, *Equus hemionus*, commonly known as the onager or the Asiatic wild ass.

The horse, *Equus caballus*, preferred more northerly latitudes. With its shaggy winter coat, its tendency to overheat despite sweating profusely, and its relatively soft hooves, the horse was at home in open steppes from central Asia to the Carpathian Basin in central Europe. On the open steppes, the horse was protected from wolves and other predators by its keen eyes, its herd instinct, and its capacity for rapid and sustained flight. Herds of wild horses dotted the steppes all through later paleolithic and neolithic times. These wild horses seldom stood more than thirteen hands high, about the size of a large pony.[1]

Just as the onager and the ass were domesticated in the Fertile Crescent and Egypt during the neolithic period, so was the horse domesticated when its natural habitat began to be cultivated.[2] The neolithic population of central Europe and the Eurasian steppe not only continued to savor horse meat, but also had a taste for mare's milk. With domestication, horses were introduced into the wooded regions of northern and western Europe, and by the end of the third millennium, the horse was a common domestic animal from France to Turkestan. At neolithic sites in the open steppe from the Ural River to Rumania, horse bones not infrequently account for approximately half of all the animal bones recovered.[3]

Like so many other of the large domestic food animals, the horse surely was often pressed into service as a pack animal. The onager and especially the ass were thus employed in the

1. On the taxonomy and the prehistory of the horse, see G. G. Simpson, *Horses: The Story of the Horse in the Modern World and through Sixty Million Years of History* (New York: Oxford Univ. Press, 1951).

2. F. Hançar, *Das Pferd in prähistorischer und früher historischer Zeit* (*Wiener Beiträge zur Kulturgeschichte und Linguistik*, vol. 11) (Vienna: Herold, 1956), presented in great detail the evidence for domestication of the horse during the neolithic and chalcolithic period in central and eastern Europe (38ff.) and in the Tripolye Culture of the Ukraine (47–81). For a more recent, although narrower, study, see S. Bökönyi, "The Earliest Waves of Domesticated Horses in East Europe," *JIES* 6 (1978): 17–76.

3. At neolithic Dereivka, on the Lower Dnieper, 24 percent of the animals attested were horses, accounting for about 60 percent of the meat consumed at the site. There is no question that these were domesticated food animals. Cf. Anthony, "The 'Kurgan Culture,' " 295: "Fifteen of the seventeen sexable horse mandible fragments from the site were those of males, and almost all of these were juveniles or young adults; there were no 'old' individuals. Such a profile would not result from predation on wild horse bands." Five hundred miles to the east of Dereivka, at neolithic sites on the Lower Volga and north of the Caspian, horses account for 55 percent of the bones of domesticated animals. See J. P. Mallory, in his reply to Anthony's article, *Current Anthropology* 27 (1986): 308.

Near East during the third millennium.[4] Because the onager
was spirited and had a nasty disposition to bite, the Sumerians
managed it with a line attached to a nose ring. Horses used as
pack animals may similarly have been managed by nose rings
and lines. And the horse, perhaps more often than the onager
or the ass, also seems to have served as a riding animal, and by
the end of the third millennium the riding of horses was apparently a common phenomenon on the open steppe.[5] There is
some evidence that in the Ukraine the bit was in use as early as
the fourth millennium,[6] but its use may not have become general in the Eurasian steppe (and remained entirely unknown in
the Near East) until the second millennium.[7]

Although such indifference to the invention of the bit might
initially appear strange, there is a reasonable explanation. A
practiced rider, on a horse that knows his hand-, knee- and
voice signals, can guide and direct the horse even if the horse
is not controlled by a bit. Third-millennium riders, then, did
not especially need the bit. For the driving of draft horses, on
the other hand, a bit is extraordinarily useful, but third-millennium vehicles were not of a type that could be efficiently

4. The evidence has been expertly and comprehensively assembled
by M. Littauer and J. H. Crouwel, *Wheeled Vehicles and Ridden Animals in
the Ancient Near East* (Leiden: Brill, 1979).

5. Anthony, "The 'Kurgan Culture,' " 295–96 and 301–303. Anthony concludes that in the early fourth millennium horses were already
being used as mounts and that this innovation resulted in profound changes
in the social and economic patterns on the steppe. On the hazards and hard-
ships of riding without stirrups, see Littauer and Crouwel, *Wheeled Vehicles*,
65–68.

6. Antler cheek pieces of bits were found associated with horse
bones at two Ukrainian sites. The carbon dates for the horse bones ranged
from 3640 to 4350 B.C. See R. Protsch and R. Berger, "Earliest Radiocarbon Dates for Domesticated Animals," *Science* 179 (1973): 235–39.

7. Stuart Piggott presented his early thoughts on the invention of
the bit in *Ancient Europe* (Chicago: Aldine, 1965), 95 and 110n. 52. For his
more recent views, see his "Chariots in the Caucasus and in China," *Antiquity* 48 (1974): 17–18, and his *Earliest Wheeled Transport*, 87–90.

drawn by horses or other equids. Why this was so is a point that must be clearly understood.

The earliest wheeled vehicles, as Piggott's lucid monograph shows,[8] were built ca. 3000 B.C. (Gimbutas's claim that there were wheeled vehicles as early as the middle of the fifth millennium is not persuasive).[9] They were sturdy and heavy, the wheels being either solid or tripartite disks cut from planks (mature oak was the favorite material). Four-wheeled wagons of this type would have weighed almost half a ton, and the two-wheeled carts several hundred pounds. Because of its ability to pull heavy loads from a yoke, the draft animal par excellence was the ox, even though a team of oxen moved at a speed of only 2 mph. The reason for the equids' inefficiency, as Commandant Lefebvre des Noëttes demonstrated long ago,[10] was the ancient method of harnessing. The "modern" horse collar, which permits a horse to throw its full weight against a load, did not appear in western Eurasia until late in the Middle Ages. In the ancient Near East and in the classical world the horse pulled against a neck strap: the heavier the load, the greater the impairment to the horse's breathing. Thus harnessed, the relatively small horse of the Bronze Age (not much

8. Much of my information I have drawn from the first three chapters of Piggott's *Earliest Wheeled Transport*. His account is not only exquisitely detailed but also highly readable.

9. See, for example, Gimbutas, "Old Europe," 7: "After the middle of the fifth millennium B.C., contacts between Old Europe and the steppe pastoralists increased. The wheel (and vehicle) also emerged at this time, which contributed to mobility and trade. Miniature models of wheels in clay are known from the Karanovo and Cucuteni cultures of the mid-fifth millennium B.C." According to Piggott, *Earliest Wheeled Transport*, 39–40, these disks occur in levels carbon dated to the late fourth and early third millennia. Whatever their date, Piggott notes that " 'wheel models' of pottery are notoriously the least reliable evidence" for wheeled vehicles, "owing to their morphological similarity to spindle-whorls."

10. Commandant Lefebvre des Noëttes, *La force motrice animale à travers les âges* (Nancy: Berger-Levrault, 1924), especially 8–12, 85–86 and 94–97.

larger than an onager or an ass) was unable to draw efficiently a load of more than a quarter of a ton.

Until the development of light vehicles, equids were of only marginal utility as draft animals. Onagers pulled both two-wheeled carts (see Fig. 2) and four-wheeled wagons in third-millennium Mesopotamia, but a team of four onagers was required to draw the bulky wagon then in use. The Ur Standard (see Fig. 3) shows a four-onager team pulling what appears to be a battlewagon, although it is likely that the wagon was meant for parade and display rather than for fighting.[11] Throughout central and northern Eurasia, heavy-wheeled vehicles have been found in third-millennium tombs, but although it is possible that a few of these vehicles were drawn by horses, the only teams of draft animals found in the tombs are oxen.[12] Given the limitations on the equid's service as a draft animal, it is not surprising that the horse had too little value to be imported into southern Europe and the Near East, where the climate was too warm for the horse to flourish. At the southernmost site in the Balkans at which horse bones have been found in third-millennium levels (Vardarophtsa, in central Macedonia), the horse may have been only a game animal.[13]

Horses were rare but not unknown in the Near East in the fourth and third millennia. Horse bones have been reported

11. This is the view, well argued, of A. Salonen, *Die Landfahrzeuge des alten Mesopotamien* (*Annales Academiae Scientiarum Fennicae*, vol. 72, fasc. 3) (Helsinki, 1951), 163. Salonen notes that in their inscriptions, Sumerian and Akkadian kings describe their armies only in terms of infantry, never mentioning the "battle-wagons." For arguments that the vehicles were used in battle, see Hançar, *Das Pferd*, 426; see also Littauer and Crouwel, *Wheeled Vehicles*, 33.

12. S. Piggott, "The Earliest Wheeled Vehicles and the Caucasian Evidence," 295ff. and map at 303.

13. The excavator, W. A. Heurtley, listed horse bones along with boar, deer, elk, goat, and ox bones. See Heurtley, *Prehistoric Macedonia* (Cambridge: Cambridge Univ. Press, 1939), 88–93, and F. E. Zeuner, *A History of Domesticated Animals* (New York: Harper and Row, 1963), 322.

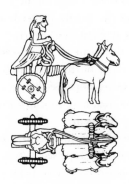

2   Copper model of two-wheeled cart, from Tell Agrab.

3   Detail of "Ur Standard."

from Norşuntepe, in eastern Anatolia, and from Tal-i-Iblis, in south central Iran, in chalcolithic and Early Bronze levels.[14] Although the eastern Anatolian specimens may have been wild horses, those at Tal-i-Iblis would undoubtedly have been domesticated animals, since the range of the wild horse apparently did not extend so far south. Domestic horses would surely have been exotic in the Fertile Crescent in the third millennium, but perhaps it would be incorrect to assume that few Near Easterners at that time had ever seen a horse. It is more likely that until the end of the third millennium, the cost, in the Near East, of using horses either as riding animals or as draft animals was so great that only an occasional rich or foolish man decided to acquire them.

At the end of the third millennium, the number of domesticated horses in central Europe seems to have increased significantly,[15] and the horse may have begun to become slightly more desirable as a riding animal in more southerly lands. There is some evidence that at the end of the third millennium the people of the Tripolye Culture, in the forest-steppe around the Dniester Valley, turned from hoe agriculture to stock raising, and it may be that in this new pastoral economy horses served both as mounts and as a source of food. However the fact is to be explained, in the period between 2000 and 1700 B.C., approximately one-fifth of the animal bones found in the Tripolye Culture settlements are horse bones, a fairly high figure for a region outside the open steppe.[16] There is also evi-

14. Littauer and Crouwel, *Wheeled Vehicles*, 24–25; P.R.S. Moorey, "The Emergence of the Light, Horse-Drawn Chariot in the Near East c. 2000–1500 B.C.," *World Archaeology* 18 (1986): 197–98.

15. Bökönyi, "Domesticated Horses," 52ff., argues that also in the northern Balkans horse-keeping did not become significant until shortly before 2000 B.C., whereas in the Ukraine it had been important all through the third millennium.

16. Hançar, *Das Pferd*, 78–79; Hançar's Table 24 presents the percentages of animal bones found in the Tripolye settlements. Although in the early third millennium, 23 percent of the bones are from the pig and only 1 percent from the horse, at the end of the millennium the distribu-

dence in the graves of the South Russian Timber-Grave Culture, spread over the open steppe between the Dnieper and the Don and across to the Caspian Sea, that a modest intensification of horse breeding occurred at the beginning of the second millennium.[17]

In Greece and in central and western Anatolia, the role of the horse in the early second millennium is uncertain, but it is important to note that the horse was at that time imported to those lands. The only domesticated equids attested for Greece and western Anatolia in the neolithic and Early Bronze periods were onagers or asses,[18] but in Middle Bronze levels there is evidence for horses at a few sites. Horse bones appear at Troy for the first time in Level VI, in fact early in Level VI (ca. 1900 B.C.).[19] These bones are found in "a quantity so exceptional as

tion is very different: horse, 19 percent; cattle, 26 percent; ovicaprid, 20 percent; pig, 4 percent; game, 29 percent. Hançar concludes that ca. 2000 B.C. the Tripolye economy shifted "vom Hackbau auf die Viehzucht," and the conclusion is probably warranted (pastoralists do not favor pigs). Although it is probable that riding horses were useful for herding, clearly the horse continued to serve mostly as a food animal: there is no need for one mounted herdsman for every two sheep or cattle.

17. Ibid., 88–122; cf. Piggott, *Ancient Europe*, 95.

18. Bones of *Equus asinus* were found at EH II and EH III Lerna. See N.-J. Gejvall, *Lerna I. The Fauna* (Princeton: American School of Classical Studies in Athens, 1969), 54, and J. H. Crouwel, *Chariots and Other Means of Land Transport in Bronze Age Greece* (Amsterdam: Allard Pierson Museum, 1981), 35. The ass was probably introduced to Greece during the third millennium. In Asia Minor the ass was common all through the Bronze Age. Onager bones were found at Çatal Hüyük in seventh-millennium levels; cf. Mellaart, *CAH* I, 1: 309. Bones of wild horse have been reported at Demirci Hüyük, in northwest Anatolia; see M. Korfmann, in *AS* 28 (1978): 17.

19. C. Blegen, J. Caskey and M. Rawson, *Troy: Excavations Conducted by the University of Cincinnati, 1932–1938*, vol. 3: *The Sixth Settlement* (Princeton: Princeton Univ. Press, 1953), 10: "One of the most important differences between the Sixth Settlement and its predecessors becomes apparent in an examination of the animal bones that were collected from the habitation deposit: for skeletal remains of horses have been identified among the material from each of the successive strata. Our systematic col-

to suggest that the horse was then an article of food,"[20] but it is likely that the builders of Troy VI also used the horse as a riding animal and as a draft animal.[21] Across the Aegean, horse bones have been found in Middle Helladic levels at Lerna and perhaps also at the Messenian sites of Nichoria and Malthi,[22] and one may assume that what few horses there were in these places were not food animals, but were acquired either as riding animals or draft animals.[23]

However much the horse had been valued as a food animal

---

lection of animal bones, layer by layer, yielded no trace of the horse from the earliest occupation of the site in Troy I to the end of Troy V. The initial stratum of Troy VI, however, produced characteristic bones of horses, and they continued to appear consistently in all the succeeding deposits."

20. H. L. Lorimer, *Homer and the Monuments* (London: Macmillan, 1950), 307.

21. Parallels from central Anatolia, as we shall see, suggest that—whatever else they were used for—the horses of Troy ca. 1900 B.C. at least occasionally pulled light carts. Blegen et al. assumed, even though no evidence had been found, that the horses of Troy VI were draft horses. Denys Page, *History and the Homeric Iliad* (Berkeley: Univ. of California Press, 1959), 57, 70, and 252, proposed that in the Late Bronze Age, Troy's reputation for the breeding of horses was known all over the Aegean world.

22. Caskey, *CAH* II, 2: 125, noted that his excavations at Lerna unearthed "bones of a few horses (*equus caballus*)" in MH levels. At Malthi, bone and skull fragments found at several locations and in several MH strata were identified as equid, although it is not entirely clear that the equid was a horse. See M. N. Valmin, *The Swedish Messenia Expedition* (Lund: Gleerup, 1938), 58, 101, 103, 108, and 138. On page 161, however, Valmin states without equivocation that in Magazine D 43–46 of MH Malthi was found "a horse tooth." One bone attributed to *Equus caballus* was found at Nichoria, on the Messenian coast; cf. Crouwel, *Chariots*, 33. Crouwel also lists (p. 33) a horse molar reported from Argissa-Magoula in Thessaly, from a context "apparently contemporary with an early stage of the Middle Helladic period."

23. In 1978 four complete horse skeletons were reportedly found at Dendra, in the Argolid, supposedly in an early Middle Helladic context (although adjacent to tombs of the Mycenaean period). Cf. *Nestor* (November 1978), 1,281 (referring to a newspaper story in *Ta Nea* of July 9, 1978). Such skeletons would not be the remains of butchered animals, but conclusions must await the publication of details.

in Europe, the Eurasian steppe, and at Troy, it is a valid generalization that in the Fertile Crescent the horse was of no interest or value except as a courser. Although from the neolithic period onward horses may from time to time have been brought to Mesopotamia, only in the Ur III period, at the end of the third millennium, does the horse appear in literary sources. The Sumerians called the horse an ANSHE.KUR, literally an "ass from the mountains."[24] The horse was also, at the turn from the third to the second millennium, sometimes referred to by Sumerian scribes as an ANSHE.ZI.ZI, apparently meaning a "speedy ass." Whatever they were called, horses were at this time prized in Mesopotamia as mounts for daredevil riders.[25] Thus, for example, in one day King Shulgi of Ur seems to have ridden—to the amazement and delight of all his courtiers—all the way from Nippur to Ur, a distance of almost eighty miles. In his hymn of self-praise, Shulgi compares himself to an ass, a mule, and a horse (as well as to a lion), and it is likely that for at least part of the trip between Nippur and Ur he had ridden a horse.[26]

To ride a horse, however, was both arduous and dangerous, and early in the second millennium a far better way was found to exploit the horse's speed: a fast-running, two-wheeled cart was hitched to a team of horses. From that point onward, horses in Mesopotamia (and in the rest of the Near East) were almost exclusively "chariot" horses. The horse was never a food animal in the Fertile Crescent in historical times and was not used for ordinary drayage. Without exception, when wagons are encountered in Near Eastern documents of the second millennium, they are drawn by oxen, asses, or mules.[27] And when

24. M. Civil, "Notes on Sumerian Lexicography," *JCS* 20 (1966): 121–22.

25. P.R.S. Moorey, "Pictorial Evidence for the History of Horse-riding in Iraq before the Kassite Period," *Iraq* 32 (1970): 36–50.

26. For the hymn, see A. Falkenstein, "Sumerische religiöse Texte, 2. Ein Shulgi-Lied," *ZA* 50 (1952): 61–91.

27. Hançar, *Das Pferd*, 488, presented the generalization as "ausnahmslos."

horses are encountered, they are almost invariably pulling chariots (the exceptions are the rare scenes of a horse carrying a rider).

Horses thus became important in the civilized world when their speed—and especially their speed as draft animals—was able to be exploited. The horse's walking speed was almost twice that of the ox. Better still was the fact that the horse, unlike the ox, had gaits other than a walk: at a trot the horse can cover almost ten miles an hour; at full gallop, it can for a few minutes move at a speed of over 30 mph. Use of the horse as a draft animal revolutionized transport and travel in the ancient world, and the revolution was scarcely less profound than the advent of the horseless carriage almost four thousand years later. The prerequisite for exploitation of the draft horse was a two-wheeled cart of much lighter construction than anything known in the third millennium. At the outset, these light carts, or "chariots," were not used for any military purposes, but were prestige vehicles of kings and high officials. In fact, quite some time seems to have elapsed between the first appearance of the horse-drawn chariot in the Near East and the advent of chariot warfare. We shall return to the chronology of the development of chariot warfare after a glance at this remarkable vehicle, and its significance, in its prime.

The War Chariot and Chariot Warfare

The design and proportions of the military chariot are familiar from paintings and reliefs of the Late Bronze Age: two-wheeled, with four or—later—six spokes to the wheel, the wheels having a three-foot diameter, the axle being positioned slightly toward the rear of the car. The chariot that grave robbers found in a fifteenth-century tomb at Egyptian Thebes in 1836 (see Fig. 4), and is now in the Museo Archeologico at Florence, was expertly built: the pole was made of elm, the felloes of ash, the axle and spokes of evergreen oak, and the

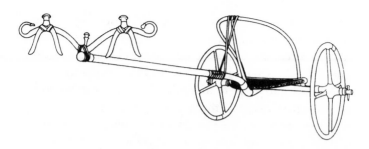

4   Chariot from tomb at Egyptian Thebes.

spoke-lashings of birch bark.[28] Occasionally, chariot wheels
were bound in bronze, but heavy materials were avoided wherever possible. So light was a good chariot in the Late Bronze
Age that a man could pick it up and carry it above his head.[29]

The manufacture and repair of chariots were evidently
highly specialized crafts. Although Near Eastern texts of the
second millennium tell us little about the subject, some details
can be learned from workshop scenes in Egyptian tombs.[30]

28. For the specifications of the Florence chariot, and for a technical
and lavishly illustrated description of chariotry in the Late Bronze Age, see
Y. Yadin, *The Art of Warfare in Biblical Lands in the Light of Archaeological
Study*, 2 vols. (New York: McGraw-Hill, n.d.), 1: 86–90 and 240–41.

29. As Diomedes thinks of doing at *Iliad* 10.505, and as several
charioteers are shown doing in Late Bronze Age paintings and reliefs. Littauer and Crouwel do not list the weight of the Florence chariot in their
otherwise meticulous description of it and other Egyptian specimens
(*Wheeled Vehicles*, 76–81), nor does Yadin (see n. 28). Hançar, *Das Pferd*,
491, reports the weight of the Florence chariot as "nur 3 kg" and general-
izes that many chariots weighed "nicht mehr als 3 bis 4 kg." These are impossible figures, which ultimately stem from a misunderstanding of an
Egyptian poem that boasts of the lightness of His Majesty's chariots. On
the other hand, the suggestion of Lefebvre des Noëttes (*La force motrice*,
24)—that the weight of the typical chariot "ne depassait vraisemblable-
ment pas 100 kilos"—is too conservative. A recently built replica of an Egyptian
chariot weighs 34 kilograms: see Piggott, *Earliest Wheeled Transport*, 89.

30. Littauer and Crouwel, *Wheeled Vehicles*, 76n.18.

Spare parts—wheels, axles, poles, and boxes—were carried along on campaigns, and the Linear B tablets have shown how large an inventory of these things a palace might keep on hand. The Rigveda assigns a high status to the woodworker, from whose skilled hand the chariot came: "he was carpenter, joiner, wheelwright in one; and the fashioning of chariots is a frequent source of metaphor, the poet comparing his own skill to that of the wheelwright."[31] In the chariot corps at Nuzi and at Hattusas, the "carpenters" seem to have enjoyed a status not much below that of the charioteers.[32]

The typical military chariot carried two men, a driver and a fighter (Hittite chariots during the period of the Empire carried three men: a driver, a shield-bearer, and a fighter). In Egypt, the Fertile Crescent, and India the chariot fighter was normally an archer (see Fig. 5), and one of the chariot's few accessories was a quiver, attached diagonally to the right side of the chariot. The chariot fighters of Egypt, about whom we are best informed, were armed with the composite bow. This weapon was far more deadly than the self bow, which was made all of wood. Composite bows, made by inserting strips of horn and sinew into grooved wood, were long (the published specimens range, unstrung, from 1.15 to 1.45 meters, or from 44 to 57 inches, measured in a straight line from tip to tip),[33] and difficult to string, but had a much greater range and effectiveness than the self bow. Although most accurate at a range of about 60 meters, the composite bow could shoot as far as 160 or even 175 meters.[34] When the composite bow was invented

31. A. B. Keith, in *Cambridge History of India* (Cambridge: Cambridge Univ. Press, 1922), "The Age of the Rigveda," 1: 100.

32. Houwink ten Cate, "The History of Warfare according to Hittite Sources," 56.

33. On the construction and measurements, see W. McLeod, "An Unpublished Egyptian Composite Bow in the Brooklyn Museum," *AJA* 62 (1958): 397–401.

34. W. McLeod, "The Range of the Ancient Bow," *Phoenix* 19 (1965): 8.

5   Detail from stone relief of Ramesses III, Medinet Habu.

is, unfortunately, a matter of dispute. Some toxophiles conclude that the composite bow was known as early as the beginning of the fifth millennium, while others find it appearing
first in the Middle Bronze Age. Perhaps it is safest to say that
although experiments with a composite bow may have occurred periodically from the chalcolithic period onward, it did
not come into common use until the middle of the second millennium.[35]

Hurrian texts from Nuzi, in northeastern Iraq, detail the
equipment of Nuzi chariots ca. 1400 B.C.[36] There the chariot

35. For the early date, see D. Collon, "Hunting and Shooting," *AS*
33 (1983): 53–54; Collon notes a fifth-millennium pot from Arpachiyah, in
northern Iraq, depicting a bow that Dr. G. D. Gaunt, of the Society of
Archer-Antiquaries, identifies as a composite bow. I find it difficult to believe that an Arpachiyah farmer-warrior of ca. 5000 B.C., before the availability of metal tools, could have constructed a weapon as complicated as a
composite bow. For a date ca. 1600 B.C. for the appearance of the composite bow, see McLeod, "Unpublished Egyptian Composite Bow," 397. An
intermediate date was championed by Yadin, *Art of Warfare*, 1: 47: on
Naram-Sin's victory stele "we have the very first representation of the composite bow in the history of ancient weapons." The enormous discrepancy in
scholarly opinions on this subject reflects the difficulty in distinguishing, in
artistic representations, a self bow from a composite bow. For a balanced
presentation of the chronological problems, see Moorey, "Emergence,"
208–10.

36. T. Kendall, "The Helmets of the Warriors at Nuzi," in *Studies*

appears to have had two quivers, each containing thirty to forty arrows. A whip and a shield were standard issue for a Nuzi chariot. In addition, either the charioteer or the chariot fighter was issued a sword, and possibly a lance. The defensive uniform consisted of a helmet and corselet, both of which were made of leather and covered with bronze scales (the helmet alone bearing from 140 to 200 scales). Presumably both the driver and the fighter wore these ponderous pieces of defensive armor (the helmet weighed about 1.85 kilograms, or 4 pounds, and the corselet more than 5 kilograms). The corselet, or breastplate, seems to have been designed specifically for chariot warfare. Although the Hittite crews seem to have included a shield-bearer, in much of the Near East the chariot driver and fighter would have had to depend entirely on body armor for protection. The corselet had the same name (*sariam* or *sharyan*) in Egyptian, Hittite, Akkadian, Hebrew, and Ugaritic, all of which languages borrowed the Hurrian "sharyan."[37]

The chariot fighters of the Hittite kings may have fought with the thrusting spear rather than with the bow. How this was managed, and especially how the warrior retracted his spear after hitting his target, is not easy to visualize. Possibly, as Oliver Gurney has suggested, the Hittite chariot fighter used both the bow *and* the spear.[38] At any rate, most of our evidence on Hittite weaponry is fairly late, and there are a few indications that during the Old Kingdom, the Hittite chariot

---

on the Civilization and Culture of Nuzi and the Hurrians in Honor of Ernest R. Lacheman, ed. M. A. Morrison and D. I. Owen (Winona Lake, Ind.: Eisenbrauns, 1981), 201–31.

37. R. de Vaux, "Hurrites de l'histoire et Horites de la Bible," *Revue Biblique* 74 (1967): 485.

38. Gurney, *The Hittites*, 106. The more widespread opinion, based largely on the Ramessid reliefs depicting the Battle of Kadesh, is that the Hittite chariot fighter used only the spear. Cf., for example, Hançar, *Das Pferd*, 490, or P.A.L. Greenhalgh, *Early Greek Warfare: Horsemen and Chariots in the Homeric and Archaic Ages* (Cambridge: Cambridge Univ. Press, 1973), 9–11.

fighters, like their counterparts in the Fertile Crescent and in Egypt, were archers.[39]

In the early days of chariotry the number of chariots was apparently quite small, as infantry continued to be the king's principal arm. In such circumstances, chariots were assigned to harry the flanks and the rear of an infantry and then, once a formation had been broken up, to pursue and kill the individual infantrymen.[40] Eventually, chariotry became the king's primary force, and tactics then required a furious rush of massed chariots against the chariots of the enemy. Whereas an infantryman required little training, and could be replaced without much difficulty, the charioteers (both the driver and the fighter) were valued professionals. Extraordinary skill was required of the driver and especially of the warrior. Amenhotep II, an unusually adept and practiced chariot fighter, boasted on a stele that from a fast-moving chariot his arrows had hit a series of four copper targets, spaced at intervals of thirty-four feet, each of the arrows piercing the target and protruding a palm's breadth out the back.[41] The chariot fighter was necessarily a strong and athletic young man, with superior hand-eye coordination.

Expertise was essential not only for fighting from chariots and for the manufacture of the vehicles, but also for the breeding and training of useful chariot horses. Tall, long-legged horses were, of course, preferred, since a horse's stride is di-

39. Houwink ten Cate, "The History of Warfare according to Hittite Sources," 56, points out that in the Old Hittite Law Code the military units that contained "archers, carpenters and LU.MESH.ISH" (translated variously as "pages," "squires," or "drivers") can only refer to chariot units. On pages 59–60, Houwink ten Cate notes that the so-called "Court Chronicle" (paragraphs 14–17) "describes the training in archery at the court of the Hittite King" in connection with the corps of charioteers.

40. S. Yeivin, "Canaanite and Hittite Strategy in the Second Half of the Second Millenium BC.," *JNES* 9 (1950): 101–107, concluded that chariotry was often kept in ambush, as a king hoped to draw the enemy infantry into an exposed position.

41. For John Wilson's translation of the stele, see *ANET*, 244.

rectly related to the length of its legs. Kings were understand-ably assiduous in acquiring the best specimens they could find. Since the Fertile Crescent and Egypt were ill-suited for the breeding of horses, kings in these areas regularly imported horses from Asia Minor. That, however, was only the first step in creating an effective chariotry. Elaborate exercise and train-ing were essential for turning an ordinary draft horse into a horse on which two men would depend for survival on the bat-tlefield. In the voluminous Hittite "horse texts" there are sev-eral references to the *LU.ashshushshani*, the "horse-training man," a respected professional.[42] We are fortunate to have a manual, preserved on a series of tablets found at Boghazköy, that spells out in exquisite and day-by-day detail a seven-month regimen for training chariot horses. The manual was written by an expert named Kikkuli, the LU.ashshushshani in charge of conditioning and training the horses of the Great King of Mitanni in the fourteenth century B.C. Although Kik-kuli dictated the manual in Hurrian, the tablets found at Boghazköy are not the original Hurrian text, but translations (one in Hittite, another in Akkadian). The fact of translation into other languages shows how great a value was put upon the expertise of a famous trainer. Let us sample the text:

> These are the words of Kikkulis, master horse-man from the land of . . . Mit⟨t⟩anni.
>
> When the groom takes the horses to pasture in the spring, he harnesses them and makes them pace three leagues and gallop two furlongs. On the way back they are to run three furlongs. He unharnesses them, rubs them down, and waters them, then leads them into the stable and gives them each a handful of clover, two handfuls of barley, and one

42. See Kammenhuber, *Hippologia Hethitica*, 6–7, and the same au-thor's "Zu den hethitischen Pferdetexten," *Forschungen und Fortschritt* 28 (1954): 119–24; cf. Hançar, *Das Pferd*, 526.

handful of chopped green grass, mixed together. When they have eaten all up, they are to be picketed.[43]

Kikkuli went on to prescribe the daily agenda for the entire seven-month regimen. Here, for example, are the instructions for the fifth day:

> Day 5. Pace two leagues, run twenty furlongs out and thirty furlongs home. Put rugs on. After sweating, give one pail of salted water and one pail of malt-water. Take to river and wash down. Swim horses. Take to stable and give further pail of malted water and pail of salted water. Wash and swim again. Give handful grass. Wash and swim again. Feed at night one bushel boiled grain with chaff.

Obviously we are dealing here with professional grooms and handlers. The expense and the trouble of all this was well worth it for a king: by the end of the seven-month program, the horses were capable of trotting long distances without tiring, and of pulling a chariot at top speed for a distance of slightly over a mile.

In the Late Bronze Age, chariot warfare was the norm

43. Translation taken from A. A. Dent, *The Horse through Fifty Centuries of Civilization* (New York: Phaidon, 1974), 57. For texts and commentary, see A. Salonen, *Hippologia Accadica* (Helsinki, 1956), and Kammenhuber, *Hippologia Hethitica*. The first tablet of the text was published by Hrozny, "L'entrainement des chevaux chez les anciens Indo-Européens au 14e siècle av. J.C.," *Archiv Orientalni* 3 (1931): 431–61. A full text of all the tablets then known, along with translation and commentary, was prepared as a doctoral dissertation at Leipzig by H. A. Potratz, *Der Pferdetext aus dem Keilschrift-Archiv von Bogazköy*, and the dissertation was subsequently published under the title *Das Pferd in der Frühzeit* (Rostock: Hinstorff, 1938). Salonen's and Kammenhuber's editions include several tablets and fragments that came to light after 1938.

throughout the Near East, and in fact a single chariot type was employed from Greece to India (the Hittite chariot was slightly larger than those in use elsewhere, but had the same design). The Egyptians of the New Kingdom created an empire with their chariot corps: the great battles of Megiddo in 1468 and of Kadesh in 1286 were essentially chariot battles. At Megiddo, Thutmose III rode in a chariot of gold. After being routed by Thutmose's charioteers, the enemy fled to the walls of Megiddo and were hoisted by ropes into the city. Thutmose claims to have captured 2,041 horses, 924 chariots (two of which were covered with gold), and—the figure is significantly low—340 men. At the beginning of the thirteenth century B.C., Ramesses II boasted that at Kadesh his chariots defeated 3,500 chariots belonging to his Hittite adversary.

Chariot warfare changed the face of society in the ancient Near East.[44] In the third millennium the kings of Egypt and of Sumer boasted more of their piety than of their military prowess, but in the Late Bronze Age the king is essentially a smiter of his kingdom's foes. In inscription and in statuary, the Egyptian pharaoh of the New Kingdom is an invincible warrior, who from his hurtling chariot discharges such volleys of arrows that no enemy can escape destruction. In this changed world, a professional military elite is conspicuous. The old militias and unprofessional levies of the third and early second millennia have been replaced by highly trained and expert charioteers. The status of these charioteers is revealed in correspondence of the period. When a king of Mitanni or of Kassite Babylon writes to the king of Egypt, he employs a formal salutation for greeting not only his "brother" the pharaoh "but also his wives, his chariots, his horses, and his chief men, usually in that order."[45]

44. Cf. R. O. Faulkner, "Egyptian Military Organization," *JEA* 39 (1953): 41: "the rise of the Eighteenth Dynasty brought with it changes in the military sphere which amounted to a revolution."

45. C. Aldred, *Akhenaten and Nefertiti* (New York: Brooklyn Mu-

Chronology

Let us now look at the chronological question in detail. Surveys of this kind become obsolete as new documents are discovered, and it is inevitable that the conclusions reached here will sooner or later need some revision.[46] It is unlikely, however, that the main lines of the present chronology will prove to be very far wrong. As mentioned above, the horse was occasionally imported to Mesopotamia in the third millennium, where it undoubtedly served as a riding animal. One would suppose that in the Near East during the third millennium the horse may also have served, in multihorse teams, as a draft animal. Our earliest *evidence* for draft horses, however, comes from the nineteenth century B.C., and is thereafter continuous. One may therefore generalize that the horse does not seem to have become important as a draft animal until after 2000 B.C.

The nineteenth-century evidence is supplied by cylinder seals and sealings from the *karum* of the Assyrian merchants at Kültepe, in central Anatolia. One cylinder seal from that ka-rum depicts a god standing upon a horse. The scene fits within the motif of a "god on a beast" (lions, stags, eagles, and bulls were favorite pedestals) common to the region throughout the Bronze Age. Since the horse on the cylinder seal is managed by a line attached to a ring through the nostrils, one may assume that at the time and place of the seal's manufacture the bit and bridle were not yet known.[47] That at least some of the horses of Kültepe in the nineteenth century B.C. were used for pulling "chariots" is shown by two sealings. The first of these, from

---

seum and Viking Press, 1973), p. 13. For the text see J. A. Knudtzon, *Die El-Amarna-Tafeln* (Leipzig: Hinrichs, 1915), 17.

46. Moorey's "Emergence" also provides a good, up-to-date survey of the chronology. I would disagree only with his statement that "the war chariot was well established in North Syria and Anatolia by the second half of the seventeenth century B.C." ("Emergence," 205), since to me the evidence indicates that the war chariot was very much a novelty in both Syria and Anatolia at that time.

47. For the cylinder seal, see Hançar, *Das Pferd*, 485–86.

Level II at Kültepe (probably 1910–1840 B.C. on the high chronology),[48] shows a team pulling a chariot in which rides a single, unarmed occupant (see Fig. 6).[49] The second Anatolian sealing again depicts one man in a chariot: he carries an ax in one hand and in the other holds the lines attached to his horses' nose rings (see Fig. 7).[50] These Anatolian sealings suggest by analogy that at least a few of the horses attested in the initial stratum of Troy VI, dating to the nineteenth century B.C., were also used as draft animals for "chariots."

Associated with the advent of the horse-drawn "chariot" in the Near East was the introduction of the bit. As the Anatolian sealings show, however, in the Near East the chariot preceded the bit: each of the several horses on the nineteenth-century sealings and cylinder seal is controlled by a single line attached to a nose ring. The occasional representations of riders from the eighteenth century B.C. also show the rider controlling his horse with the nose-ring-and-line mechanism (the rider is also equipped with a stick).[51] Although a rider, sitting astride his mount, would have had little difficulty in controlling the animal's movements precisely, it is not known how a driver could guide a team of draft horses without the assistance of the bit.

48. For arguments supporting that dating, see H. Lewy, *CAH* I, 2: 710. The date is correlated with the reign of Erishum I at Ashur. In the chronological tables at the end of the same volume, the editors of the *CAH* date Erishum I some forty years later than did Lewy.

49. As J. Morel's drawing of the seal impression indicates, the ancient artist had difficulty representing the horses (which look like hooved dogs) but clearly showed each animal managed by a single line attached to a nose ring.

50. On this sealing, which comes from an unpublished tablet in the Metropolitan Museum in New York, cf. Littauer and Crouwel, *Wheeled Vehicles*, 51 and fig. 29.

51. Ibid., 65ff. The authors note (p. 66) that "the riders are always male, often either naked or lightly clad, riding astride and bareback. . . . The rider is usually shown seated well back, sometimes with knees sharply drawn up." Although King Zimri-Lim of Mari seems to have enjoyed riding a horse, his palace prefect criticized such behavior, either because it was undignified or because it was dangerous (see ibid., 67–68).

6   Detail from cylinder seal impression, Kultepe.

7   Detail from cylinder seal impression.

Clearly the nose-ring-and-line mechanism would not have been satisfactory for a team of horses galloping at full speed, and representations of horses with slit nostrils[52] may attest to the hazards of the system.

As indicated above, the bit may have been known in the Eurasian steppe quite early.[53] Its use may not, however, have become widespread in the steppe until the second quarter of the second millennium. In the sixteenth century B.C., cheek pieces for teams of horses suddenly appear in the steppes between the Dnieper and Kazakhstan.[54] Also suggesting that the bit was an innovation (although not, of course, an invention) of the second quarter of the second millennium is the fact that in the third quarter of that millennium the inhabitants of the steppe experimented rather rapidly and radically with diverse types of cheek pieces.[55] At any rate, the bit does not seem to have made its way from the steppe to the lands south of the Caucasus until the late eighteenth or early seventeenth century. From eighteenth- or seventeenth-century Syria come several seals and one sealing with chariot scenes. Each chariot horse in these scenes is controlled by two lines that can therefore be properly described as "reins." Although the type of

52. Ibid., 83.

53. Ibid., 61n. 59, refer to "pairs of metal loops, presumably cheekpieces, some with traces of leather on them, from sites of Maikop culture of later 3rd mill. B.C." Still earlier bits made of organic material have also been reported from the Dniester and Don basins and were probably used for controlling ridden animals (ibid., 25). The earliest evidence north of the Caucasus for bits certainly associated with draft horses are cheek pieces, along with pairs of horse skeletons, found in the Timber Graves north of the Caspian Sea. The graves are dated ca. 1700 B.C. On them, see M. Gimbutas, " 'Timber-Graves' in Southern Russia," *Expedition* 3 (1961): 14–20.

54. E. E. Kuz'mina, "Stages in the Development of Wheeled Transport in Central Asia during the Aeneolithic and Bronze Age (On the Problem of the Migration of Indo-Iranian Tribes)," *Soviet Studies in History* 22 (1983): 96–142. The Russian original of this article appeared in *Vestnik Drevnej Istorii* in 1980.

55. Kuz'mina, "Stages," 121.

headstall cannot be detected in such miniature scenes, it is probable that the reins were attached to a bit.[56]

The obvious prerequisite for a fast-moving cart was the spoked wheel. In Europe and in the Near East, wheels were invariably solid disks during the third millennium, but early in the second millennium spoked wheels began to appear.[57] Since disk wheels were very heavy (a wheel with a one-meter diameter typically weighed well over a hundred pounds), the development of a spoked wheel was a historic innovation. Although we do not know how the earliest spokes were constructed, the spoked wheels of the Late Bronze Age required expert and sophisticated woodworking, with both the felloes and the spokes being bent from heated wood.[58]

From Cappadocia and from Chagar Bazar in northeastern Syria come our earliest depictions of the spoked wheel. Both of

56. Littauer and Crouwel, *Wheeled Vehicles*, 61 and figs 33, 34, and 36. The authors discussed the dates of these Syrian sealings and seal with Professors Edith Porada and Briggs Buchanan and concluded that all three belonged "to the 18th–17th centuries B.C." (*Wheeled Vehicles*, 51, with n. 14). For the classification, see B. Buchanan, *Ancient Near Eastern Seals in the Ashmolean Museum* (Oxford: Oxford Univ. Press, 1966), 165ff., and Porada's review of that book in *Bibliotheca Orientalis* 27 (1970): 13. For a comprehensive study of bits in the ancient Near East, see H. A. Potratz, *Die Pferdetrensen des Alten Orient* (Rome: Pont. Ist. Stud. Or., 1966).

57. In several discussions of the subject, a third-millennium cylinder seal from Tepe Hissar, in northwestern Iran, is described as depicting a spoked wheel. The "spokes" on the Tepe Hissar seal, however, look very much like the slats that held together the solid wooden wheels found in third-millennium levels at Susa. Cf. P.R.S. Moorey, "The Earliest Near Eastern Spoked Wheels and their Chronology," *PPS* 34 (1968): 430–32.

58. Littauer and Crouwel, *Wheeled Vehicles*, 79: "To form the spoke, a single piece of wood, somewhat more than twice the length of each spoke and half its thickness, was bent sharply at the nave, turning back at a 90° angle (on four-spoked wheels) or a 60° angle (on six-spoked ones) to form the complementary halves of sister spokes, these sections being glued back to back the length of the spoke." Wet rawhide was bound around the spoke-halves at the nave, and as the rawhide dried it bound the halves tightly together. Finally, the rawhide was covered with lashings made of birch bark, which waterproofed the spoke.

the Anatolian sealings mentioned above portray two-wheeled "chariots" with four-spoked wheels. In addition, a Kültepe cylinder seal (also from the nineteenth century B.C.) shows a four-wheeled wagon drawn by equids that have been supposed to be horses, and the wagon's wheels appear to be spoked. At Chagar Bazar, 150 miles northwest of Ashur and near the headwaters of the Habur River, terracotta figurines of equids (again, presumably, horses) were found in a context dating ca. 1800 B.C., and among the figurines was a fragment of a terracotta model of a wheel that is indisputably multispoked.[59] A slightly later representation of a spoked wheel occurs in a seal impression on a clay tablet from Sippar,[60] the tablet dating from the fourteenth year of Hammurabi's reign (1779 B.C.). The Akkadian word for spoke (*tirtitu*) is a loan-word, borrowed from some people outside Mesopotamia. On the other hand, in texts from the eighteenth century B.C., the word used for the horse-drawn "chariot" was *narkabtu*, the same Akkadian word that in earlier centuries had been used for any two-wheeled cart.[61]

From shortly after 1800 B.C., Akkadian texts at Chagar Bazar refer to more than a score of horses (in a variety of three-

59. See Hançar, *Das Pferd*, plate 23B for the cylinder seal, and Plate 26A for the terracotta model. Lefebvre des Noëttes, *La force motrice*, 13–18, dated this cylinder seal to the middle of the third millennium, and so could not observe that the spoked wheel was a fairly late innovation in Mesopotamian history.

60. H. H. Figulla, *Cuneiform Texts from Babylonian Tablets in the British Museum XLVII* (London: British Museum, 1967), no. 22, plate 14. Cf. Moorey, "Earliest Near Eastern Spoked Wheels," 431, and Littauer and Crouwel, *Wheeled Vehicles*, fig. 31 and 51.

61. A. Salonen, "Notes on Wagons and Chariots in Ancient Mesopotamia," *Studia Orientalia* 14, 2 (Helsinki: Societas Orientalis Fennica, 1950), 1–8. Salonen points out (p. 6) that since *narkabtu* originally referred to any two-wheeled cart, the precise term for a war chariot was *narkabat tahazi*; another two-wheeled vehicle, manifestly unsuited for warfare, was the *narkabat shepa*. In conventional usage of the later periods, however, "narkabtu" regularly stood for the war chariot.

horse and two-horse teams) and to their grooms.[62] Another tablet of the same date, found in the archives at Mari, is a letter from Shamshi-Adad I, the Great King of Ashur, to his lackadaisical son, Iasmakh-Adad, petty king at Mari. In his letter, Shamshi-Adad writes that for the New Year festival at Ashur, which he has fixed for the sixteenth of the month Addar, he wishes to have a team of horses and a chariot; Iasmakh-Adad is ordered to dispatch the animals and the vehicle to Ashur.[63] It is revealing that so great a king as Shamshi-Adad did not have horses and a chariot in his own city. At a slightly later date, but still within the first half of the eighteenth century B.C., Zimri-Lim (who had become Great King at Mari) sent a request for white chariot horses to Aplachanda, king of Carchemish (two hundred and fifty miles to the northwest). Aplachanda replied with a letter explaining that although white chariot horses were not available, he would see to it that some bays or chestnuts would be secured for Zimri-Lim.[64]

In short, early in the eighteenth century B.C., one could occasionally see, in the northern tier of the Fertile Crescent, horses trotting along a road from one city to another, drawing a "chariot" (that is, a two-wheeled cart, the wheels being spoked and the entire vehicle being of relatively light construction). But the scene was exceptional, and it is important to appreciate the fact that at least in the Fertile Crescent the horse and the chariot did not yet have any military value. The early horse-drawn chariot may not have been quite as light as those of the Late Bronze Age, but it was not for lack of speed that

62. Gadd, "Tablets from Chagar Bazar and Tell Brak," 22ff. Cf. Salonen, *Die Landfahrzeuge des alten Mesopotamien*, 46.

63. W. von Soden, "Das altbabylonische Briefarchiv von Mari," *Die Welt des Orients* 1 (1948): 201–202.

64. E. Weidner, "Weisse Pferde im Alten Orient," *Bibliotheca Orientalis* 9 (1952): 157–59. The key phrase in the letter is *sisu pishutum sha narkabtim*, which Weidner (p. 158) translates as "weisse Pferde für den Streitwagen." The Akkadian *narkabtim*, however, need not have the military connotations of the German word.

the chariot had only peaceful uses ca. 1800 B.C. For Near Easterners of the time, after all, it would have seemed to roll with
breathtaking speed.

The simplest explanation for both the rarity of the chariot
and its employment in nonmilitary contexts is that in the
eighteenth century B.C. an effective means of chariot warfare
had not yet been devised. As we have seen, there is positive
evidence that the bit was not yet in use in the Near East in the
early eighteenth century. It is also possible that the composite
bow was still a rarity at this time, although here the argument
is *e silentio*.[65] If, as is likely, the chariot began to be used for
hunting soon after its development, several generations of
charioteers may have tried various devices to better guide and
control their horses. At the same time, chariot archers may
have experimented with self bows and composite bows before
perfecting a dependably lethal weapon (construction of the
composite bow was an intricate business, and a good bow was
five to ten years in the making).[66] The earliest evidence for the
chariot's use in hunting comes from a Syrian cylinder seal dating from the eighteenth or seventeenth century B.C. The horses
in this scene are evidently controlled by bits: the driver himself
shoots the bow, having tied the reins around his hips.[67]

For more than a century after the time of Shamshi-Adad and
Zimri-Lim, the horse may have remained an extraordinary
spectacle in Mesopotamia, used only for rapid transportation,
for hunting, for ceremony, or for royal recreation and amuse-
ment. In our copious documentation from the Age of Hammurabi, there are no references to chariot forces anywhere in
the Fertile Crescent (needless to say, the horse is not mentioned
in the Code of Hammurabi). Nor is there a representation of
the light chariot in the monumental art of the age, a fair

65. The earliest preserved specimen comes from outside a Seventeenth Dynasty tomb in Egypt. Cf. McLeod, "Egyptian Composite Bow,"
397n. 4.

66. Ibid., 400.

67. Littauer and Crouwel, *Wheeled Vehicles*, 63 and fig. 36.

amount of which has survived (one would have expected, for example, that the chariot would appear in the frescoes of the Mari palace).

For Anatolia, matters are less clear. The "Anittas Text" indicates that when Anittas captured Salatiwara he found in that city (or possibly encountered in battle there) forty teams of horses.[68] Anittas is known to have been a formidable king in central Anatolia ca. 1800 B.C. The "Anittas Text" comes down to us in three scribal copies (all in the Hittite language), one from the sixteenth century B.C. and two from the thirteenth.[69] The forty "chariots" that those forty teams mentioned in the text imply[70] may have been parade or prestige vehicles: we have seen that the king of Chagar Bazar, ca. 1800 B.C., had a stable of more than twenty horses, comprising various two- and three-horse teams. A difficulty for translators is that in the "Anittas Text" the reference to the teams stands between a reference to a fourteen-hundred-man garrison and a reference to silver and gold, and it is not clear whether the text presented the teams as contributing to the defense of Salatiwara, or as part of the plunder that Anittas took from the town.[71] In analyzing the several scribal copies of this text, Houwink ten Cate

68. For a transcription and translation of the text, see E. Neu, *Der Anitta-Text* (*Studien zu den Bogazköy-Texten*, 18) (Wiesbaden: Harrassowitz, 1974), 10–15.

69. Ibid., 3 and 6.

70. Where there are teams of horses there must also be "chariots," although in the "Anittas Text" only in Copy B, from the thirteenth century, are chariots (GISH.GIGIR.MESH) explicitly mentioned; this copy also omits the numeral "forty."

71. See Neu's translation of lines 64–71 of the document (*Der Anitta-Text*, 15):

Noch im selben Jahr zog ich gegen [ ] [Salatiua]ra zu Felde.
Der Mann von Salatiuara machte sich zusammen mit seinen
    Söhnen (Leuten?) auf und ging
[ent]gegen; sein Land und seine Stadt (ver)liess er,
und er besetzte den Fluss Hulanna.
Ne[shas   ] umging [ihn]

inclines toward the conclusion that—whatever the sixteenth-
and thirteenth-century scribes may have thought—the original
author of the text presented the teams as part of the booty taken
out of Salatiwara and not as part of the the city's defenses.[72]
Houwink ten Cate also inclines toward the wider conclusion
that ca. 1800 B.C. chariots were not used at all in Anatolian
warfare. On the other hand, as Erich Neu's translation suggests, it may be that the horses of the "Anittas Text" pulled
war chariots. Even if that could be established, however, we
still would not know how to imagine the king of Salatiwara
employing his battle chariots. To imagine them as drawn by
bit-controlled horses, and as carrying archers armed with composite bows, would almost certainly be anachronistic. We
must leave the matter in uncertainty. It is possible that ca.
1800 B.C. a few Anatolian kings had begun experimenting
with the chariot in battle. But if such experiments did occur,
they evidently were unsuccessful, since for the next century and
a half, nothing more is heard about war chariots.

The effective use of chariots in battle, for which the bit was
undoubtedly a prerequisite, does not seem to have begun until
well into the seventeenth century. Unfortunately, we have very
little literary evidence on this period, and no contemporary references to chariot warfare. Yet there are grounds for supposing
that the chariot was used in battle in Egypt ca. 1650 B.C. In
his excavations at Tell el Ajjul (ancient Gaza), Sir Flinders Petrie discovered bronze bits in a level that he identified as "Hyksos," and that today is usually dated to the seventeenth century
B.C.[73] The earliest evidence for the horse in Egypt during his-

---

und zündete seine Stadt an, und [   ] jene ei[n],
die *Einschliessung* der Stadt (bestand in) 1400 Fusstruppen,
und 40 Pferdegespanne, Si[lber (und) Gold
jener aber hatte (mit)geführt, und er war (davon)gegangen.

72. Houwink ten Cate, "The History of Warfare according to Hittite Sources," 59 and 80–81n.66.

73. For a full discussion of "die Hyksostrense," see Hermes, "Das
gezähmte Pferd im Alten Orient," 379–81. Hermes dated the bits to ca.

torical times is a horse skeleton, found by W. B. Emery in 1959, from Buhen, a fortress near the Second Cataract.[74] The skeleton was found on the brick rampart of the Middle Kingdom fortress that was destroyed between ca. 1680 and 1640 B.C.[75] The horse was presumably killed during the destruction of the fortress in the *hyksos* wars. The Buhen horse had apparently for much of his life been controlled by a bit, for an observant excavator noted that "the wear on one tooth was caused by a bit."[76] Additional evidence for the horse in *hyksos* Egypt comes in the form of two horse teeth found in the Delta, in a context of ca. 1650–1600 B.C.[77] Most Egyptologists are persuaded that chariot warfare was brought to Egypt by the Great Hyksos, who seem to have established a regime over most of Egypt in the middle of the seventeenth century B.C. The Great Hyksos certainly had chariotry when they were expelled from Egypt ca. 1550 B.C., for Kamose's account of his victory refers to "their horses" confined within their camp.[78]

1700 B.C., a somewhat earlier date than is now preferred. Piggott, "Chariots in the Caucasus and in China," 74, assigns them to the seventeenth century. Littauer and Crouwel, *Wheeled Vehicles*, 87n. 59, would put the Gaza bits still later, but do not confront Hermes's arguments.

74. The skeleton was first published by J. Clutton-Brock, "The Buhen Horse," *Journal of Archaeological Science* 1 (1974): 89–100.

75. If we follow Bietak, "Problems of Middle Bronze Age Chronology: New Evidence from Egypt," we would date the destruction closer to the end than to the beginning of this period.

76. Littauer and Crouwel, *Wheeled Vehicles*, 56. For a very clear photograph of the teeth, see Clutton-Brock, "The Buhen Horse," fig. 2. Cf. Clutton-Brock's remarks on pages 92–93: "The excessive wear on the lower left second premolar (the lower right second premolar is missing) establishes that the horse was not kept as a curiosity or as a valued member of a menagerie. It was ridden or driven with a bit which would have been made either of bone or bronze. According to Littauer (pers. comm.) this is the earliest material evidence for the use of the bit." The teeth indicate that at its death the Buhen horse was about nineteen years old (Clutton-Brock, pp. 91–92).

77. Littauer and Crouwel, *Wheeled Vehicles*, 56.

78. See John Wilson's translation of the document, *ANET*, 233

There is also reason to believe, it seems, that chariots played an important role in the battles and raids of Hattusilis I in the second half of the seventeenth century. The skeleton of a stallion has been found at Osmankayasi, near Hattusas, in a seventeenth- or sixteenth-century context.[79] It is true that chariots are rarely mentioned in the better known documents of the Hittite Old Kingdom (they do not appear at all, for example, in the Edict of Telipinus). According to Houwink ten Cate's survey, however, the expression " 'foot-soldiers and charioteers' . . . occurs rather often in the Old Hittite fragmentary historical texts."[80] And in the Old Kingdom, the expression for "army" (the Sumerogram ERIN.MESH) seems to have stood for "a complete army . . . consisting of both infantry and chariotry." The chariot forces of the earliest Great Kings at Hattusas were undoubtedly small when judged by later standards. For example, Tudhaliyas II, who reigned during the second half of the fifteenth century B.C., reports without much fanfare that after a victorious campaign he brought back to Hattusas, and settled there, "10,000 infantrymen and 600 chariot-teams, together with their drivers and masters."[81] By ca. 1440

---

col. A. A very few Egyptologists believe that the Egyptians already had the chariot by the time of the *hyksos*'s arrival, and that the various *hyksos* intruders learned of chariotry from the Egyptians. Such a reconstruction is based on presumptions rather than on evidence, whether textual or archaeological. From the ample documents of the Middle Kingdom, it is clear that when the Second Intermediate Period began, the horse-drawn chariot was still unknown in Egypt, and it is also clear that at the end of that period chariotry was established. King Ahmose evidently had chariots of his own, for even before he attacks the *hyksos* capital at Avaris, he rides in a chariot (see the tomb inscription of Ahmose the crew commander, tr. Wilson, *ANET*, 233 col. B).

79. Littauer and Crouwel, *Wheeled Vehicles*, 56. This stallion resembled the Buhen stallion both in size and in type; both horses were small by today's standards (they stood 1.45 and 1.50 m. at the withers; today 1.47 m. is the upper limit for a "large pony"), but "they are rather big by ancient criteria" (ibid., 57).

80. "The History of Warfare according to Hittite Sources," 57.

81. For this excerpt from the "Tudhaliyas Annals," see Neu, *Der Anitta-Text*, 18.

B.C., it would thus appear, the Hittite kings commanded a chariotry numbered in the hundreds. In contrast, an epic text known as "The Siege of Urshu" tells us how one of the early Great Kings of Hatti (almost certainly, in this context, Hattusilis I) deployed "eighty chariots (*narkabat*) and eight armies" around the city of Urshu. The same epic ascribes thirty chariots to a Hurrian city opposed to the king.[82]

Although not numerous, the chariots of Hattusilis I and his successor, Mursilis I, seem to have been crucial to the triumphant careers these two kings enjoyed. Hattusilis's selection of Hattusas to serve as his capital suggests a reliance on chariots: Hattusas was an abandoned, unwalled citadel overlooking a vast plain (to the north, the plain extended to another ridge, fifteen miles from Hattusas). Even more suggestive are the long-distance raids for which the first two Great Kings of Hatti were famous. As we have seen, Hattusilis traveled almost three hundred miles to sack Alalakh on the Orontes, and his successor Mursilis made the amazing march to Babylon. It is difficult to imagine that long-distance overland raids through hostile lands (both Hattusilis and Mursilis were attacked by kings from the cities of Hurri) could have been conducted without chariots. Relevant here is the saddle boss from the yoke of a chariot found at Alalakh. Woolley discovered the boss in the leveling layer (Alalakh VI–V) just above the ruins of the palace destroyed by Hattusilis I (the archives of Alalakh, it is worth noting, do not indicate that Alalakh itself had chariotry).[83] The pankus convoked by the first Great Kings of Hatti, I would assume, included a small but indispensable corps of charioteers.

That the light chariot was in existence several centuries before 1650 B.C. is quite clear. And it is even possible that some Anatolian kings tried to use chariots on the battlefield as early

---

82. For the text, see Güterbock, "Die historische Tradition bei Babyloniern und Hethitern," 114–25; both of the references occur on the reverse side of the tablet, at lines 5 and 26; cf. also line 11 for an unclear reference to *narkabati*.

83. Moorey, "Emergence," 205.

as 1800 B.C. The essential point, however, is that chariot tactics (specifically, the use of the chariot as a fast-moving and effectively guided platform for an expert archer) seem not to have been used until the seventeenth century B.C. In his study of the early textual references to chariot warfare, Houwink ten Cate concludes that "the first incontestable example would be those in texts referring to the time of Hattusilis I and Mursilis I."[84] It is not unlikely that Hattusilis I and the Amorite and Hurrian princes who imposed their *hyksos* regime upon Egypt were chiefly responsible for drawing attention to the possibilities of chariot warfare.

Although our chronological framework is tentative and admittedly fragile, it may be useful to present it in concise form:

> End of third millennium: proliferation of the domesticated horse, and increased use of riding horses, in Eurasian steppe; Shulgi of Ur imports riding horses into Mesopotamia

> Nineteenth century B.C.: invention of the spoked wheel; development of a light, horse-drawn "chariot"

> Early eighteenth century B.C.: in the Fertile Crescent, horse-drawn "chariots" sought by kings for rapid transportation and for display; in Anatolia, possible experiments with chariots in battle

> Late eighteenth or early seventeenth century B.C.: introduction of the bit to the Near East; chariot used in hunting

> Middle decades of seventeenth century B.C.: with aid of small chariot corps, *hyksos* chiefs and Hattusilis I make selves Great Kings; advent of chariot warfare

> 1468 B.C.: approximately two thousand chariots clash at Battle of Megiddo

84. "The History of Warfare according to Hittite Sources," 59.

The New Warfare

Provenance of the Chariot and of Chariot Warfare

Of the specialists on the horse and chariot in the ancient world, a significant number have come to the conclusion that the chariot was developed in the highlands of eastern Anatolia (I here use "Anatolia" in the widest possible sense, including all of Asiatic Turkey, the northwestern tip of Iran, and the Soviet republics of Armenia, Azerbaijan, and Georgia). Gertrud Hermes, in articles published in the mid 1930s, showed definitively that the chariot was not perfected in northern Europe, as earlier historians had supposed.[85] Her review of the evidence pointed to eastern Anatolia as the most likely place for the chariot's development. That surprising conclusion was not accepted initially,[86] but subsequently was endorsed in several hippological studies. Most importantly, Franz Hançar, after canvassing all possibilities in exhausting detail, reached the conclusion that the horse-drawn chariot originated in the highlands of eastern Anatolia, especially Armenia and Transcaucasia.[87] Specialized studies on horses and chariots in the Aegean and the Near East have concurred with the findings of Hermes and Hançar. Thus Fritz Schachermeyr, in his study of Mycenaean chariots, found that their trail led "auf die Bergländer Armeniens."[88] And in 1963 Albrecht Goetze matter-of-factly observed that the evidence points "to the Ararat region as the place where the chariot was, if not invented, certainly perfected."[89]

On the other hand, among Indo-Europeanists and among

85. For Hermes's articles in *Anthropos*, see Ch. Three, n. 3.

86. J. Wiesner, "Fahren und Reiten in Alteuropa und im Alten Orient," *Der Alte Orient* 38 (1939) (reprinted under separate cover [Olms: Hildesheim, 1971]; my page references are to the Olms reprint). Weisner maintained—although in a somewhat revised form—the old view that the chariot was brought into the Near East by invaders from the north.

87. Hançar, *Das Pferd*, 472–535.

88. F. Schachermeyr, "Streitwagen und Streitwagenbild im Alten Orient und bei den mykenischen Griechen," *Anthropos* 46 (1951): 712.

89. A. Goetze, "Warfare in Asia Minor," *Iraq* 25 (1963): 125.

archaeologists whose concern is prehistoric Europe and Asia, one still encounters the view that it was in the lands north of the Caucasus that chariotry began. This view, which was in some danger of being quashed altogether by Hançar's weighty study, has lately been bolstered by scientific findings: carbon dating has shown beyond any doubt that not only the domesticated horse but also the bit and the spoked wheel appeared quite early in the lands—all of them without written records for the Bronze Age—of southern Russia and eastern Europe. The debate has able protagonists on both sides. Thus while Mary Littauer and Joost Crouwel conclude that the chariot was developed "in the Near East itself" and was not brought into the Near East by "Indo-European-speaking steppe tribes,"[90] Stuart Piggott and Alexander Häusler continue to believe that the chariot originated somewhere in what Piggott refers to as the "technological *koine*" that stretched from Slovakia to the Urals.[91]

It will be helpful here to repeat a distinction made by both Littauer and Piggott. The word "chariot" has, for most scholars, a military connotation,[92] especially when the word is used in Bronze Age contexts. That is understandable, since in our written sources from the Bronze Age the chariot is almost exclusively a military vehicle, and since much of the artistic evidence from the Near East and Greece also features the war chariot. In parts of the Bronze Age world, however, the chariot

90. Littauer and Crouwel, *Wheeled Vehicles*, 68. In their rather brief "Note on Origin of Chariot" (pp. 68–71), the authors are concerned only with the distinction between "the Near East" and Eurasia north of the Caucasus.

91. Cf. Häusler, "Neue Belege," 675–76. For Piggott's most recent discussions, see his "Chinese Chariotry: An Outsider's View," in *The Arts of the Eurasian Steppelands*, ed. P. Denwood (Colloquies on Art and Archaeology in Asia, no. 7) (London: 1978), 32–51, and also his *Earliest Wheeled Transport*, 103–104.

92. In this regard, English speakers are better off than their German-speaking colleagues, for whom *Streitwagen* must inevitably denote a military vehicle.

seems to have had no military use. In these areas it was what Piggott[93] has called a "prestige vehicle," used for ceremony, for recreation, for display, or for a relatively comfortable and dignified form of rapid transport. The appearance of these non-military chariots in the Near East, as we have seen, antedates by at least two centuries the advent of effective chariot warfare. Where the "chariot" in the broad sense was first developed and produced is obviously one question, and where chariot warfare began is another. Both need to be addressed.

It is, perhaps, barely possible that the chariot in the broad sense—a light vehicle, with two spoked wheels—was invented somewhere in the vast area, north of the Near East, between the Carpathian Basin and the Urals. The Pontic steppe (and other treeless steppes) apparently can be ruled out entirely,[94] but other parts of the koine cannot. The argument in support of this thesis makes reference to the undeniable facts that the wild horse was native to the entire area under consideration, and that by the beginning of the second millennium the domesticated horse was common to all of the cultures found therein. For a more pointed argument, one can refer to the handful of sites, scattered over the whole of the horse-breeding koine that stretched from central Hungary to the Aral Sea, where bits made from bone or antler have been found in levels from the early second, the third, and even the fourth millennia. This argument, however, is less conclusive than it may initially seem, since most of these bits (or, more exactly, these cheek pieces) can hardly attest to the presence of "chariots" or any other wheeled vehicle drawn by horses. For example, six antler bits were found in fourth-millennium levels at Dereivka (on the Lower Dnieper); but since wheeled vehicles are not attested at so early a date, the bits must have controlled ridden horses. The direct evidence for early "chariots" in central Eur-

93. Piggott, *Earliest Wheeled Transport*, 90 and 95.
94. So Häusler, "Neue Belege zu Geschichte von Rad und Wagen im nordpontischen Raum."

asia is in fact extremely limited. In 1972, while excavating a Bronze Age cemetery near the town of Rimnikski, on the Sintashta River in the Urals, Soviet archaeologists uncovered five graves containing the decayed traces of vehicles that quite clearly deserve to be called "chariots" (the vehicles had two wheels, with ten spokes to the wheel). So far as chronology is concerned, "a date before or around the middle of the second millennium BC for the chariot-burials . . . would seem appropriate."[95] We have already noted the slightly earlier, although less direct, evidence for "chariots" on the steppe: pairs of horse skeletons found in the Timber Graves along the Lower Volga, the graves dating to ca. 1700 B.C.

The only other evidence of any kind for early "chariots" in the lands north of the Near East comes from the other end of the horse-breeding koine: in Hungary and eastern Czechoslovakia, Bronze Age graves have yielded pottery models of spoked wheels, and the graves have been carbon dated to the first half of the second millennium. That the modelers had two-wheeled rather than four-wheeled vehicles in mind cannot be proven, but unambiguous evidence for two-wheelers is not far away. At Trebisov, in eastern Slovakia, a decorated pot quite clearly shows four vehicles, each with two wheels (the wheels having four spokes), and each drawn by a team of horses. The pot came from a cremation grave dated shortly after 1500 B.C.[96]

Although the evidence for "chariots" in the horse-breeding koine is not quite so early as the cylinder seals from Kültepe, it must be conceded that "chariots" made their appearance in southern Russia and eastern Europe at about the same time that they were being sought by kings in the Near East. In the steppes above the Caucasus and the Caspian Sea there is evidence that in the sixteenth century B.C. "chariot" teams were

95. S. Piggott, "Bronze Age Chariot Burials in the Urals," *Antiquity* 49 (1975): 289.

96. Piggott, *Earliest Wheeled Transport*, 92–94.

in use in widely scattered communities.[97] Wherever the invention of the spoked wheel occurred, it very clearly was followed by a remarkably rapid diffusion of the "chariot," from the Danube to the Urals, and from the headwaters of the Volga to the Persian Gulf.[98] That is not to say, of course, that the "chariot" was a commonplace throughout the entire area. One would suppose that in the steppe, where domesticated horses were so plentiful, there were more "chariots" in the eighteenth century B.C. than there were in Mesopotamia or Syria, but even in the north it is likely that the "chariot" was at that time a rare and prestigious vehicle.

Whether it was the technique of chariot manufacture that was diffused, or whether the vehicles themselves were traded over long distances from some central region where they were made is not certain. Probability, however, and the little evidence that we have, both point to the second alternative. Neither the wood nor (we must suppose) the woodworking skills necessary for the making of chariots were available in most of the Eurasian steppe and the Fertile Crescent. If the environment of the North Pontic steppe in the second millennium B.C. was roughly the same as in modern times (and there is no evidence to the contrary), the timber necessary for the manufacture of any vehicle—whether wagon, cart, or chariot— "would have to be sought in either the Woodland Steppe zone

97. Kuz'mina, "Stages in the Development of Wheeled Transport in Central Asia," 120.

98. In discussing the origins of the tripartite disk wheel, Piggott (*Earliest Wheeled Transport*, 63) makes a good case for the "diffusionist" theory, and against the theory of independent indigenous developments ("Switzerland and Sumer can hardly have invented, independently and simultaneously, the tri-partite disc wheel around 3000 BC"). By way of analogy, Piggott points to the rapid diffusion of the riding horse among American Indians, from the Carribean to northwestern Canada, after being introduced by the Spaniards. The diffusion of the "chariot" through most of Eurasia was apparently even more rapid than the diffusion of the tripartite wheel.

to the north or the Caucasus to the east."[99] Mesopotamia and Syria were even less self-sufficient in the matter of chariotry, since these areas lacked not only the necessary wood but also horses. The letters of Shamshi-Adad of Ashur to his son, and of Aplachanda of Carchemish to Zimri-Lim of Mari, show that in the Fertile Crescent, at least, rich and powerful men of the eighteenth century B.C. had to arrange for "chariots" and chariot horses to be brought from distant places, lying somewhere to the north of the Fertile Crescent. Let us review the credentials of Armenia, or eastern Anatolia, as a center from which chariots and, when necessary, chariot horses might have been exported.

During the Upper Paleolithic period, horses evidently were not nearly so common in Armenia as they were in the Eurasian steppe. For the fourth and third millennia, three sites, all near Elazig, have yielded skeletal evidence for domesticated horses,[100] and one gathers that before 2000 B.C. the inhabitants of Armenia did not consider the horse an especially desirable domesticated animal. In later times, however, by Near Eastern standards Armenia was a veritable land of horses. As far back as they reach, literary sources show that eastern Anatolia was famous for its horses. Strabo, who was a native of Pontic Amasia, observed (11.13.7) that Armenia was a superlative "horse-pasturing" country. The Persian kings, he said, used to obtain many of their "Nesaean" horses from Armenia. These "Nesaeans" were famous all through classical antiquity: Herodotus (7.40) reported that they were the biggest, and Aristotle (*Hist.Anim.* 9.48) that they were the fastest horses known. Strabo passes on the story that the Persian kings kept fifty thousand mares in their Nesaean herds in Media and Armenia, and elsewhere (11.14.9) he tells us that every year the satrap of Armenia would send twenty thousand colts to the

99. Ibid., 56.
100. J. Mellaart, "Anatolia and the Indo-Europeans," *JIES* 9 (1981): 137.

Persian king. In the sixth century B.C., Ezekiel (27:14) declared that the Phoenicians of Tyre, who were accustomed to having the best of everything, got their horses from Togarmah. This Togarmah, or Til-Garimmu, was "on the border of Tabal," in southwestern Armenia.[101] The Assyrians remarked on the horses and horsemanship of Urartu, the lands around Lake Van, Lake Urmia, and Mt. Ararat: so, for example, Sargon II in his account of his eighth campaign (714 B.C.).[102] Tiglath-Pileser I, at the end of the twelfth century B.C., was one of the first Assyrian kings to campaign in Armenia. He claimed to have collected there as booty twelve hundred horses along with two thousand cattle.[103]

The earliest reference to the horses of Armenia may be the letter, mentioned above, that Aplachanda of Carchemish sent to Zimri-Lim of Mari ca. 1800 B.C. Horses were not bred in Carchemish, and Aplachanda therefore had to send to a place called Charsamna in order to obtain the chariot horses that Zimri-Lim requested. Weidner noted that Charsamna was mentioned in documents from Kültepe and from Boghazköy (he also noted that it must have long remained an equid emporium, since a Neo-Assyrian gazetteer describes it as "the mountain of horses").[104] Although precision is impossible, it is almost certain that Charsamna lay somewhere in eastern Anatolia, and it is possible that it lay in the Uzun Yayla District, east of Kayseri.[105]

101. For the location of Til-Garimmu, see Sennacherib's inscriptions in D. D. Luckenbill, *Ancient Records of Assyria and Babylonia* (Chicago: Univ. of Chicago Press, 1927), vol. 2, nos. 290 and 349.

102. Cf. ibid., no. 158: "The people who live in that district are without equal in all of Urartu in their knowledge of riding-horses. For years they had been catching the young colts of (wild) horses, native to his wide land, and raising them for his royal army."

103. Ibid., vol. 1, no. 236.

104. Weidner, "Weisse Pferde," 158.

105. Otten, *s.v.* "Harsumna" in *RLA* (4: 126), describes the name only as "an Anatolian placename" (he notes that one of the Mari letters mentions Charsamna in conjunction with Kanesh and Hattusas). For the

Because of the lack of written records for the area, archaeology has always been an important source of evidence for both the horses and the vehicles of ancient Armenia. Even in the early decades of this century, hippological surveys presented Armenia as something of a bonanza in this respect. Here were found bronze bits, the earliest known antler snaffle, vehicles of various types, and much ancient harnessing. All of the artifacts came from graves, most of which were dug for humans, but a good many of which were specifically intended for horse burials. If one surveyed all of the archaeological evidence for the use of horses in western Asia, one specialist concluded, "so stellt sich etwa Transkaukasien als sein geographisches Zentrum dar."[106] The hippological record of Armenia as it was known in the early 1950s was meticulously presented in Franz Hançar's massive survey.[107] I select here three illustrative examples. Horses that were "valued personally" by their owners were given elaborate burials, with grave goods that occasionally included gold.[108] The "Transcaucasian snaffle bit" was technologically superior to (and more effective than) other ancient bits; it attests to the primacy of the area in the breeding of high-spirited horses and its priority in the development of superior and more effective harness and gear.[109] A stele of ca. 800 B.C., found to the east of Lake Van, marks the spot where Arshibini, an obviously long-legged horse belonging to King Menua, jumped thirty-seven feet.[110]

Until recently there has been little material evidence for the horse in Armenia and Transcaucasia before the first millennium

---

more specific location, see Kammenhuber's review (*Hippologia Hethitica*, 36 and n. 143) of knowledgeable guesses; the Uzun Yayla location, favored by Kammenhuber, was proposed by F. Cornelius.

106. Hermes, "Das gezähmte Pferd im alten Orient," 387–88.

107. Hançar, *Das Pferd*, 123–93 ("Grenz- und Brückenland Kaukasien").

108. Ibid., 180–81.

109. Ibid., 182–85.

110. Ibid., 181.

B.C. This is in part, I suppose, because in the period of the Early Transcaucasian Culture (third millennium) the domesticated horse was not yet of much importance, and because for much of the second millennium the material record for Armenia is very limited. It is clear, however, that even before horse breeding became important to them, the peoples of ancient Armenia had a long tradition of wheeled transport. In the last several decades, in fact, Soviet archaeologists have confirmed the importance of Armenia, or more precisely of the chalcolithic and Bronze Age civilization of the Kura-Araxes valleys, in the development of wheeled vehicles, including—possibly—the chariot. Shortly before World War II, a great number of kurgans, or barrow graves, were hastily excavated in the Trialeti steppe, and these graves threw considerable light on the development of the ox carts and wagons in use in the Early Transcaucasian Culture. More spectacular (and better published) have been the excavations of barrow graves in a flood plain below the village of Lchashen at the southern shore of Lake Sevan (see Fig. 1). In conjunction with a hydroelectric project in the 1950s, the level of Lake Sevan was significantly lowered, and the plain with its graves thus came to light. Because the plain had been under water for almost three thousand years, the waterlogged contents of the Lchashen graves were relatively well preserved. For our purposes, the significant contents were the twenty-three wheeled vehicles buried with the deceased as grave goods. These were of several types: four-wheeled wagons with disk wheels, two-wheeled and A-frame carts, and light spoked-wheel passenger carts or "chariots."

Unfortunately, the only carbon test thus far conducted on a Lchashen vehicle is not as helpful as it might be. The vehicle chosen for the test was apparently a "chariot," but the published report is somewhat vague on this point. At any rate, the test yielded a date of ca. 1500 B.C. (± 100 years).[111] On the

111. Piggott, *Earliest Wheeled Transport*, 77–78: "A single radiocarbon date of 1200 ± 100 bc was obtained from 'wood remains of ritual

basis of the evolution of the wagon types at Lchashen and in the Trialeti steppe of Georgia, Stuart Piggott made a strong case that it was here, in the Kura-Araxes culture, that wheeled vehicles were first used; and that from this region their use spread to Mesopotamia and to central Anatolia, and eventually to Europe.[112] Many of these wagons seem to date from the third millennium, and presumably all were ox-drawn.

In a 1974 study,[113] Piggott turned his attention to the spoked-wheel vehicles from Lchashen, and to the evidence for horses at the site. Although complete horse skeletons were not found, several graves contained "heads-and-hoofs" burials or hide burials. The principal funerary animal, however, was certainly the ox, for almost all of the Lchashen graves included oxen. Aside from the limited skeletal evidence for horses, several of the Lchashen graves yielded bronze bits (six of them from a single barrow) and modeled horses. As for the two "chariots," obviously horse-drawn, Piggott not only noted their general similarity to the military chariots of the Near Eastern Late Bronze Age, but also pointed to remarkable parallels between the Lchashen two-wheelers and chariots known from Shang and Chou Dynasty China. The parallels, Piggott found, are "too specialized to be dismissed as coincidental," and he suggests that the vehicle was brought from Armenia eastward to Ferghana, possibly by the people known to philol-

chariot from burial' at Lchashen: if 'chariot' is taken literally in a translation of the original Russian, this would be from Barrow 9 or 11, but it could represent a less specific 'vehicle.' In calibrated form it would be *c.* 1500 BC."

112. Piggott, "Earliest Wheeled Vehicles." In reviewing the Transcaucasian evidence in *Earliest Wheeled Transport*, 66–70, Piggott is somewhat more conservative, noting that a carbon test has dated one of the Trialeti wagons slightly later than the archaeological evidence had suggested. In this most recent publication, too, however, he sees the Kura-Araxes region as pivotal in the development of wheeled transport. He notes, for example, that in the Trialeti wagons "even the gauge or wheel-track spacing appears to be settling towards a norm which was to be perpetuated throughout European antiquity" (ibid., 68).

113. Piggott, "Chariots in the Caucasus," 16–24.

ogists as Tocharians.[114] The spoked-wheel vehicles from Lchashen, however, are in one respect sui generis. They do not appear to have been military vehicles. With an open front, and rails at the sides and back, they seem to have been used simply for transportation. They are, then, "chariots" in the broad sense and perhaps not unlike the "chariots" sought by kings and chieftains throughout much of Eurasia in the nineteenth and eighteenth centuries B.C. Structurally, the Lchashen two-wheelers seem to belong to a type anterior to the typical Late Bronze Age military chariot. The axle is positioned under the middle of the "chariot" body, whereas throughout the Near East from the fourteenth century onward, chariot axles were positioned toward the rear. The Lchashen graves also contained miniature bronze models of chariots, and these conform to the normal military type: they have rear axles, and a box closed in front and open in the back.[115]

The Lake Sevan "chariots" were made in Armenia, since the combination of woods used in their construction (elm, oak, beech, and pine) would not have been available outside the Armenian highlands. Both the "chariots" and the other vehicles provide impressive testimony that the woodworking skills requisite for the manufacture of chariots were highly developed in Armenia. The elements are regularly joined by mortice-and-tenon, or dowel, construction. One vehicle had been elaborated with "no less than 12,000 mortices; large and small, round and square. The tilt framework in this wagon had 600 such slots or mortices alone."[116] Although it is possible that

114. Ibid., 19.
115. Littauer and Crouwel, *Wheeled Vehicles*, 78.
116. Piggott, "Earliest Wheeled Vehicles," 289. Cf. Burney, *The Peoples of the Hills*, 106: "The Lchaschen wagons and carts give proof of the skill in woodworking of the craftsmen of this region. Oak and elm were the woods most used for the wheels, axles and draught-poles, the yokes being of oak and the framework of the arched roof of the pliable yew; beech and pine were also used. The wagon with wickerwork sides from Barrow 11 at Lchaschen is typical in its dimensions, and demonstrates the immense labour which went into the manufacture of these vehicles: mortice-and-tenon or dowelled joints were used exclusively, with pegs and treenails; this wa-

carpenters and wheelwrights in Mitanni, Hatti, or the Fertile Crescent were equally accomplished, the likelihood is that at least in the first half of the second millennium they were not. As we have seen, when spoked wheels first appear in the Near East, they appear in those outposts of Near Eastern civilization—Kültepe and Chagar Bazar—closest to Armenia.

Further evidence for the primacy of the lands south of the Caucasus in the development of the chariot comes from thousands of rock carvings found in the Syunik region of Armenia, at an altitude of 3,300 meters. Although the carvings are, of course, not readily dateable, they "are considered to cover a period from the fifth through the second millennium B.C.,"[117] and they seem to show a development from wagons to spoked-wheel carts (many of them ox-drawn) and horse-drawn "chariots."[118] In short, it may be that many of the innovations that occurred in wheeled vehicles during the third and early second millennia occurred in Transcaucasia. Perhaps the spoked wheel originated here, as an improvement designed for the ox cart; and perhaps only after light, spoke-wheeled vehicles had been developed did the cart drivers begin to substitute horses for oxen, and to breed horses on a scale that until then had been found only north of the Caucasus. We may tentatively conclude that the chariot was developed in Armenia, and that the reason why it was developed there is that the making of wheeled vehicles was all along—from the very beginning of wheeled transport—a specialty of that region.

Let us now turn to our second question: can the development or the perfection of chariot warfare be traced to any one region? Here one must begin with the negative observation that nowhere in the Eurasian steppe is there any evidence whatever for

gon was made out of seventy pieces with twelve thousand mortices of varying size, round and square."

117. M. A. Littauer, "Rock Carvings of Chariots in Transcaucasia, Central Asia and Outer Mongolia," *PPS* 43 (1977): 243.

118. Ibid., 251, Littauer suggests that these spoked two-wheelers were carts, meant merely for transportation, rather than military chariots. See her figs. 1–7 for the relevant carvings.

chariot warfare, whether in the middle of the second millennium B.C. or at a later date. Horses were, of course, important in warfare on the steppe, but the typical steppe warrior was the mounted archer.[119] In Asia Minor, on the other hand, as early as ca. 1800 B.C., Anittas of Kushshara may have encountered chariots on the battlefield when he fought against the king of Salatiwara, which seems to have lain somewhere to the east of Kültepe. The earliest certain references to war chariots ascribe them to Hattusilis I and Mursilis I, the first Great Kings of Hatti, and to the cities of Hurri against whom these Great Kings fought.

In the sixteenth century, by which time chariot warfare had matured, the practitioners of the new art seem to have come mainly from the lands north of Assyria. The Hurrians, whose association with chariotry has been remarked by many scholars, were originally at home somewhere in the mountainous country just above Mitanni, and the Kassites seem to have come to Mesopotamia from the northern Zagros. The Aryans we shall look at in detail in the next chapter. Here it is sufficient to note that whether their original "home" was in Armenia, or whether they merely passed through Armenia as a stage in a Volkswanderung, they emerged from eastern Anatolia as expert chariot warriors.

The period in which effective chariot warfare began, the seventeenth century B.C., is unfortunately so poorly documented that one can do little more than speculate about the role eastern Anatolia may have played in that historic episode. We have seen that Hattusilis I seems to have employed a small but effective chariotry, and one can hardly avoid the conclusion that both his chariots and his charioteers came from somewhere in eastern Anatolia (there is no reason to think that the vehicles and their crews, any more than the horses, could have come from Mesopotamia or Syria).

---

119. On the mounted archers of the steppe, for which archaeological evidence is available from the late second millennium onward, see Hançar, *Das Pferd*, 551–63.

Where the *hyksos* chiefs who took over Egypt ca. 1650 B.C. may have gotten their chariots and charioteers is not known, but eastern Anatolia is not an unlikely source. The most direct evidence for the importance of Armenia in the development and manufacture of military chariots in the Late Bronze Age comes from Egyptian tombs. Since Egypt lacked the necessary woods, one assumes that the pharaohs regularly purchased from abroad either finished chariots or—after Egyptian woodworkers had perfected their skills—the requisite chariot wood. A tomb inscription from the reign of Amenhotep II declares that the wood for His Majesty's chariot was brought from "the country of Naharin" (Mitanni).[120] Since Mitanni itself was not wooded, we may suppose that the material came from the mountains to the north of Mitanni. In the case of the fifteenth-century chariot now in Florence's Museo Archeologico, studies of the wood done more than fifty years ago concluded that the chariot was made in Armenia, or quite precisely in the mountainous area bounded on the east by the Caspian, and on the south and west by a diagonal line extending from the southern shores of the Caspian to the Black Sea coast in the vicinity of Trebizond.[121] If Egypt was to some extent dependent upon eastern Anatolia for its chariotry during the Eighteenth Dynasty, there are grounds for suspecting that when chariot warfare first came to Egypt, it came from Armenia.

120. N. de Garis Davies, *The Tomb of Ken-Amun at Thebes* (New York: n.p., 1930), plate 22; cf. O'Callaghan, *Aram Naharaim*, 134.

121. For the ecological definition, see H. Schaefer, "Armenisches Holz in altägyptischen Wagnereien," *Sitzungsberichte der preuss. Akad. der Wissenschaften* (1931), 730ff. K. H. Dittmann, "Die Herkunft des altägyptischen Streitwagens in Florenz," *Germania* 18 (1934): 249–52, likewise concluded that the vehicle came from Armenia-Transcaucasia. Birch bark is the most important diagnostic item, since birch does not appear south of Armenia. Littauer and Crouwel, *Wheeled Vehicles*, 81, suggest that since birch bark is "easily transportable," the Florence chariot may have been built in Egypt. However, since the birch lashings were necessarily applied while still green, perhaps it is more likely that the finished chariot came from Armenia.

SIX

The Evolution of Opinion on PIE Speakers and the Horse

In the middle of the nineteenth century, most philologists and historians believed that "the Indo-Europeans" introduced the horse and horse-drawn vehicles into the Near Eastern and Mediterranean world. This belief was based on several observations. Horses and chariots were prominent, first of all, in the Rigveda and the *Iliad* and seemed to have been featured in a number of early Indo-European myths and rituals. On the other hand, the horse did not seem to appear in the art and inscriptions of Old Kingdom Egypt or, so far as it was known, of early Mesopotamia. Philologists observed that in Sanskrit, Greek, and Latin the word for horse had evolved from a Proto-Indo-European ancestor (reconstructed as *ekwos), and that the various Indo-European languages shared a remarkable number of words relating to wheeled vehicles: the English words "wheel," "yoke," "wain," and "axle" all derive from Indo-European roots. The Sanskrit word for chariot (*ratha*) was related to the Latin *rota* and the Germanic *rad*.

The belief that the draft horse was brought to the civilized world by the Indo-Europeans, however, was undermined late in the nineteenth century. When the polymath Victor Hehn was banished to central Russia, his interests turned from classical philology to wider questions of cultural and natural history; perhaps the most important product of his new interest was his pioneering study of the "migration" of plants and animals from Asia to Europe, published in 1870.[1] In his chapter

---

1. V. Hehn, *Culturpflanzen und Hausthiere in ihrem Übergang aus Asien*

on the horse, Hehn argued that in ancient times the horse was not used for pulling plows or heavy vehicles, and he concluded that although it occasionally served as a riding animal, it could not have become important until the invention of the chariot. That invention, Hehn reasoned, must have occurred after the Egyptian Old Kingdom, and he attributed it to "the Assyrians." Hehn proposed that the Indo-Europeans, like the Hyksos and the Egyptians, learned of the chariot from Assyria. Prior to their borrowing of the chariot, Hehn assumed, the Indo-Europeans would have valued the horse primarily as a source of meat, and because fermented mare's milk was a powerful intoxicant.

Arguments such as these convinced many scholars that the early Indo-Europeans knew the horse only as a food animal and, occasionally, as a riding animal. Thus Isaac Taylor concluded that "the common Aryan name for the horse must have referred to it as the object of the chase, and has no more significance than the existence of common names for the wolf and the fox."[2] In his important study of Indo-European prehistory, Otto Schrader observed that the chariotry the Aryans celebrated in the Rigveda had been learned from the Babylonians, and that in the Indo-European homeland the horse had been valued only as a source of meat and milk.[3] And Herman Hirt's definitive

---

nach Griechenland und Italien, sowie in das übrige Europa: Historisch-linguistische Skizzen (Berlin: Borntraeger, 1870). The work went through several German editions and was translated into Russian and English. The English translation is entitled *Cultivated Plants and Domesticated Animals in their Migration from Asia to Europe: Historico-Linguistic Studies* (London: Sonnenschein & Co., 1885) and in 1976 was reprinted as vol. 7 in the series, *Amsterdam Classics in Linguistics* (E.F.K. Koerner, general editor). For a general assessment of Hehn's career, see J. P. Mallory's "Victor Hehn: A Bio-bibliographical Sketch," pp. ix–xvi in the 1976 reprint.

2. Taylor, *The Origin of the Aryans*, 76.

3. O. Schrader, *Sprachvergleichung und Urgeschichte. Linguistisch-historische Beiträge zur Erforschung des indogermanischen Altertums* (Jena: Costenoble, 1883), 344–45. An English translation of Schrader's book was published in 1890.

Die Indogermanen concurred that the Indo-Europeans in their homeland knew the horse only as a food animal, and that only when they came into the civilized world did they begin to see that their food animal could also serve as a draft animal.[4] The early Indo-Europeans' wheeled vehicles, Hirt reasoned, were ox-drawn.[5] In his "archaeological answer" to the Indo-European question, Gustav Kossinna did not discuss the horse at all.[6]

This modest or minimal association between the Indo-Europeans and the horse seems to have appealed especially to scholars who located the Indo-European homeland in northern Europe—in Germany, Scandinavia, or the Baltic coast between East Prussia and Estonia. On the other hand, that the horse was quite important in early Indo-European society was one of the tenets of a small but promising school of thought that identified the Indo-European homeland with southeastern Europe or southern Russia. This identification, proposed by Otto Schrader in the later editions of his *Sprachvergleichung und Urgeschichte*, made the "original" Indo-Europeans pastoralists rather than agriculturalists and assigned them a vast homeland in the steppes from the Carpathians to the Caspian. Although the "south Russian hypothesis" was not popular with Indo-European philologists and archaeologists at the beginning of this century, it did receive a rather favorable hearing from orientalists and historians. Breasted, for example, regarded as "established fact" that ca. 2000 B.C. Aryans were pasturing their herds east of the Caspian, while their centum relatives occupied the lands from the Caspian to the Danube. For all of these Indo-Europeans, Breasted believed, "chief among their domes-

---

4. Hirt, *Die Indogermanen*, 1: 191 and 289.

5. Ibid., 354–55.

6. G. Kossinna, "Die indogermanische Frage archäologisch beantwortet," *Zeitschrift für Ethnologie* 34 (1902): 161–222. Kossinna's essay, which discusses only pottery and other material remains, symbolizes the extent to which the Indo-European question had become an archaeological question by the beginning of this century.

ticated animals was the *horse.* . . . They employed him not only for riding but also for drawing their wheeled carts."[7] Like several other scholars who emphasized the association between the Indo-Europeans and the draft horse, Breasted largely ignored the hippological argument that until the invention of the chariot, the horse would have been of little value as a draft animal.

V. Gordon Childe's *The Aryans* (1926) promoted the "south Russian hypothesis," using both archaeological and philological arguments. Not entirely a coincidence was Childe's assurance that the horse was "a specifically Aryan animal" and "the Aryan animal par excellence"[8] (Childe, of course, used the word "Aryan" as a synonym for "Indo-European"). The horses in which Childe's Aryans delighted were mostly riding horses, although occasionally used as draft animals. On the other hand, Childe's influential book did not make more than a passing reference to the chariots of the "Aryans," and encouraged the notion that in early Indo-European society the domesticated horse had a wide and general utility.

At about the same time that Childe was writing *The Aryans*, however, other scholars were beginning to assert once again that chariots and chariot warfare had been brought to the Near East by Indo-Europeans. This old view, which had faded in the late nineteenth century, was revived with the discovery of the Hittites, of the Aryans of Mitanni, and of the Kikkuli text. By the 1930s, eminent orientalists and historians—Hartmut Schmökel, Albrecht Goetze, Eduard Meyer, and Oswald Spengler among them[9]—were convinced that the chariot had indeed been brought to the Near East by Indo-Europeans. The new consensus, in fact, was that the Indo-European invasions of the civilized world had been successful primarily because the

7. Breasted, *Ancient Times*, 174; the italics are Breasted's.
8. Childe, *The Aryans*, 57 and 83.
9. For Spengler's contribution, see his "Der Streitwagen und seine Bedeutung für den Gang der Geschichte," *Dei Welt als Geschichte* 3 (1937): 280–83.

Indo-Europeans brought the horse-drawn chariot with them from their northern homeland, whether in the Eurasian steppe or in northern Europe. Most scholars by the late 1930s were agreed that toward the end of the third millennium the Indo-Europeans had pioneered driving and fighting from horse-drawn chariots.

Closer hippological analysis, however, indicated that the consensus needed revision on one or two central points. Gertrud Hermes's study of the supposedly neolithic and Early Bronze Age antler and bronze bits of Europe[10] showed once and for all that the "tamed" horse was a late-comer to northern Europe, and by so doing, it eventually contributed to the demise of the "northern European hypothesis." Equally sobering was Hermes's conclusion that the chariot originated south of the Caucasus, in eastern Anatolia. Despite these conclusions, however, Hermes not only accepted the view that the early Indo-Europeans were pioneers of chariot warfare, but refined it: she argued brilliantly that the Indo-European movements were not mass migrations of pastoralists or agriculturalists, but conquests by relatively small groups of charioteers.[11]

It is instructive to see how Hermes reconciled her findings about the provenance of the chariot with her insistence that the chariot was indispensable for the Indo-European conquests. In her reconstruction, the original Indo-Europeans inhabited the steppe from the Black Sea to the Caspian and there developed a special dependency upon the draft horse. About 2000 B.C., some Indo-Europeans from the steppe crossed the Caucasus, bringing their favorite animal with them. In their new location they came into contact with Hurrians and other peoples on the periphery of the Near East and so had access to a far more advanced craftsmanship and technology than they had known in the steppes. The light chariot was one of the first fruits of the

10. The title of her article ends with a question mark: "Das gezähmte Pferd im neolithischen und frühbronzezeitlichen Europa?"

11. "Das gezähmte Pferd im alten Orient," and "Der Zug des gezähmten Pferdes durch Europa."

symbiosis of Indo-Europeans with Hurrians and other civilized peoples, as the Indo-Europeans recognized that with a sufficiently light vehicle their horses could very profitably be put to military use. Very soon after 2000 B.C., the Indo-Europeans perfected chariot warfare in eastern Anatolia and thereupon began their conquest of much of Europe and Asia. The first Indo-European conquest occurred when the Hittites headed westward from Armenia to central Anatolia. Several centuries later—ca. 1600 B.C.—another group of Indo-European charioteers descended upon the Aegean: it was at this time and in this way that the Greeks came to Greece.[12] On "the coming of the Greeks," Hermes was, I think, entirely correct; but when she wrote there was very little sympathy (and not much of an argument) for dating that event to 1600 B.C.

Hermes's main thesis, unfortunately, incorporated and promoted the misconception that long before the invention of the chariot the Indo-Europeans were uniquely dependent upon the horse, both as a riding animal and a draft animal. This misconception, as we have seen, was encouraged by the writings of Childe and other proponents of the "south Russian hypothesis." According to Hermes, the chariot was not built until the Indo-Europeans came into contact with Near Eastern technology. What was distinctive about Proto-Indo-European society in the third (and even in the late fourth) millennium, as she saw it, was the "tamed" horse per se: the Proto-Indo-Europeans, with their antler and bronze bits, were "tamers of horses" long before they invented the chariot. Hermes thought that in the Indo-European homeland the tamed horse was both ridden and driven: the early Indo-Europeans pioneered the use of the draft horse, hitching it to disk-wheeled wagons and carts.[13]

12. Hermes, "Das gezähmte Pferd im alten Orient," 373–75. At n. 26 on page 374, Hermes finds it "unverständlich" that in searching for evidence for "the coming of the Greeks" most scholars ignored the shaft graves, the tholos tombs, and the monumental architecture of the Mycenaeans, and turned instead to a scrutiny of the pottery.

13. Ibid., 393–94.

Her articles thus helped to disseminate the idea, now accepted in most Indo-Europeanist scholarship, that the PIE speakers were especially dependent upon the domesticated horse (or, stated the other way round, that the domesticated horse was somehow peculiar to the PIE-speaking community, and that this peculiarity antedated the chariot by centuries or even millennia).

Once the notion took root that the Indo-Europeans were a horse-taming race, the question arose whether they rode their horses or drove them. Josef Wiesner, fighting a rear-guard action, insisted that the Indo-Europeans were surely not riders: no evidence linked the Aryans, the Greeks, or the Hittites to equitation, whereas a great deal of evidence showed that these peoples used the horse as a draft animal. And because the Indo-Europeans were drivers rather than riders, Wiesner urged, one could be quite certain that their homeland was in northern Europe, and not in the Eurasian steppe (where equitation was traditional and indisputable). More specifically, Wiesner located the homeland in the Schnurkeramik and Battle Axe Culture of central and northern Europe. There, he concluded, the Indo-Europeans had begun harnessing their horses to plows and wagons during the third millennium.[14] The wave of Indo-European invaders who came to Greece and Anatolia soon after 2000 B.C., Wiesner supposed, had the draft horse but not the chariot. Approximately four centuries later, other Indo-Europeans who had been living in the lowlands of eastern Europe[15] began to drive southward. One group headed southwest toward the Lower Danube and the Aegean, and the other headed for the Caspian, eventually reaching Persia and India. It was this second wave of Indo-European invaders, Wiesner concluded, that brought the chariot to the civilized world. As for the place of its invention, Wiesner hesitated between the Baltic

14. Wiesner, "Fahren und Reiten," 23–24.
15. Ibid., 41.

coast and "die grossen Tieflandsgebiete von der Nordsee bis zum Schwarzen Meer."[16]

But Wiesner's reconstruction, along with the entire thesis of a northern European Urheimat for the Indo-Europeans, was soon out of favor. The ever more popular view was that the prehistoric PIE speakers rode their horses, and that they rode them in the Eurasian steppes. Wilhelm Schmidt described the PIE speakers as a rider folk of central Asia, whose association with the domesticated horse preceded by thousands of years their invention of the chariot and their first migrations.[17] What one pictured was a society rather like that of Herodotus's Scythians, a nation of horse-riding pastoralists. One could even go on to describe the character of these Indo-European nomads, their "passion de la vitesse et leur goût du risque."[18]

While the Indo-Europeans' association with the domesticated horse continued to grow, their association with chariotry was all but dissolved in the 1950s. Although Hermes had argued as early as 1936 that the chariot originated south of the Caucasus, twenty years passed before anyone ventured to draw from that thesis a fairly obvious (although ultimately—I believe—an erroneous) conclusion: if chariot warfare arose south of the Caucasus, the PIE speakers could not have been responsible for it, since the Indo-European homeland did not lie south of the Caucasus. This was the conclusion—eminently

16. Ibid.,43–44.

17. W. Schmidt, *Rassen und Völker in Vorgeschichte und Geschichte des Abendlandes*, 2 vols. (Lucerne: Stocker, 1946). For a summary of his views, see Schmidt's "Die Herkunft der Indogermanen." Although Schmidt did credit the Indo-Europeans with the introduction of chariot warfare, what interested him most was the Indo-Europeans' immemorial association with the domesticated horse. Schmidt concluded that the Indo-European homeland must have been located near the place where horses were first domesticated. This place he identified as the steppes of central Asia, where he supposed ("Herkunft," 314–15) that evidence for the domesticated horse went back as far as the ninth millennium.

18. E. Delebecque, *Le Cheval dans l'Iliade* (Paris: Klincksieck, 1951), 226.

logical, it appeared at the time—put forward by Franz Hançar in his *Das Pferd in prähistorischer und früher historischer Zeit*, published in 1956. Like Hermes (and on the strength of a far more thorough sifting of the evidence), Hançar concluded that the chariot originated in eastern Anatolia, or Armenia. Unlike Hermes, however, Hançar regarded such a provenance as incompatible with the view that the PIE speakers had pioneered chariot warfare. As he saw it, the evidence for the chariot's development in the Near East, and above all in eastern Anatolia, "eliminates from the pages of history the image of an invincible wave of Indo-European chariots, everywhere overwhelming the land."[19] In place of the PIE speakers, Hançar suggested the Hurrians as the people responsible for perfecting and disseminating chariot warfare.

Hançar's conclusions were immediately reinforced (and given wide currency among orientalists) by Annelies Kammenhuber. This respected Hittitologist, whose publications include not only the definitive edition of the Kikkuli treatise but also a monograph on the Aryans in the Near East,[20] clearly and emphatically denied that chariot warfare in the Near East was introduced by Indo-Europeans.[21] Kammenhuber believed that the Kikkuli treatise confirmed Hançar's suggestion (which had been based almost entirely on archaeological evidence) that the

19. The argument is developed especially at pages 525–35 of *Das Pferd*. Although acknowledging Indo-European exploitation of (and expertise in) chariot warfare, Hançar emphatically rejected the view that the Indo-Europeans were instrumental in perfecting it, or that the Indo-Europeans were responsible for bringing it to the Near East. The Near Eastern data "streichen die Vorstellung der alles Land siegreich überrollenden indogermanischen Streitwagengeschwader . . . aus dem Geschichtsbild" (p. 525).

20. Kammenhuber, *Hippologia Hethitica*, and *Die Arier im Vorderen Orient*. Kammenhuber's publications on the subject began with her "Philologische Untersuchungen zu den 'Pferdetexten' aus dem Keilschriftarchiv von Boghazköy," *Münchener Studien zur Sprachwissenschaft* 2 (1952): 47–120.

21. In her own words (*Die Arier*, 238), her several studies have demonstrated that "man die Arier endgültig nicht mehr für Pferd und Wagen im Vorderen Orient verantwortlich machen kann."

PIE speakers learned their chariotry from the Hurrians. It was the Hurrians, Kammenhuber insisted, who brought the art of chariot warfare to its highest point of development. For Kammenhuber, as for Hançar, the crucial fact was that chariotry was an indigenous development in the Near East, and of course both scholars assumed that the Indo-European homeland lay not in the Near East but north of the Caucasus.

Such, in brief outline, has been the evolution of assumptions about PIE speakers, the horse, and the chariot. As a result of all this, there is today—among scholars in several disciplines—a general and vague impression that the domesticated horse was at a very early date uniquely important in Proto-Indo-European society, that the PIE speakers were somehow especially dependent upon the wheeled vehicle (whether ox-drawn or horse-drawn is usually unclear), but that they very likely were not responsible for the development of chariot warfare. The rival orthodoxies on the location of the Indo-European homeland are beneficiaries of this hazy association of domesticated horses and wheeled vehicles with PIE speakers: since in both the Ukraine and the Carpathian Basin there is ample evidence for the domesticated horse and the wheeled vehicle, these two regions have seemed to have the best credentials as the Indo-European Urheimat. Since the domesticated horse, rather than the horse-drawn war chariot, is now center stage in both linguistic and archaeological scholarship on the Proto-Indo-Europeans, it is no surprise that most Indo-Europeanists assume that the Proto-Indo-European homeland must have lain somewhere in the "horse-breeding koine" of southern Russia and eastern Europe.

The association of the PIE speakers with the domesticated horse has encouraged some scholars to assume that evidence for horse sacrifices, or for the ritual importance of the horse, is reliable evidence for the presence of an Indo-European language.[22] In its simplest and most extreme form, the identifi-

22. J. Maringer, "The Horse in Art and Ideology of Indo-European

cation of Indo-Europeans with the domesticated horse expresses itself in the assumption that when one finds evidence for domesticated horses (even when they were nothing but food animals), one has found evidence for Indo-Europeans. Thus Homer Thomas, in looking for archaeological evidence that in the second half of the third millennium an Indo-European language was already being spoken in southeastern Europe, observes that "the horse, which the philologist has long associated with the Indo-Europeans, offers further evidence that these invaders were Indo-Europeans."[23] Similarly, in rounding up "data which prove the presence of ethnic Indo-Europeans," Gamkrelidze and Ivanov give pride of place to "the remains of domesticated horses."[24] In so doing, the linguists were merely echoing James Mellaart, who presented horse bones as "archaeological evidence" that there were "Indo-European speakers" in Anatolia in the middle of the fourth millennium.[25]

A less extreme version of the association between PIE speakers and the horse is the assumption that the "tamed" horse, which is to say the horse used as a riding animal or a draft animal, was peculiar to Proto-Indo-European society. The belief that PIE speakers pioneered the taming of horses and introduced the wheeled vehicle to Europe is imbedded in the foundation of Gimbutas's "Kurgan hypothesis": her Proto-Indo-Europeans who invade Europe in the middle of the fifth millennium are "horse-riding pastoralists from the Pontic steppes," who bring with them ox-drawn wagons (the more likely possibility is that wagons did not exist until ca. 3000 B.C.).[26] By

---

Peoples," *JIES* 9 (1981): 177–204; J. P. Mallory, "The Ritual Treatment of the Horse in Early Kurgan Tradition," ibid., 205–26.

23. Thomas, "Dating the Indo-European Dispersal in Europe," 200.

24. Gamkrelidze and Ivanov, "Problem," 179.

25. Mellaart, "Anatolia and the Indo-Europeans," p. 137.

26. Gimbutas, "Old Europe in the Fifth Millennium B.C.: The European Situation on the Arrival of Indo-Europeans," in *The Indo-Europeans in the Fourth and Third Millennia*, ed. E. C. Polomé (Ann Arbor, Mich.: Ka-

arguing that the domesticated horse appeared in the Ukraine before it came to the Balkans, one scholar supposes that he is confirming Gimbutas's theory that the PIE speakers came from the Ukraine,[27] while another assumes that the Carpathian Basin's priority over the Ukraine in the production of wheeled vehicles points to the Basin as the probable homeland.[28] The confusion is further confounded by Gamkrelidze and Ivanov, who suppose that in their Armenian homeland the PIE speakers were hitching wheeled vehicles to draft horses as early as the fourth millennium.[29]

In the interest of clarification, let us recall a few points made in Chapter Five. Throughout the immense area to which the wild horse was native, the domesticated horse is attested in the neolithic and chalcolithic periods. By the end of the third millennium, the domesticated horse was so common that in a number of sites, from central Europe to central Asia, more than half of the bones recovered by archaeologists were horse bones. That the PIE speakers had a word for horse is of almost no significance, since every people living in or near the horse's natural habitat must have had such a word. There is, in short, no reason to believe that third-millennium PIE speakers were any more dependent upon the horse as a food animal than were

---

roma Publishers, 1982), 18. Most recently, see Gimbutas, "Primary and Secondary Homeland of the Indo-Europeans," 188: "the horse was introduced to Europe by the Kurgan people in the second half of the 5th millennium B.C." Gimbutas's attribution of wheeled vehicles to these early Kurganites has drawn criticism from Indo-Europeanists as well as archaeologists. Edgar Polomé, "Indo-European Culture, with Special Attention to Religion," in *The Indo-Europeans in the Fourth and Third Millennia*, ed. Polomé, 160, asks how it is possible to posit an Indo-European migration into Europe ca. 4400 B.C. "if the cartwright's trade postdates the first migrations by more than a millennium."

27. Bökönyi acknowledges Gimbutas's encouragement in his introduction to "Domesticated Horses."

28. Häusler, "Neue Belege," 675–76.

29. Gamkredlidze and Ivanov, "The Ancient Near East and the Indo-European Question," 12–13.

other Eurasian societies. And there is no justification for interpreting the bones of a domesticated horse as evidence for the presence of an Indo-European language.

Nor is there any reason to suppose that the "tamed" horse, or a horse controlled by a bit, was peculiar to Proto-Indo-European society. Childe, Hermes, and Wiesner assumed that it was, and the assumption is by now perhaps ineradicable, but it is unfounded. If one supposes that the PIE speakers used the bit to control riding horses, we must counter that the riding of horses was not characteristic of any of the Indo-European peoples who are *known* from the second millennium: neither the Bronze Age Greeks, nor the Aryans of India, nor any of the Aryans attested in Near Eastern texts had any reputation as riders. If, on the other hand, it is argued that for the PIE speakers the bit was important because it enabled them to use the horse as a draft animal, the response must be that prior to the invention of the spoked wheel—early in the second millennium—the horse's value as a draft animal was insignificant. In short, there are no grounds at all for supposing that in the fifth, fourth, or third millennia Proto-Indo-European society was distinguished by the employment of tamed horses.

The matter of wheeled vehicles is somewhat different. Here we must first make a distinction between the use of the vehicles and their manufacture. Throughout most of the third millennium, the use of ox-drawn carts and wagons was widespread, from the Persian Gulf and central Asia to Denmark. Not all societies, it is true, found wheeled transport practicable. On the Greek mainland, wheeled vehicles are not attested for the Early and Middle Bronze periods,[30] nor is there evidence for them in Egypt or the southern Levant at that time. In Syria and Mesopotamia, carts and wagons were employed from 3000 B.C. onward, although by far the most common means of transportation continued to be the pack animal, moving either singly or in caravan. In the forested regions of Eurasia, on the

30. Crouwel, *Chariots*, 54–58.

other hand, wheeled vehicles seem to have been considerably more numerous than they were in the Near East. The land of the PIE speakers may have been one of many in which ownership of an ox-drawn vehicle was not restricted to the very wealthy.

The manufacture of wheeled vehicles was more localized than their use. Although the Sumerians knew both the four-wheeled wagon and the two-wheeled cart, there is no evidence that they built the vehicles. As Piggott's *Earliest Wheeled Transport* shows, carts and wagons were built in those areas where oaks and other large hardwood trees were available. South of the Armenian mountains all such trees were scarce, and many species did not grow at all; on the mountains of Lebanon there were cedars and other conifers, but these are softwood trees. North of the Black Sea, the peoples of the open steppe presumably had to acquire from forested regions the vehicles of which they were so fond.

It is therefore likely that in the third millennium the PIE speakers' accomplishments as cartwrights and wainwrights distinguished them from many other societies. That the PIE speakers did manufacture wheeled vehicles is indicated by their vocabulary: the inherited Indo-European terms for wheel, yoke, wain, axle, and other vehicular elements suggest that the PIE speakers' self-sufficiency in this respect must have begun almost at the very beginning of wheeled transport (had it not, one would expect to find the PIE speakers borrowing words along with the object for which they stood). If they had neighbors whose lands produced no large hardwood trees, the PIE speakers would almost certainly have had a specialty of sorts in the manufacture of ox-drawn vehicles. Such a specialization may be deduced, but it cannot be demonstrated from the evidence now available.

In summary, there is no reason to think that before the invention of the "chariot" the PIE speakers were unusually dependent upon the domesticated horse. Nor would they have been remarkable for their use of the ox-drawn vehicle, although it is quite possible that many of them were specialists in its manufacture. What seems to have been the most distinctive feature of Proto-Indo-European society, it will be argued in the following chapter, appeared only in the last generations of that society: expertise in building, driving, and fighting from chariots. Nineteenth-century scholars suggested the association between Indo-Europeans and the draft horse in part because they noticed that chariot warfare and chariot racing were important in the Rigveda, the *Iliad*, and the common mythology of the Indo-European peoples. For many scholars in the early twentieth century, the Indo-Europeans' association with chariot warfare was confirmed by the Kikkuli treatise and the discovery of Aryan charioteers in the Near East.

The association between PIE speakers and chariot warfare, however, has been chronically blurred and obscured. The notion that what was peculiar to Proto-Indo-European society was the domesticated horse per se (and, possibly, the wheeled vehicle) is a misconception that for the last fifty years has sent investigators down false trails. We must once again focus the argument on its original object—the chariot.

SEVEN

PIE Speakers
and the Beginnings of
Chariot Warfare

During the last fifty years, as I have shown in Chapter Six, the PIE speakers' association with chariot warfare has been obscured and then denied. In broad outlines, the general opinion that prevailed on this topic in the 1930s seems to have had more validity than does the one that prevails today. It is perhaps not a paradox that this regress has been accompanied by a daunting increase in detailed information (archaeological especially) on chariotry and other wheeled vehicles, as well as on the prehistory of Europe and the Eurasian steppe, and on the Bronze Age of Greece and the Near East.

In order to understand the deterioration of opinion on our topic, we must begin by noting that part of the foundation for the 1930s consensus was defective. A major defect even in Hermes's perceptive and valuable reconstruction was the chronology upon which it was built. Hermes erroneously placed the dawn of chariot warfare ca. 2000 B.C., more than three hundred years too early, because in her day most Assyriologists were still dating the Age of Hammurabi to the late third millennium, and Mursilis's sack of Babylon to the beginning of the second (Hermes accepted Meyer's date—1926 B.C.—for that event). For many scholars, the early date worked out well enough for explaining the Hittite nation's invasion of central Anatolia at the turn of the second millennium as well as the Greeks' invasion of Greece ca. 1900 B.C., although for the more meticulous it was somewhat puzzling that there was no evidence for the chariot in Greece for the first three centuries after the invasion (Hermes's conclusion that the Greeks came to Greece ca. 1600 B.C. was generally ignored).[1] Even more irritating was the fact that the chariot did not seem to have come to Egypt until the seventeenth century B.C. A "culture gap" had to be postulated in order to explain Egypt's laggardly situation, and it seemed that "adoption" of the horse-drawn chariot must have been a fairly slow and optional affair.

When Sidney Smith, Ernst Weidner, and William Albright revised Mesopotamian chronology, lowering Hammurabi by three hundred years, the date for the beginning of chariot warfare was (for those who followed these things closely) correspondingly lowered. What happened to Egypt in the seventeenth century became more intelligible thereby, but the Hittite and Greek invaders at the beginning of the second millennium were left without chariots. If orientalists had it right that chariot warfare did not appear until the seventeenth century B.C., and if prehistorians of Greece were correct in concluding that the Greeks came to Greece ca. 1900 B.C., then one had to concede that at least some of the Indo-Europeans had managed their invasions quite successfully without the chariot. All the more did this seem true when the Hittites were considered: if the Hittite nation came to Asia Minor before 1900 B.C. (and the Kültepe tablets certainly seemed to prove that the Hittite nation was in central Anatolia by that time), then both of the earliest Indo-European invasions occurred without the benefit of the chariot. These chariotless invasions, of course, could not have been effected by small companies of conquerors. They obviously were mass migrations, which by sheer numbers overwhelmed the indigenous populations of Greece and central Anatolia.

That is more or less the picture that Josef Wiesner proceded

1. For example, Schmidt, "Die Herkunft der Indogermanen," 315–16, supposed that the invention of the chariot ca. 2000 B.C. made it possible for the Indo-Europeans to begin their westward thrust from central Asia: the Hittite invasion of Asia Minor and the Greek invasion of Greece (ca. 1900 B.C.) were the first fruits of the new invention.

to draw: ca. 2000 B.C., Indo-Europeans who used the horse as a draft animal, but did not yet have the chariot, came en masse from northern Europe to Greece and Asia Minor.[2] In the sixteenth century B.C., a second wave of Indo-Europeans, with the chariotry that they themselves had recently invented, came from the Indo-European homeland to join their Indo-European cousins at Mycenae and Hattusas,[3] and they came as well to Mitanni, to various cities in the Levant, and to India.[4] What motivated the Indo-Europeans to migrate southward, both in the earlier and the later wave, had never seemed a serious question, and Wiesner (like most of his predecessors) disposed of it with one short sentence: perhaps the climate in the homeland had changed for the worse.[5]

Since Wiesner's time, most scholars have abandoned the belief that PIE speakers introduced the chariot to the civilized

2. In fact, Wiesner was not aware of any reference to chariotry in the Hittite texts from the Old Kingdom and accordingly concluded that the Hittites did not adopt chariotry until the period of the Empire. Cf. "Fahren und Reiten," 23–24.

3. On the relationship of the charioteering Indo-Europeans to the original Greek and Hittite invaders of the twentieth century B.C., cf. ibid., 38: "In Mykene kann dieses Herrentum [i.e., the sixteenth-century charioteers], das sich in neuem Formengut und neuem Brauchtum äussert, in seinem Kriegsgeist an die Tradition der ihm rassisch verwandten Streitaxtleute anknüpfen, in Kleinasien an das ältere Reich der Hethiter. So vollzieht sich überall ein jäher Aufstieg zu kultureller und politischer Grösse."

4. Ibid., 37–44. Curiously, Wiesner did not concern himself much with chronological matters; he apparently followed the old chronology that dated Hammurabi to the end of the third millennium (on page 41, for example, he places the Kassite invasion of Mesopotamia in the eighteenth century B.C.). This might have spoiled his thesis, had he known of the tablets and cylinder seals that show that the chariot was already known in Mesopotamia in Hammurabi's time. However he came to them, Wiesner's ultimate chronological conclusions—that the migrations of the charioteers occurred in or shortly before the sixteenth century B.C.—were approximately on target.

5. Ibid., 44: "Den Grund für den Aufbruch dürfen wir vielleicht in schweren klimatische Veränderungen suchen."

world (their introduction of chariotry into India is conceded, but that episode is seen as anomalous rather than typical). While Indo-Europeanists, following Childe's, Hermes's, and Wiesner's unfortunate lead, generally persist in the belief that the domesticated horse was from early on (well before the invention of the chariot) uniquely important in Proto-Indo-European society, they have for the most part given up Hermes's and Wiesner's quite valid insistence that the Indo-Europeans played a central role in the development and spread of chariot warfare.[6] Most ancient historians, too, if they have explored the origins of chariot warfare, have also fallen away from the belief that the war chariot was perfected by the PIE speakers.

The main reason for this apostasy has been the majority view of hippologists and archaeologists that chariot warfare was indeed developed and perfected south of the Caucasus (a conclusion that is almost certainly correct), and the insistence of an eminent Hittitologist that the Aryans had nothing to do with the advent of chariot warfare in the Fertile Crescent and Anatolia (a conclusion that, as we shall see, rests on invalid arguments). Historians who have been diligent enough to read the specialists' arguments, and have concluded that chariot warfare did not originate in Europe or the Eurasian steppe, naturally enough have seen the chariot's eastern Anatolian provenance as an argument *against* assigning to chariotry the leading role in "the Indo-European invasions." Much less has the apparent Anatolian origin of the chariot encouraged the belief that chariot warfare was pioneered by the PIE speakers, since until now there has been no serious argument that the Indo-European

6. Some scholars who have, almost incidentally, credited the PIE speakers with the chariot have had little regard for chronology. Gamkrelidze and Ivanov, for example, make references to draft horses and chariots in third- and fourth-millennium contexts (cf. "Migrations," 61 and 75). Gimbutas, "Old Europe," 19, notes that the Indo-Europeans' "principal gods carry weapons and ride horses or chariots," but she does not add that these theological vehicles could not possibly have been envisaged by Kurgan pastoralists in the fifth, fourth, and early third millennia.

homeland could have been in Anatolia. In abandoning Wiesner's generalization that the chariot was invented in an Indo-European homeland somewhere in the lowlands between the Black Sea and the North Sea, or on the Baltic, historians have had to credit the chariot either to Hurrians or to anonymous "peoples of the hills" whom historians have hitherto imagined in Bronze Age Armenia.

We must now trace the ambivalent progress of scholarship, to see how the connection between PIE speakers and the war chariot was severed by authoritative conclusions, and thus to assess present opinion on the matter. Hançar's argument, first of all, was essentially archaeological and was limited to a demonstration that the chariot appeared south of the Caucasus before it came either to Europe or to the Eurasian steppe. That the PIE speakers had nothing to do with the introduction of chariot warfare was simply an inference that Hançar drew, based on his conclusion about the provenance of chariot warfare and on his assumption that the Indo-European homeland lay north of the Caucasus.

Far more damaging to the association between Indo-Europeans and chariotry has been Kammenhuber's argument, for it claims that documentary evidence—and in particular the Kikkuli treatise—rules out the possibility that Aryans were instrumental in bringing chariot warfare to the Near East. Many of Kammenhuber's conclusions about the Kikkuli treatise are philological and are generally accepted and valuable. She showed, first of all, that the Aryan terms in the Kikkuli treatise were "fossils," and she reasonably drew the conclusion that when the Kikkuli treatise was written, the Aryan language was not a spoken language in Mitanni.[7] Her studies also left no

7. The Aryan terms are glosses. That is, the Hittite text presents an instruction in Hittite terms, and then for good measure adds the Aryan "technical term." Kikkuli's instructions for the eighty-third day, for example, direct the trainer to trot the horses for about two and a half miles, and then to gallop them for one mile. The text gives us (Kammenhuber, *Hippologia Hethitica*, 80–81): "he lets them trot for half a *danna* and twenty *iku*,

doubt that the Kikkuli treatise had been translated into Hittite from a Hurrian text by Hurrian scribes, several of whom had a less than perfect knowledge of Hittite. The few Aryan terms in the treatise, Kammenhuber argued (and here, too, she is convincing), indicate that the Aryan speakers of Mitanni had not come to Mitanni from India (as scholars had hitherto believed), but were on their way *to* India; for these Aryans spoke the still undifferentiated Aryan out of which both the Indian and the Persian varieties of Aryan would develop. Kammenhuber also made the useful point that Aryan *ashwash* is not likely to have been the source of the word for horse in Egyptian, Hurrian, and three Semitic languages (Akkadian, Aramaic, and Hebrew).[8]

From these particular conclusions Kammenhuber drew some wider historical conclusions, not all of them sound. If the Near Eastern peoples did not borrow the Aryan word for horse, she reasoned, it is not likely that the Aryans anticipated the Near Eastern peoples in utilizing the draft horse. That there may never have been an Aryan text of the Kikkuli treatise, and that there were no Aryan speakers in Mitanni in Kikkuli's time,

---

and then gallops them for another twenty iku, which is the *aika vartanna*." Whereas in Hittite, danna and iku were as familiar as are miles or kilometers in English, the term "aika vartanna" was exotic. In Aryan it meant, literally, "one turn" (cf. the Latin *vertere*). The Hurrian and the Hittite texts preserved the Aryan terms, Kammenhuber cogently suggests, because the terms had become venerable (ibid., 293: "aus Pietätsgründen").

8. Ibid., 236–37. It is likely that all these languages (including Proto-Indo-European) borrowed their words from yet another linguistic community. On the Semitic loan-words, cf. the entry *sisu(m)* in the Meissner-Von Soden *Akkadisches Handwörterbuch*. On the entire question, see especially Goetze's review (*JCS* 16 [1962]: 34–35) of Kammenhuber's *Hippologia Hethitica*. What eventually became the normal Hittite word for horse, on the other hand, may have been borrowed from the Aryans toward the middle of the second millennium. Goetze points out that although we cannot be certain how the Hittites vocalized the word for horse (cuneiform Hittite always employs the Sumerogram ANSHE.KUR), it was probably similar to the Aryan "ashwash"; for in "Hieroglyphic Hittite" the word for horse was *ash(u)a*.

suggested to Kammenhuber that Aryan speakers had *never* ruled Mitanni: the few Aryan words and names attested in Mitanni in the fifteenth and fourteenth centuries B.C. can be explained as the result of contact made when Aryans, on their way to India, passed along the Hurrians' eastern frontier. It was during that passage, Kammenhuber proposed, that the Aryans learned about chariots from the Hurrians, and in return, the Hurrians borrowed a number of words, names, and gods from the Aryans. Having expunged the Aryan princes from Mitanni, Kammenhuber did the same for the Levant: the Aryan names one finds there, she argued, were borne by Hurrians, among whom Aryan nomenclature was in vogue. As for the maryannu, Kammenhuber emphasized the Hurrian suffix of the word and identified the warriors as Hurrian.[9] The Kassites, finally, borrowed neither words nor gods from the Aryans.[10] In short, Kammenhuber argued that the supposed incursion of Aryan charioteers into the Near East at the beginning of the Late Bronze Age was a myth. Although her conclusions on this matter have encountered occasional criticism, they remain quite influential.[11]

Let us examine Kammenhuber's thesis that Mesopotamia (rather than Anatolia) was the place where chariotry originated, and that the Hurrians were the people who brought the art of chariotry and horse breeding to its highest level. Her argument for Mesopotamia's priority over Anatolia has two points, the first of which is that the Akkadian word "narkabtu"

9. *Die Arier*, 220–23.

10. Ibid., 47ff. On pages 58–60, Kammenhuber attacks the conclusions that Mayrhofer, in *Die Indo-Arier im Alten Vorderasien*, had come to about the Aryan origin of some of the Kassite color terms for horses.

11. One of Kammenhuber's first and most respected converts was I. M. Diakonoff; see his "Die Arier im Vorderen Orient: Ende eines Mythos," *Orientalia* 41 (1972): 91–120. Her principal antagonist has been Manfred Mayrhofer. Mayrhofer's *Die Indo-Arier im Alten Vorderasien* was much criticized in Kammenhuber's *Die Arier*, and Mayrhofer responded in *Die Arier im Vorderen Orient—ein Mythos?* (Oest. Akademie der Wiss., Phil.-hist. Sitzungsberichte, Bd. 294, Abhandlung 3) (Vienna, 1974).

and the Sumerogram GISH.GIGIR (both of which usually denote a chariot in second-millennium texts) occur in a number of texts from the third and early second millennia.[12] The argument makes no mention of the fact that "narkabtu" and GISH.GIGIR originally stood for any two-wheeled cart, including the solid-wheeled cart drawn by oxen (which is the only kind of two-wheeled cart attested for third-millennium Mesopotamia). Secondly, Kammenhuber read a chariot into the Hymn of Shulgi (Shulgi does not specify whether his speedy horse was ridden or driven).[13] On the basis of these two arguments, she concluded that before 2000 B.C. the Sumerians had developed not only the chariot, but chariot warfare. Her argument makes no reference to artistic representations, to spoked wheels, or to archaeological evidence of any kind.

Nor is there much to be said for the thesis that the Aryan speakers, while lodging on the outskirts of Mitanni, learned about chariot warfare from the Hurrians. The thesis, of course, supposes that the Aryans were at the time embarked upon a massive pastoral Volkswanderung, migrating from the fertile lands of eastern Europe (Kammenhuber assumed that the Indo-European homeland lay west of the "beech tree line" from Königsberg to the mouth of the Danube)[14] toward the Zagros Mountains and the Persian desert. According to Kammenhuber's reconstruction, upon reaching the fringes of Mesopotamia, the Aryans quickly and completely learned the art of chariotry from the Hurrians. Such adept students did the Aryans prove to be that within a few decades they not only were able to use their newly acquired skills to conquer India, but also came to be regarded by many Near Easterners (and even by their Hurrian instructors) as experts in the arts of chariotry and horse breeding. Thus, although conceding that by the middle of the second millennium the Aryan speakers enjoyed a remarkable

12. Kammenhuber, "Zu den hethitischen Pferdetexten," 120, and *Die Arier*, 237.

13. *Hippologia Hethitica*, 11–12.

14. Ibid., 15.

reputation as charioteers, Kammenhuber refused to credit them with having pioneered the art.

Kammenhuber recognized, of course, that it was remarkable that the Aryans, who knew nothing about chariots when they arrived in the Near East, were so suddenly transformed into charioteers par excellence. She therefore advised that further investigations would be necessary to explain the about-face, and to determine why, for instance, Aryan terms for hippological subjects enjoyed such prestige among Hittite and Hurrian scribes.

> What is the basis for this prestige? Why in the Kikkuli treatise do the Hurrians use for "laps" terms that they had taken over from the Aryans? What help in the training of horses could the Hurrians of Mitanni expect from the Aryans, since the Hurrians themselves had known the horse and chariot longer than had the Aryans: could it be that the Aryans, after their contact with Mesopotamia had taught them to hitch chariots to their horses, so quickly gained so much experience as horse trainers that the Hurrians of Mitanni regarded and accepted them as teachers?[15]

The questions arise, of course, only because of the *parti pris* that the Aryans knew nothing about chariots until they encountered them in the "Gebirgszonen um Babylon."[16]

Kammenhuber's strained attempt to dissociate the Aryan speakers from the development and dissemination of chariotry goes against the grain of most of our evidence. It overlooks the fact, first of all, that effective chariot warfare began at the very time that the Aryans began to make their presence felt. Kammenhuber was able to ignore this synchronism because she assumed that chariot warfare in its full elaboration began when

15. *Die Arier*, 239.
16. Ibid., 238.

the first "chariot" was hitched to a team of horses (or even when the first horse ran from Nippur to Ur). As we have seen, effective chariot warfare began some two centuries after the appearance of the first "chariots," and four centuries after Shulgi of Ur delighted in the speed of his horse.

Secondly, even the evidence in the Kikkuli treatise works against Kammenhuber's thesis. The Aryan horse-training terms in the treatise, it is argued, were glossed not because the Aryan language was still in use in Mitanni in Kikkuli's day, but because they were traditional and venerable terms which "aus Pietätsgründen" the Hurrian scribe felt compelled to include. So far so good. One must go on to ask, however, how it happened that Aryan horse-training terms came to be held in such reverence by the Hurrians. One cannot suppose that after the Aryans had learned the Hurrian art of chariotry, and had added to it a few elaborations of their own, they wrote Aryan treatises on the breeding and training of chariot horses. Being illiterate, Aryan speakers must in person have brought such terms as *aika vartanna* to the attention of the Hurrians. In other words, Aryan-speaking charioteers must at one time have resided in Mitanni. What is more, these Aryan-speaking charioteers were so highly respected that not only their hippological terms but even their gods were taken over by the Hurrians. Quite clearly, the Aryan glosses in the Kikkuli treatise cannot be explained as Hurrian borrowings from a nomadic people passing along Mitanni's frontier.

Other considerations are still more damaging to Kammenhuber's argument. With its focus on vocabulary, and its emphasis on the Hurrian prototypes from which the Hittite "horse texts" must have been copied, it leaves out of consideration some fairly obvious contradictory evidence from further afield. Essentially, Kammenhuber argued that scholars' association of Aryans with chariotry is based on nothing more than a mistaken derivation of Near Eastern words for horse from the Aryan word "ashwash," and an anachronistic retrojection from the undeniable fact that the Aryans of the Rigveda were avid

charioteers. Now, it is remarkable that nowhere in *Hippologia
Hethitica* or *Die Arier im Vorderen Orient* did Kammenhuber deal
with (or even mention) the chariots of Bronze Age Greece.
That is a large omission (although in fairness it must be added
that the Greek chariots were also overlooked by the reviewers
of her books). Early in the sixteenth century B.C., as we shall
see in Chapter Eight, the Aryans' linguistic counterparts in
Greece were using chariots of the same type as those in use in
the Near East, and as those described in the Rigveda. It is not
likely that these Proto-Greek charioteers had learned to use
their vehicles while moving past a Hurrian frontier; but it is
virtually certain that the people who Indo-Europeanized
Greece "knew the chariot when they first entered Greece."[17]
The Greek analogy suggests that ca. 1600 B.C., Aryan speakers, too, were already masters of the art of charioteering, and
that it was they who brought the art to the Hurrians of Mitanni. At any rate, no discussion of the relationship of the Aryan speakers to chariotry is worth very much unless it also takes
into account the chariots of Mycenaean Greece. Kammenhuber's thesis, so widely influential, rests upon a faulty foundation.

Since highly specialized monographs—dealing either with
the Aryans in the Near East or with horses and chariots in the
Near East—have denied that the PIE speakers were responsible
for the development of chariot warfare,[18] it is hardly surprising
that the once-popular belief has been renounced by many historians, especially if they have read Kammenhuber's conclusions without testing her arguments. Thus, for example, Diakonoff advises his readers that

> another formerly widespread opinion now dis-
> proved, is that the Indo-Iranians . . . arrived in the

17. Wyatt, "The Indo-Europeanization of Greece," 107.

18. Littauer and Crouwel, *Wheeled Vehicles*, are the most recent authorities to have denied that the Indo-Europeans perfected chariot warfare.
Like their predecessors, they are forced to this conclusion by their perception that the chariot originated south of the Caucasus, and their assumption
that the Indo-European homeland lay north of the Caucasus.

Near East and in India . . . as conquerors possessing a new technique of movement on light horse-
drawn chariots and the tactics of horse-chariot battle still unknown to the peoples of the countries
which they invaded. It has now been established
that in the Near East the horse was domesticated
already in the 3rd millennium B.C. . . . Not only
in mountain regions but also in Mesopotamia
horses were harnessed to war-chariots already in the
21st to 18th centuries B.C.[19]

With such a perception of what has been "disproved" and what
has been "established," and supposing that Sumerians were using horse-drawn chariots in battle as early as the Ur III period,
Diakonoff predictably concludes that the Indo-European
movements "must not be seen as victorious expeditions of conquerors." Instead, Diakonoff is quite sure, we must imagine
the Indo-European movements as migrations of "pastoral agriculturalists over the spring grass in the course of a number of
generations."

Although Kammenhuber's (and—to a lesser extent—Hançar's) specialized monographs are in part responsible for the
current orthodoxy, there have been other reasons for rejecting
the thesis that chariotry played a crucial role in the Indo-European movements. Initially, racist presuppositions impeded
some historians from assigning much importance to the chariot
in these movements. Believing in the existence of an "Aryan"
race, and in the superiority of that race, they were not inclined
to attribute the Indo-Europeans' success to a gadget (even
Hermes allowed that the Indo-Europeans' rise to power was
rooted in their moral qualities as well as in their chariots). The
reaction to Aryanism was equally uncongenial to the idea that
the PIE speakers began as charioteering conquerors. In such a
picture, after all, especially if one gave it only a superficial
glance, one was embarrassed to see that the PIE speakers still

19. Diakonoff, in *CHI*, 1: 46.

looked like a *Herrenvolk*, lording it over Semites, Hurrians, and the pre-Indo-European inhabitants of Europe. Another school of thought was not averse to seeing the chariot as one of several means by which the PIE speakers prevailed, but was not inclined to believe that mastery of chariot warfare had motivated them to embark on their expeditions. Such an explanation seemed too simplistic, and perhaps too romantic. Better were explanations that spoke of economic developments and imbalances, of demographic pressures, or of factors too abstract to be disproven.[20]

It is time to put the PIE speakers back in their chariots. In favor of such a revision is the thesis, newly constructed by Gamkrelidze and Ivanov, that the Proto-Indo-European language was "initially" spoken south of the Caucasus, somewhere in the area now covered by northeastern Turkey, the northwestern tip of Iran, and the Soviet republics of Azerbaijan, Georgia, and Armenia. Gamkrelidze and Ivanov based their argument primarily on linguistic evidence and analyses, and on the relationship of the Indo-European to the Semitic and the Caucasian language families. If we disregard their assumptions (and their too hastily drawn conclusions) about the chronology and nature of "the Indo-European invasions," we are left with an eminently usable thesis about the location of the

20. D'iakonov, "On the Original Home of the Speakers of Indo-European," 149–51, argues that a Proto-Indo-European homeland in the northern Balkans is more likely than a homeland in Armenia because the northern Balkans are more fertile than Armenia. The argument begins with the statement that the PIE speakers would never have migrated had they not been forced to do so by external circumstances. Overpopulation, D'iakonov contends, must have been the principal factor. And overpopulation "can be explained only by an unusual percentage of children's survival, and consequently, by the growth of food production, especially such nutritious foods as meat, dairy products, vegetables, wheat, and so on" (p. 149). The Armenian plateau and Transcaucasia, however, could not have produced great quantities of these foods. "The plateau itself consisted of isolated, poorly connected mountainous valleys: the slopes were completely covered with forests unfit for cattle pasture" (p. 151).

Indo-European homeland. As the concluding section of Chapter Five has indicated, what evidence we have about the provenance of chariot warfare fits exactly with the thesis that early in the second millennium the PIE speakers lived in Armenia.

The argument works both ways. Just as Gamkrelidze and Ivanov's thesis strengthens the likelihood that chariot warfare originated in Armenia, so does that likelihood strengthen the linguists' thesis. Perhaps it is theoretically conceivable that the PIE speakers pioneered rapid and comfortable transportation by "chariot" in a homeland located in the forest-steppe or the open steppe above the Black Sea, or possibly in the Carpathian Basin. Although there is no direct evidence for the spoked wheel north of the Caucausus before the middle of the second millennium,[21] one would suppose that light and spoked-wheel "chariots" were known in the horse-breeding koine at least as early as ca. 1700 B.C. (the date of the Timber Graves containing teams of slaughtered draft horses, and of the models of spoked wheels in the Slovakian and Hungarian graves). But that chariot *warfare* was perfected in the lands north of the Caucasus is not suggested by any evidence, and is in fact quite unlikely, since there is no period in which chariot warfare is attested for the Eurasian steppe. Our earliest evidence for chariot warfare comes from Anatolia. If the PIE speakers were in large part responsible for the development of chariot warfare, eastern Anatolia is a far more likely Indo-European homeland than either the Carpathian Basin or the Pontic steppes.

There is another, and more important, reason for reviving the old notion that the Indo-European "invasions" were in fact conquests by charioteering peoples. This is the erosion of evidence for Indo-European invasions at the very beginning of the second millennium. As we have seen, the argument for dating the arrival of the Greeks to 1900 B.C. has disintegrated, and there are no grounds whatever for moving that arrival back still

21. Piggott, "Bronze Age Chariot Burials in the Urals," 289; Littauer and Crouwel, *Wheeled Vehicles*, 70.

further, to 2100 B.C. Secondly, it is now quite clear that there was no "Hittite invasion" of central Anatolia in the twentieth century B.C. And we have seen that—whatever the relationship between Proto-Anatolian and Proto-Indo-European might have been—the presence of Proto-Anatolian speakers in Hatti at the beginning of the second millennium implies nothing about "Indo-European invasions." Finally, what evidence there is suggests that the Aryan incursion into India took place no earlier than the middle centuries of the second millennium. Thus, it is time to abandon the belief that Indo-Europeans, in massive Volkswanderungen, began invading and taking over other peoples' lands at the end of the third and the beginning of the second millennium.

Let us turn to the facts. Aside from the Proto-Anatolian names in the Kültepe tablets, the earliest possibly Indo-European names that come to the historian's attention occur in a Hittite document, known as the "Legend of the Cannibals," dating to ca. 1600 B.C.: three cities in Hurri (perhaps, but not necessarily, synonymous with Mitanni) were at that time ruled by men with what look like Aryan names—Urutitta, Uwagazzana, and Uwanta.[22] And we may infer that at some time before the establishment of the Eighteenth Dynasty (ca. 1550 B.C.) there had come to the Levant the ancestors of those maryannu princes whose Aryan names are so striking in the Amarna correspondence. The very names of the PIE speakers who appear in these early texts are redolent of horses. The name of the greatest of the Great Kings of Mitanni, Tushratta (or Tush-rata), meant something like "having the chariot (rata) of terror." Bardashwa, the name of at least four individuals in fifteenth-century Nuzi, meant "possessing great horses," and Biridashwa (prince of Yanuamma) was "he who owns a grown horse." The name of Zurata, prince of Accho, can be translated as "one who owns a good chariot."[23]

22. Güterbock, "Die historische Tradition," 108–109; cf. Albright, "New Light," 30, and Drower, in *CAH* II, 1: 420–21.

23. P. E. Dumont, "Indo-Iranian Names from Mitanni, Nuzi and

It is not only individual PIE speakers whose association with chariotry is conspicuous. In most of the Near East, two equestrian professional classes were designated by Aryan loan-words: the *marya* in Egyptian and Akkadian texts was a charioteer or chariot fighter, and the LU.ashshushshani of the Hittite texts was a horse trainer. The only convincing explanation for the loan-words is that the first charioteers and the first horse trainers in the Fertile Crescent and central Anatolia had been Aryans.

More ambiguous, but perhaps equally significant, is the evidence supplied by comparatist scholarship on Indo-European ritual and mythology. Indo-Europeanists have long been aware of the remarkable similiarities in the Vedic ritual known as the Ashvamedha and the early Roman ritual of the October Horse. In both societies, a two-horse chariot race was held annually, and the horse on the right side of the winning team was sacrificed to the war god.[24] The ritual parallels are here so striking that most Indo-Europeanists have concluded that a common ceremony lies behind the Vedic and the Roman traditions.[25]

Syrian Documents," *JAOS* 67 (1947): 251–53; O'Callaghan, *Aram Naharaim*, 56–63.

24. In Rome the sacrificiant was the Flamen Martialis. W. W. Fowler, *The Roman Festivals of the Period of the Republic* (London: Macmillan, 1916), 241–50, was led by Frazer to see the October Horse as an agricultural rather than a military animal, and the ceremony as originating in "the simple rites of the farm." The horse slain by the spear of the Flamen Martialis was originally a "farm horse," who had shared the farmer's spring and summer labors. Roman farm horses, alas, are as imaginary as unicorns. For a Macedonian ritual in which "horses in armor" were sacrificed as a lustration for the army, see Polybius 23.10.17.

25. Cf. P. E. Dumont, *L'Asvamedha* (Paris: Geuthner, 1927), 23; G. Dumezil, *Archaic Roman Religion* (Chicago: Univ. of Chicago Press, 1970), 216. For an archaeological argument to the contrary, see Mallory, "Ritual Treatment of the Horse in Early Kurgan Tradition." Mallory denies a Proto-Indo-European source for the two ceremonies, on the grounds that "a notional date of c. 4000–2500 B.C." for the Proto-Indo-European community is too early to accommodate a ritual featuring a chariot race: "no matter how striking the ritual parallels, the archaeological evidence does

Also relevant are the "Heavenly Twins," which nineteenth-century scholars discovered in Indic, Greek, Baltic, and Celtic mythologies. The twins, as has frequently been noticed, "are more or less directly connected with the standard horse-unit of Bronze Age horse domestication, the pair of yoked horses drawing the swift, two-wheeled chariot."[26] The Heavenly Twins lie behind the Greek Dioscuri and the Vedic Ashvins (literally "owners of horses") and are in some respect the quintessential Indo-European heroes. The evidence for the myth, in five of the language branches of Indo-European, "is of such a nature that it remains one of the most striking single justifications for the comparative study of Indo-European mythology."[27] The earliest reference to the twins occurs in the treaty that Matiwaza of Mitanni made with Suppiluliumas of Hatti in the fourteenth century B.C. There the twins are referred to as the *nasatyas*, an epithet that as charioteers they often bear in the Rigveda.[28] The twins seem to have begun as the ideal chariot crew: an unbeatable driver and an invincible fighter.[29]

Early nineteenth-century scholars were on the right track in sensing an association between the war chariot and the early

not support the ascription of paired draught (vehicles) or chariots to the PIE period." The argument illustrates the danger of relying upon an archaeologically based chronology (and especially Gimbutas's chronology) for the Proto-Indo-European community and dispersal.

26. C. Grottanelli, "Yoked Horses, Twins, and the Powerful Lady: India, Greece, Ireland and Elsewhere," *JIES* 14 (1986): 125. That the Heavenly Twins were also a part of Germanic mythology was the thesis of D. J. Ward's *The Divine Twins: An Indo-European Myth in Germanic Tradition* (Berkeley: Univ. of California Press, 1968); see Ward's summary paper, "An Indo-European Mythological Theme in Germanic Tradition," in *Indo-European and Indo-Europeans*, ed. Cardona et al., pp. 405–20.

27. Ward, "An Indo-European Mythological Theme," 405.

28. P. Thieme, "The 'Aryan' Gods of the Mitanni Treaties," *JAOS* 80 (1960): 315: "Within Vedic religion . . . the *Nasatyas* appear again and again as heavenly charioteers."

29. On the twins' association with chariotry, see also S. O'Brien, "Dioscuric Elements in Celtic and Germanic Mythology," *JIES* 10 (1982): 117–36.

Indo-Europeans. Unfortunately, the relationship between the Indo-European conquests and the advent of chariot warfare has been obscured by the march of scholarship (often in opposite directions) in the several pertinent disciplines. The original error was perhaps the failure, in discussions of the advent of the draft horse, to make a distinction between the chariot and disk-wheeled vehicles. Orientalists early on confused the matter by constructing a faulty chronology for early Mesopotamian history. A bogus "coming of the Greeks" at ca. 1900 B.C. severely distorted the larger picture of what the PIE speakers did, and when. And in much of the recent literature on the subject, the horse, rather than chariot warfare, has come to be regarded as a distinguishing feature of Proto-Indo-European society.

All the Indo-European movements of the Bronze Age that we *know* about are takeovers, date no earlier than ca. 1600 B.C., and are associated with chariot warfare. To "the coming of the Greeks" we shall return in the next chapter. In anticipation, it will here be sufficient to say that the evidence from Greece, which regularly has been held to contradict the association of chariot warfare with the Indo-European movements, strongly supports such an association. In short, mastery of chariot warfare explains sufficiently and cogently what the PIE speakers (and their charioteering neighbors) were able to do in the middle centuries of the second millennium B.C., and why they did it.

Each of the takeovers itemized in Chapter Four seems to have been accomplished by charioteers. The PIE speakers were most active in these takeovers, but other language communities were also involved. As we have seen, the *hyksos* princes who established a regime over most of Egypt in the seventeenth century were apparently Amorites from the Levant and had Hurrian associates. Hurrian speakers, in fact, seem to have been second only to PIE speakers as a factor in the seventeenth- and sixteenth-century upheavals (the extent to which Hurrian speakers were involved in the armies and palaces of the Levant at the time of the Egyptian New Kingdom has already been noted). Still another linguistic community that bettered itself during the upheavals was the Kassite: soon after 1600 B.C., Kassite speakers took over much of southern Mesopotamia. Perhaps in eastern Anatolia there were several language communities in which chariot warfare became an accomplished art: the Proto-Indo-European would have been by far the largest of these communities, but Kassite speakers and some of the more northerly (and less urbanized) Hurrian speakers were evidently also much involved.

The Aryans whom we meet in Mitanni were closely associated with chariotry. This is evident in their personal names (which frequently were compounds of *-ashwa* or *-rata*) and in the Aryan imperial dynasty's dependence on maryannu. In the Amarna correspondence of Amenhotep III and IV are thirteen letters that Tushratta sent to the Egyptian kings, and horses figure prominently in them. The king of Mitanni not only attached to his letters a greeting to the Pharaoh's horses and chariots, but also sends teams of outstanding horses as gifts to his "brother."[30] It was in fourteenth-century Mitanni that Kikkuli dictated his Hurrian treatise on the breeding and training of chariot horses. Amid the infinite detail, as we have seen, the texts provide us with technical terms in the Aryan language for the "turns" and courses in which the chariot horse needed to be exercised. The only credible explanation for the Aryan terms in the treatise is that the Hurrians had learned about chariotry from Aryan-speaking experts.

The Kassite-speaking conquerors of Babylon were notorious charioteers. Of the few dozen Kassite words that are known, a high proportion are words for parts of a chariot or for the kinds and colors of horses.[31] Kassite horses had personal names, usually theophoric, in which the goddess Minizir was often the

30. For excerpts and references, see Hançar, *Das Pferd*, 477–78.
31. In Balkan, *Kassitenstudien*, pages 11–40 are given over entirely to a category that the author designates as "Pferdetexte." On pages 123–30, Balkan presents the known personal names of Kassite horses and the Kassite vocabulary for chariotry and the parts of a chariot.

divine element. As summarized by Margaret Drower, "the Kassite kings appear to have come to power as leaders of a powerful, but perhaps quite small, aristocracy who wrote elegant letters full of compliments to each other and were expert and enthusiastic horsebreeders."[32]

The maryannu of the Levant were regularly charioteers and chariot warriors. Although by the end of the fourteenth century B.C. most of the maryannu in the Levant had Semitic names, at the beginning of the Late Bronze Age the majority must have spoken either Hurrian or Aryan: the word "maryannu" is an Aryan-Hurrian hybrid.[33] Since the status and obligations of the maryannu tended to be hereditary,[34] it is likely that after a few generations the Aryan speakers were assimilated to the Semitic- or Hurrian-speaking population. So close is the association between the maryannu and chariotry that some analyses have concluded that the word was a technical term for "professional chariot forces" (on this analysis the corresponding term for professional infantrymen, many of whom were Hurrian, was SA.GAZ or *hapiru*).[35]

Among yet another group involved in a takeover, the Aryans of India, charioteering was an obsession. The relatively late Mahabharata as well as the earlier Rigveda are much concerned with chariotry. In the Mahabharata, two rival chariot forces battle for supremacy. The mythical charioteers of the Rigveda were, in the words of Stuart Piggott, nothing else but

> the Aryans themselves, magnified to heroic proportions. The greatest god of the *Rigveda* is Indra, to

32. Drower, *CAH* II, 1: 440.

33. Cf. O'Callaghan, "New Light on the *maryannu* as Chariot-Warriors."

34. A. F. Rainey, "The Military Personnel of Ugarit," *JNES* 24 (1965): 19–20. At Ugarit, each *marya* was given a land-holding and payment in silver.

35. W. Helck, *Die Beziehungen Aegyptens zu Vorderasien im 3. und 2. Jahrtausend v. Chr.* (Wiesbaden: Harrassowitz, 1962), 530; cf. H. Cazelles, "The Hebrews," in *Peoples of Old Testament Times*, ed. D. J. Wiseman, 14.

whom about one quarter of the hymns are addressed, and he is the apotheosis of the Aryan bat-
tle-leader: strong-armed, colossal, tawny-bearded,
and potbellied from drinking, he wields the thun-
derbolt in his more godlike moments, but fights
like a hero with bow-and-arrows from his chariot. . . . He is a cattle-raider, and above all he is
the destroyer of the strongholds of the enemy.[36]

Piggott goes on to quote from the Rigveda (1.53) a hymn that
may show us the ethos of the Proto-Indo-European charioteer
in the middle of the second millennium B.C.:

With all-outstripping chariot wheel, O Indra, thou
far-famed, hast overthrown the twice ten kings of men
With sixty thousand nine and ninety followers . . .
Thou goest on from fight to fight intrepidly,
destroying castle after castle here with strength.[37]

So much detail does the Rigveda provide about chariots, Piggott noted, that "a modern coach-builder could probably turn
out a passable replica of Indra's vehicle."[38]

We may end this chapter by placing the PIE speakers' takeovers into the chronological sequence set up in Chapter Five.
The earliest of the takeovers seems to have followed by a few
decades the apparent use of chariots by Hattusilis I in Hatti
and by the *hyksos* in Egypt in their acquisition of Great Kingships. I would suggest that the example of Hattusilis, and of
the amurru and Hurrian princes who established their *hyksos*
regimes in Egypt, may have inspired the charioteering peoples
of eastern Anatolia to think new and ambitious thoughts. A
community that had seen a number of its maryannu enlist to

36. S. Piggott, *Prehistoric India* (Harmondsworth: Penguin, 1950),
260.
37. Ibid., 261.
38. Ibid., 258.

help a foreigner establish himself as lord of Hatti, or of most of Egypt, would not long have overlooked the opportunities that beckoned. It is reasonable to suggest that in the land occupied by the PIE speakers, and in neighboring lands (where, for example, Kassite and Hurrian may have been spoken), whole charioteering communities decided to wait no longer for offers of employment, but to leave home for foreign adventures, and to subjugate societies more advanced but more vulnerable than their own.[39]

39. It is noteworthy, in this connection, that many of the less desirable regions of Armenia witnessed a drastic decline in population during the second millennium. Settlements that had flourished in the period of the Early Transcaucasian Civilization, and that would be resurrected in the Urartian period, were entirely abandoned in the second half of the second millennium. According to Burney, *Peoples of the Hills*, 86, "this decline was particularly marked in the bleaker highlands, such as the regions of Erzurum and Van, where the Early Trans-Caucasian culture lingered on, to be followed by a long dark age when nomadism may have predominated. There seems to have been an abandonment of sites in the plains and elsewhere, most clearly illustrated by the hiatus at such sites as Armavir and Garni between the Early Trans-Caucasian occupation and that of the Iron Age or of the classical period." Armavir and Garni lie a short distance west of Lake Sevan.

When and under what circumstances Armenian, a *satem* language, established itself in Armenia remain difficult questions. It is generally believed, however, that much of the evolution of Armenian did not occur within Armenia itself, and specialists have tended to describe the first Armenian speakers in the area as invaders from the west, with linguistic affinities to Thracian and Phrygian (on the fragile foundations for this description see Baldi, *An Introduction to the Indo-European Languages*, 79–81). As late as the ninth and eighth centuries B.C., a non-Indo-European language, Urartian, was spoken in at least a part of what would one day be Armenia.

EIGHT

The Coming of the Greeks

Their bones show that the men buried in the shaft graves at Mycenae were big men, taller and broader than the typical inhabitants of Middle Helladic Greece.[1] The men were also charioteers. That is an old fact, known since Schliemann found the graves. What has only recently become apparent is that these charioteers buried at Mycenae were among the pioneers of their art. Gertrud Hermes supposed that Mursilis and his charioteers made their expedition to Babylon more than three centuries before the Shaft Grave Dynasty was established. We now know that the occupants of Grave v must have been young men when Mursilis sacked Babylon. And since the discovery of Grave Circle B (made by the Greek Archaeological Service in 1951, and published in 1973),[2] it has become evident that it was within the lifetime of the first shaft-grave princes that Hattusilis ruled in Hatti and that effective chariot warfare began.[3]

1. Cf. O.T.P.K. Dickinson, "The Shaft Graves and Mycenaean Origins," *BICS* 19 (1972–1973): 146.

2. G. Mylonas, *Grave Circle B at Mycenae* (in Greek) (Athens: Greek Archaeological Service, 1973).

3. Mylonas dated the majority of the tombs in Grave Circle B to the MH period, but in his critical review of Mylonas's publication (*JHS* 96 [1976]: 236–37), Dickinson makes a persuasive case against Mylonas's chronology. Most of the burials in Grave Circle B seem to belong to the sixteenth century B.C., with only a very few (and these the poorest) dating to the end of the seventeenth. Nevertheless, it does appear that the earliest of the warrior graves in Circle B fall within a few decades of the origins of effective chariot warfare.

The chariots in which the charioteers of Mycenae delighted were of the same kind that swept the world from Egypt to India at the beginning of the Late Bronze Age, and it is as likely as such things can be that Greece was taken over by charioteering invaders ca. 1600 B.C. Possession of horses and chariots seems to have been not an incidental, but a fundamental feature of Shaft Grave Mycenae, enabling the Mycenaeans to do whatever else they did. In retrospect, it appears that the coming of the charioteers was an event fraught with no less significance for Greece than for India. The chariot, as William Wyatt has observed, is sufficient evidence that it was ca. 1600 B.C. that a form of Proto-Indo-European came to Greece.[4] It was then that Greek history began.

Testimony to the Mycenaean lords' charioteering comes from the well-known stelai that stood on the grave circles, each stele marking a single burial.[5] Two sculptured stelai were

4. Wyatt, "The Indo-Europeanization of Greece." See especially his summary on page 107: "My conclusion is inextricably bound up with the chariot: if a chariot, or evidence for a chariot, is found in Greece dating from before 1600, then my argument will lead me to assume that the Greeks can have arrived at that earlier date."

5. Exactly where each of the eleven stelai found by Schliemann originally stood is not entirely clear, but most of those of importance to us came from Grave V. The definitive publication of Grave Circle A is Georg Karo's *Die Schachtgräber von Mykenai*, 2 vols. (Munich: Bruckmann, 1930 and 1933). The conventional dates for the graves of Grave Circle A range through the sixteenth century B.C.: Graves II and VI are regarded as the earliest (first half of the century), Graves IV and V are dated to the middle of the century, and Graves I and III ca. 1500 B.C. For a good description of Grave Circles A and B, see Chapter IV ("The Shaft-Graves," 82–110) of Emily Vermeule's *Greece in the Bronze Age* (Chicago: Univ. of Chicago Press, 1964). Fritz Schachermeyr, "Streitwagen," thoroughly discussed the evidence for chariots in Late Helladic Greece, but from an odd angle; his unconventional thesis in this article is that the Greeks (who by 1600 B.C., he supposed, had been in Greece for several centuries) learned of the chariot because some of them went to Egypt to participate in the native Egyptians' revolt against the Hyksos. The definitive work on Mycenaean chariots is now Joost Crouwel's *Chariots*.

found at Grave Circle B and eleven at Grave Circle A. Unfortunately, the scenes on only six stelai can be confidently reconstructed. On five of the six (Stelai I, IV, V, VIII, and IX), a charioteer is depicted.[6] The grave-circle reliefs are crude and primitive (they are among the earliest preserved portrayals of the chariot), but perhaps for that very reason they testify that for the men buried beneath the stelai nothing in life had been more important than charioteering. Nor should there be any doubt that the chariot was important to them because it helped them to kill. Although Mylonas argued that the stelai portray chariot racers,[7] it now appears that all six of the intelligible stelai portray combat: men fighting lions, or men fighting against other men.[8]

The stelai are not the only evidence for charioteering found in Grave Circle A. A gold ring found in Shaft Grave IV carries an engraving of a chariot, pulled by horses at full gallop; in the chariot are two men, one of them an archer taking aim at a stag (see Fig. 8).[9] Fully as interesting, although not so immediately obvious, are four small bone objects from Grave IV. These discoid objects (each with three studs protruding from one face) seem to comprise two pairs and were identified as the cheek pieces of horse bits in a 1964 article.[10] Although the identification was not immediately accepted, it now seems secure.[11]

6. See Crouwel, *Chariots*, plates 35–39.

7. G. Mylonas, "The Figured Mycenaean Stelai," *AJA* 55 (1951): 134–47, and *Mycenae and the Mycenaean Age* (Princeton: Princeton Univ. Press, 1966), 93ff.

8. Crouwel, *Chariots*, 119–20, makes the argument against Mylonas's interpretation. From Crouwel's plate 37, for example, it is evident that what Mylonas called the "rocky landscape" of a race course is in fact the prone and helmeted body of a fallen enemy. And on two other stelai, Mylonas's "umpires" turn out to be armed, and one "appears to be aiming a spear at the chariot."

9. Ibid., plate 10 (the scene is also used as a cover illustration for Crouwel's book); Lorimer, *Homer and the Monuments*, fig. 38 (p. 311).

10. A. M. Leskov, "The Earliest Antler Psalia from Trakhtemirova," *Sov. Arkh* (1964, 1), 299–303 (in Russian).

11. Piggott, *Earliest Wheeled Transport*, 100–101. Although Lit-

8   Detail of gold ring from Mycenae, Shaft Grave IV.

The Grave IV cheek pieces fit into a series of bone and antler bits found from Hungary to the Urals and have bronze counterparts in the barrows at Lchashen, in Soviet Armenia, described in the final section of Chapter Five.[12]

That in the Aegean the chariot loomed large in the imagination during the sixteenth and fifteenth centuries (the LH I and II periods) is shown by glyptic art. An amethyst cylinder seal found in a tholos tomb at Kazarma (in the Argolid), and dated to the LH IIA period, portrays a single occupant in a chariot drawn by lions.[13] A sealing from Ayia Triada in Crete depicts another charioteer, lashing his team forward.[14] On a seal found on the floor of the Vaphio tholos (LH IIA), the chariot

tauer and Crouwel, "Evidence for Horse Bits from Shaft Grave IV at Mycenae?" *Praehistorische Zeitschrift* 48 (1973): 207–13, initially rejected the identification, a close and unambiguous parallel from southwestern Russia has since been discovered. For Crouwel's present and modified position, see his *Chariots*, 105. Cf. also Piggott, "Chariots in the Caucasus," 18.

12. Piggott, "Chariots in the Caucasus," 18.

13. Crouwel, *Chariots*, 122–23; in Crouwel's Catalog (pp. 157–73) the Kazarma seal appears as G 1 (for illustration, see his plate 9).

14. Ibid., 122 (in Crouwel's Catalog, G 8; plate 16). The sealing perhaps dates from the LM IB period.

driver is accompanied by a fighter who seems about to hurl a long spear.[15]

From a later date, there survive many fragments of frescoes that portrayed scenes of chariots and perhaps chariot warfare. Schachermeyr concluded that at both Mycenae and Tiryns, chariot scenes were the favorite subject of artists of the LH II and III periods.[16] In the LH III palace at Mycenae the megaron was decorated with a great frieze—running for seventeen meters on the north wall and part of the west wall—in which chariots seem to have played a very prominent part.[17] In the famous Boar Hunt Tableau at the Tiryns palace, dating to ca. 1300 B.C., the chariot is not the principal subject, but is still important: one of the most famous of all LH fresco fragments shows two ladies of the court setting out for the hunt in a chariot. Discoveries now being made indicate that a very similar fresco decorated a palace at Orchomenos: here, too, a boar hunt was the subject of the fresco, and chariots figured prominently in the action.[18] And a military chariot appears in a poorly preserved wall painting at Pylos.[19]

A wealth of other archaeological evidence, all of it now conveniently assembled in Crouwel's book, makes it quite clear how central the horse-drawn chariot was to the society of Mycenaean Greece. The skeletal evidence for horses is limited, but growing. The most dramatic discoveries, although still not well published, have been made in tholos tombs at Marathon (dating ca. 1425 B.C.) and at Dendra: in the dromoi of these

15. Ibid., 123 (G 3; plate 11).

16. Cf. Schachermeyr, "Streitwagen," 722: "Kein Zweifel, dass nun die Streitwagenszenen bereits den Vorzug errungen haben vor fast allen anderen Darstellungsstoffen."

17. For discussion, see Crouwel, *Chariots*, 129–32 (Catalog W 1–12; plates 82–86).

18. Remains of a palace, apparently of LH IIIA date, were found at Orchomenos in 1985; on the fresco fragments, see H. W. Catling's summary in *AR 1984–85*, 31.

19. Crouwel, *Chariots*, 132 (Catalog W 35).

early tholoi were found the complete skeletons of teams of horses.[20] Archaeologists have also discovered or identified a surprising number of bronze bits from the LH period. In addition, the horse and chariot appear frequently in terracotta figurines and in vase paintings all through the Mycenaean Age.[21]

The literary evidence on the horse in Heroic Greece is perhaps more familiar than the archaeological. With or without chariots, horses are prominent in many of the myths: the stories of Bellerophon and Pegasus, Phaëthon, the Lapiths and Centaurs, the Trojan Horse, Pelops's chariot race, and others. The importance of horses to the heroes of the *Iliad* is sometimes overlooked but can readily be verified by attentive reading.[22] Heroic names—Hippolytus, Hippodamia, Leucippus (almost a mythological "John Doe")—are in themselves an index of the horse's value in Mycenaean times.[23] It is no surprise that after surveying the literary evidence, Edouard Delebecque described Heroic Greece as "la civilisation du cheval."[24]

The military importance of the chariot in the Late Helladic Aegean is established above all by the Linear B tablets. Scribes at both Knossos and Pylos inventoried parts of chariots (especially pairs of wheels) in one set of tablets and whole chariots in another. At Knossos both sets of tablets were found in the

20. On this and other osteological evidence, see ibid., 34–35; although found in 1958, the Marathon skeletons have not yet been published. The Dendra discoveries were made in 1976 and also await publication.

21. All of the artistic evidence has been meticulously cataloged, and most of it illustrated, by Crouwel in ibid.; on pages 101–109 he describes and classifies the bronze bits.

22. For documentation, see especially Delebecque, *Le Cheval dans l'Iliade*. Cf. also Greenhalgh, *Early Greek Warfare*, 7–8; G. J. Stagakis, "Odysseus and Idomeneus: Did they have Charioteers in Troy?" *Historia* 27 (1978): 255–73; Stagakis, "Homeric Warfare Practices," *Historia* 34 (1985): 129–52.

23. For a full list of the hippophoric names in the Trojan War, see Delebecque, *Le Cheval dans l'Iliad*, 43.

24. Ibid., 45.

west wing of the palace, in what has inevitably been called "The Room of the Chariot Tablets." One Mycenologist has estimated that the Knossos palace had available a thousand pairs of wheels, and well over three hundred chariot bodies.[25] Even John Chadwick, who believes that one class of the Chariot Tablets is merely a batch of scribal exercises (why the lords of the palace would have found such tablets valuable enough to keep is not clear), estimates that the Greek masters of Knossos had at least two hundred chariots at their disposal.[26] At Pylos, Blegen found the "wheel tablets" but not the tablets totaling the complete chariots. The "wheel tablets" indicate that the palace at Pylos had on hand "at least two hundred pairs of wheels, and no doubt the figure was very much larger."[27]

Although there can be no denying that chariots were at the heart of Late Helladic armies, it unfortunately must be admitted that we do not know how the chariots were used. The details of chariot warfare in Mycenaean Greece (as in most lands other than Egypt) are not documented and are therefore a matter of considerable controversy among specialists. As we have seen, an occasional LH cylinder seal or ring depicts an archer or a spearman in a chariot, but chariot warfare does not appear in these miniature scenes. Chariots are a commonplace in the *Iliad*, but they do little more than carry the heroes to and from the battlefield. In one of the few passages that describes fighting from a chariot (*Iliad* 8.118ff.), Diomedes and Nestor in one chariot bear down upon Hector and Eniopeus in another, and from his chariot Diomedes hurls a javelin at Hector (he misses Hector, but kills Eniopeus). Thus, one might sup-

25. M. Lejeune, "La civilization mycénienne et la guerre," in *Problèmes de la Guerre en Grèce Ancienne*, ed. J.-P. Vernant (Paris: Mouton, 1968), 49.

26. J. Chadwick, "The Organization of the Mycenaean Archives," in *Studia Mycenaea. Proceedings of the Mycenaean Symposium, Brno*, ed. A. Bartoněk (Brno: Universitas Purkyniana Brunensis, 1968), 17; Crouwel, *Chariots*, 127–28, does not find Chadwick's characterization persuasive.

27. Greenhalgh, *Early Greek Warfare*, 11.

pose—despite the fact that it is uncommonly difficult to hurl anything while standing flat-footed in a moving vehicle—that in Mycenaean Greece the chariot fighter relied mainly on his throwing-spears or javelins. But there are other possibilities. Fritz Schachermeyr reasonably assumed that chariot warfare in the Aegean paralleled what is known for New Kingdom Egypt (and for most of the East): the pharaoh's chariot fighters were archers, armed with the composite bow.[28] It has also been suggested that in LH Greece the chariot fighters relied primarily on thrusting-spears (their chariots would have charged in massed formations).[29]

Knowledgeable scholars have also periodically proposed that in Heroic Greece the chariot was indeed mostly a conveyance, exactly as Homer describes it, used to transport spearmen on and off the battlefield.[30] This hypothesis may contain a partial truth. It may very well be that toward the end of the second millennium, by which time new styles of fighting (especially, perhaps, the transition from thrusting-spears to throwing-spears) were making chariotry obsolete, the chariot was little more than a prestige vehicle in which a *basileus* might ride to and from the battlefield. P.A.L. Greenhalgh has shown very clearly that in Archaic Greece noblemen regularly rode horses to the battlefield, where they would dismount and join their poorer comrades as foot soldiers, and has argued that this prac-

28. Schachermeyr, "Streitwagen," nowhere stated how he imagined the Greeks fighting in their chariots, but his thesis—that the Greeks learned chariot warfare in Egypt—makes bowmen of them.

29. Greenhalgh, *Early Greek Warfare*, 7–18; Greenhalgh assumes that the Hittites used chariots in the same fashion. One might object, however, that the evidence on Hittite chariot tactics is so limited that it does not provide a very solid analogy.

30. J. K. Anderson, "Homeric, British and Cyrenaic Chariots," *AJA* 69 (1965): 349–52; M. Littauer, "The Military Use of Chariots in the Aegean in the Late Bronze Age," *AJA* 76 (1972): 145–57; Anderson, "Greek Chariot-Borne and Mounted Infantry," *AJA* 79 (1975): 175–87; Crouwel, *Chariots*, 126–27.

tice began during the Dark Age.[31] It may be, then, that for at least the first century or two of the Dark Age, the chariot had served very much as the riding horse served in the Archaic period.

That possibility, however, does not help us to visualize how the chariot was used in Greece when the chariot was still militarily effective—before the end of the LH IIIB period. As Greenhalgh has argued, the Late Helladic chariot was necessarily much more than a taxi. The alternative view—that in the Late Helladic period chariots were indeed nothing more than battle-taxis—appeals for support to the bronze corselet discovered at Dendra, in the Argolid, in 1960 (the corselet was found in a tomb that dates from shortly before 1400 B.C.). According to this argument, the corselet is so bulky and restrictive—it consists of fifteen pieces of plate armor—that an infantryman encased in it would have needed to be hauled to the scene of the battle, and deposited in front of the enemy, by a chariot. One might object, however, that the corselets known from the Near East were regularly worn by chariot personnel, not by men who fought on foot,[32] and the same seems to have been true in the Aegean.[33] And one would also suppose that, had transport been their objective, the Mycenaeans would have devised more commodious personnel carriers, capable of delivering not just a solitary warrior but an entire platoon to the critical point of the battle.[34]

31. The third chapter (pp. 40–62) of Greenhalgh's *Early Greek Warfare* makes the argument that the *hippeis* of the later Dark Age were horse-owning infantrymen, and the fifth and sixth chapters (pp. 84–145) focus on the "mounted infantry" of the Archaic Period.

32. The Nuzi corselets were not plate armor, but were covered with bronze scales. Nevertheless, one would suppose that the function of the corselet was the same in Greece as it was in Nuzi ca. 1400 B.C. On the parallels between the Nuzi helmets and Mycenaean helmets, see Kendall, "The Helmets of the Warriors at Nuzi," 224–31.

33. The Linear B tablets from Knossos record the issue of numerous corselets, apparently to chariot crews. See Crouwel, *Chariots*, 124–25.

34. The Dendra corselet has been a problem since its discovery, but

Adding to our confusion about chariot tactics in Late Helladic Greece is some ambiguity about archers in Mycenaean warfare. It was once believed, because of the battle descriptions in the *Iliad*, that the Mycenaeans did not use the bow in battle. That belief has been undermined not only by the Linear B tablets' references to large stores of arrowheads,[35] but also by reanalyses of artifacts that Schliemann found in the Mycenaean

---

has more often been interpreted as the armor of a charioteer than of an infantryman. In *Early Greek Armour and Weapons from the End of the Bronze Age to 600 BC* (Edinburgh: Edinburgh Univ. Press, 1964), A. M. Snodgrass concluded that "such ponderous apparatus can only have been worn by chariot-borne warriors, fighting actually *in* their chariots rather than merely *from* them in the Homeric manner" (p. 35). Reviewing Snodgrass's book in *Antiquity* 42 (1968): 69, Sylvia Benton agreed: "Fancy trying to walk under the Greek sun in a red-hot panoply of that weight. Surely it would only have been worn in a chariot." Crouwel disagrees, contending that no one enclosed in such armor could have stretched a bow or thrown a spear from a chariot. Noting that a man wearing the Dendra corselet would not have needed a shield, Crouwel concludes (p. 127) that the warrior "would have had both hands free to handle his weapons. At the same time, his mobility on the ground would have been minimal, and he would surely have needed a vehicle to convey him any distance once he was armed. The development of this type of body-armour presupposes the availability of chariots, and may even have given a new impetus to their military use. The vehicles would then have functioned as carriers to and from the battlefield." I find it much more credible that the Dendra corselet was worn by one of the chariot crew, whether the fighter or the driver. The Nuzi charioteers seem to have managed adequately in their twelve-pound corselets. That Homer himself knew far less about chariotry than had his remote predecessors is indicated by the fossilized formulas for chariots in the *Iliad*; on these see Page, *History and the Homeric Iliad*, 280n.63.

35. For the relevant tablets, along with chests of arrowheads (and the carbonized debris of arrow shafts) found at Knossos, see Sir Arthur Evans, *The Palace of Minos*, vol. 4, pt. 2 (London: Macmillan, 1935), 836ff. These Knossos "Armoury" tablets referred to enormous lots of arrows (6,010 in one lot, 2,630 in another), and the chests corroborated the figures. According to Evans (p. 837), "there seems to be some probability that these 'Armoury' chests were made to contain 10,000 arrows." We are obviously dealing here with archers who were something other than hunters or sportsmen.

shaft graves.[36] In addition, it appears that Homer's few formulas for bows and arrows are "the residue of a much larger system" that earlier bards had employed.[37] Finally, bronze arrowheads appear rather suddenly in Greece in LH I levels (in EH and MH levels all arrowheads are of stone). The conclusion is quite inescapable that the bow was much more important in Late Helladic warfare than was once thought.[38]

As for the type of bow used by the Mycenaeans, Helen Lorimer insisted that although the Minoans knew the composite bow, the Mycenaeans were familiar only with the self bow.[39]

36. In Grave VI, Schliemann found grooved stone objects whose purpose has only recently been discovered: they were meant for smoothing and polishing arrow shafts; see H. G. Buchholz, "Der Pfeilglätter aus dem VI. Schachtgrab von Mykene und die helladischen Pfeilspitzen," *Jahrbuch des Deutschen Archäologischen Instituts* 77 (1962): 1–58. The archers on the Silver Siege Rhyton from Grave IV have long been known, but archers on another silver vessel (a krater) from the same grave were not recognized until the 1950s. The krater, which had crumbled into a multitude of fragments, was reconstructed by Ch. Karousos after World War II. For the publication, see A. Sakellariou, "Un cratère d'argent avec scène de bataille provenant de la IVe tombe de l'acropole de Mycènes," *Antike Kunst* 17 (1974): 3–20. Two archers, along with spearmen (both archers and spearmen are on foot), are engaged in battle.

37. Page, *History and the Homeric Iliad*, 279n. 63. For a comprehensive study of the subject, see W. McLeod, "The Bow in Ancient Greece, with Particular Reference to the Homeric Poems" (Ph.D. diss., Harvard University, 1966); for summary, see *HSCP* 71 (1966): 329–31.

38. The argument is well made by R. Tölle-Kastenbein, *Pfeil und Bogen im alten Griechenland* (Bochum: Duris Verlag, 1980), 24–26 and 41–42. Tölle-Kastenbein also presents, in tabular form, the types of arrowheads attested for Bronze Age Greece; it is remarkable how many of these types appeared at the beginning of the Late Helladic period. Robert Avila, *Bronze Lanzen- und Pfeilspitzen der griechischen Spätbronzezeit* (Munich: Beck, 1983), 117, observes that bronze arrowheads first appear in Late Helladic levels, but he attributes the shift to "dem gesteigerten Wohlstand" of the Argolid Greeks in the sixteenth century B.C. (on the circularity of this argument see below). Because of their size, Avila believes that most of the fourteen types of arrowhead attested for the LH period were used as *Kriegswaffen*.

39. Lorimer, *Homer and the Monuments*, 276–305, remains the most influential discussion of the bow in Minoan and Mycenaean times. Lorimer

Lorimer's analysis is still widely accepted, even though its foundation is now eroded: Lorimer erroneously assumed that the Linear B tablets that Evans found in the "Armoury" at Knossos were Minoan documents.[40] Ventris's decipherment of the tablets as Greek ought to transfer the composite bow from Minoan to Mycenaean hands. As for the fifteen adjectives that Homer applies to the bow, "none of them need refer to a self bow; none is inappropriate for a composite bow."[41]

Although it is likely that the bow was very important in Mycenaean chariot warfare, it must be conceded that the particulars of combat in Mycenaean Greece are not sufficiently known to permit us to picture the fighting with any confidence. It is possible (although unlikely, given the difficulties of throwing anything from a moving vehicle) that Greek chariot fighters threw javelins from their vehicles, or that—attacking in a formation of massed chariots—they ordinarily relied

---

knew of two Mycenaean representations of the bow and found that "in both cases it is unmistakably of European type" (p. 278; a "European" bow is a self bow). One of the two representations is on the gold ring from Shaft Grave IV, the other is on the blade of the Lion Hunt Dagger. Apparently, Lorimer found the size of these two bows, relative to the men who wield them, too small to have been composite bows; but it should be pointed out that the Mycenaean artists in both cases had a great deal of trouble putting things in proper scale (the lion, on the Lion Hunt Dagger, is taller than the men who are attacking him). Nor is it clear how Lorimer decided that of the several Mycenaean artifacts depicting bowmen only two were truly "Mycenaean." According to Lorimer, the archers on the Silver Siege Rhyton are using bows that are "certainly composite," but the archers are not Mycenaean (279n. 4).

40. Several of these tablets are inventories of goat horns, and Evans reasonably concluded that these inventories were kept in the "Armoury" because the horns were needed for construction of composite bows (see Evans, *Palace of Minos*, vol. 4, pt. 2, 833–34 ("Materials for Horn-Bows"). Lorimer, like Evans, assumed that the Armoury Tablets were written in the Minoans' language and reflected Minoan weaponry. Professor Emmett Bennett assures me that the pertinent tablets are in "classic Linear B."

41. Thus the summary in *HSCP* 71 (1966): 330, of McLeod's "The Bow in Ancient Greece, with Particular Reference to the Homeric Poems."

upon thrusting-spears. But it is also possible that, like their counterparts in Egypt, Mitanni, and India, Late Helladic chariot fighters were archers, armed with composite bows. And it must be conceded that the tactics that had been employed by the first generation of charioteers in Greece were not necessarily the same as those in use at the end of the Late Helladic period.

That the chariot, however used, was of central importance in Late Helladic Greece is obvious. Less obvious is the link between the arrival of the chariot in Greece and the arrival of Proto-Indo-European. The language and the vehicle arrived together. Wyatt has shown in detail that in early Greek (the Linear B tablets and the Homeric epics) the technical terms for the parts of a chariot were all Indo-European words, derived from "an Indo-European technical vocabulary."[42] Included here, of course, are the more general vehicular terms, the Greek words for wheel, yoke, and axle. That, however, is only the beginning, and Wyatt focused his argument upon the words that are specific to the light, spoked-wheel cart: the spoke, the felloe, the nave, the cab, the rail, and the chariot itself in diverse forms (the "carriage," the assembled chariot, the unassembled chariot). For all of these objects the early Greeks had Indo-European terms. As Wyatt has stated, "we may therefore conclude that the IE invaders of Greece knew the chariot when they first entered Greece, and may assume that they arrived with or on them."[43] Chariot warfare, along with "the Greeks," came to Greece ca. 1600 B.C.

The first charioteers at Mycenae were apparently the rulers of a considerable state, possibly extending beyond the Argolid. The clearest index of their position and power in the sixteenth century, before a palace at either Mycenae or Tiryns was built, is the enormous wealth of the shaft graves. The earliest of these contained little besides the skeletons of very large men. By the middle of the sixteenth century, however, the charioteers en-

42. Wyatt, "The Indo-Europeanization of Greece," 104.
43. Ibid., 107.

joyed such a glittering opulence that one must imagine them
lording it over a vast area in which were many productive communities. Let us glance at Emily Vermeule's catalog of the contents of a single grave, Grave IV. One of the richest graves of
all, Grave IV held the skeletons of three men and two women—
and more than four hundred gifts for the dead. In it

> there were three gold masks; two gold crowns;
> eight gold diadems or headbands; at least twenty-
> seven swords and sixteen more sword pommels of
> ivory, gold, alabaster, and wood; at least five dag-
> gers and six more pommels; sixteen knives; five "ra-
> zors"; five gold vases; ten or eleven silver vases;
> twenty-two bronze vases; three alabaster vases; two
> faience vases; eight clay vases; two gold *rhyta*; three
> silver *rhyta*; two ostrich-egg *rhyta*; two engraved
> gold rings; two silver rings; three gold armbands;
> at least one gold necklace with animal links; one
> gold-and-ivory comb; one large silver figure-of-
> eight shield. From the funeral clothes of these five
> people came 683 engraved gold discs and miscella-
> neous repousse ornaments, gold foil cutouts in the
> shape of cult buildings . . .[44]

and on and on. Looking only at the beads, for example, we note
not only beads of amethyst and other precious stone, but no
less than 1,290 of amber. Such were the contents of Grave IV.
Altogether, the shaft graves yielded treasures unmatched in the
history of archaeology. We are obviously dealing here with rulers whose dominion was wide and complete.

In contrast to the immensely powerful and wealthy center
that Mycenae was under the Shaft Grave Dynasty, before 1600
B.C. Mycenae was not a center at all. Middle Helladic Mycenae
had been inhabited, for sherds of the period have been found
there, but whatever settlement there was must have been thor-

44. Vermeule, *Greece in the Bronze Age*, 89.

oughly unremarkable. Then, ca. 1600 B.C. the place was chosen to serve as a fortress-capital. The choice was evidently based on the strategic advantages of the site, remarked upon by observers from Schliemann to the present: it commands the Argive plain as well as the routes from the plain to the Isthmus of Corinth. Eventually, the place required fortification walls, but the wisdom of the charioteers' choice is manifested in the fact that for four hundred years, without discernible interruption, the site provided security for rulers of the Mycenaean kingdom.

The kind of event that occurred in the Argolid ca. 1600 B.C. fits squarely within the category of takeovers described in the preceding chapter. Just as charioteers appropriated thrones and states throughout the East, so PIE-speaking charioteers invaded Greece and took over for exploitation the population they found there. Although circumstances must have varied considerably from one land to another, the rudiments of the pattern were apparently similar in the takeover of northwestern India by the Aryans, of southern Mesopotamia by the Kassites, of Egypt by the *hyksos*, of Mitanni by Aryans, and of many small Levantine states by Aryan and Hurrian *maryannu*. All of the takeovers occurred within a few generations after the perfection, around the middle of the seventeenth century B.C., of chariot warfare and the demonstration of its possibilities by Hattusilis I and by the *hyksos* who set themselves up in Egypt.

It has occasionally been argued, and more often assumed, that the first shaft-grave charioteers were natives of Greece, descended from Greeks who had been in the Aegean since ca. 1900 B.C. In a naive form, this argument supposes that chariot warfare evolved in Greece itself. That possibility is, of course, excluded by the evidence (most fully and recently presented by Littauer and Crouwel in *Wheeled Vehicles and Ridden Animals in the Ancient Near East*) that the light chariot was known in central Anatolia and Syria at the beginning of the eighteenth century B.C., and by the fact that to date we have no archaeological evidence for wheeled vehicles of any kind in Early or

Middle Helladic Greece.[45] Most important of all is the fact (long acknowledged by specialists) that the chariots of Late Helladic Greece are in all essentials parallel to those of the Near East. Wiesner's thesis—that Indo-Europeans from the north brought the chariot simultaneously to Greece and to the Near East early in the sixteenth century—has been rendered untenable by the evidence that the horse-drawn chariot was known in the Near East well before that time. As both Schachermeyr and Crouwel have plainly said, the chariots used by the first shaft-grave princes came to Greece from the east.

The manner of their coming, however, is variously understood. Thus A. W. Persson and Fritz Schachermeyr proposed that Greek soldiers of fortune went from the Aegean to Egypt early in the sixteenth century B.C. to assist the Egyptians in expelling the Hyksos. It was in Egypt, Persson and Schachermeyr believed, that these Greeks were introduced to chariot warfare, and after their mission in Egypt was accomplished, they came back to Greece and built chariots for themselves and their countrymen.[46] Frank Stubbings put forward a variant of

45. Crouwel, *Chariots*, 54–58. From the Bronze Age Aegean only one representation of a wheeled vehicle other than a chariot has come to light: a terracotta model of a wagon, dating to the early second millennium, was found at Palaikastro in Crete. Despite the archaeological *argumentum e silentio*, however, the pre-Greek inhabitants of Greece undoubtedly did build a modest number of carts and wagons. Wyatt, "The Indo-Europeanization of Greece," 104–106, notes that although the Greeks' technical terms for chariot elements came from Indo-European roots, their wagon nomenclature was non-Indo-European. The implication is that although the first Greeks in Greece built their own chariots, they depended upon the indigenous population for wagons and utilitarian carts. These could not have been numerous, since most of Greece was mountainous and deficient in large hardwood trees. As Crouwel notes, the use of wheeled transport in Greece was relatively limited until very modern times, and one may assume that throughout antiquity, wagons and carts were far rarer in Greece than they were in most of Eurasia.

46. The thesis was proposed by A. W. Persson, *New Tombs at Dendra near Midea* (Lund: Gleerup, 1942), 178–96, and is at the heart of Schachermeyr's "Streitwagen." Although many of Schachermeyr's observa-

this analysis. Pointing out that Middle Helladic Greeks would have been of little value to the Egyptians as allies against the Hyksos, Stubbings proposed that the shaft-grave princes *were* Hyksos, who after their expulsion from Egypt were given shelter by the Greeks of the Argolid.[47] Both theses run into chronological difficulties, since the shaft-grave charioteers must have come to Greece several decades before the establishment of the Eighteenth Dynasty in Egypt. In addition, both theses assume that the Mycenaean chariots derive from Egypt, but that assumption is not well founded. Schachermeyr argued at great length that the Late Helladic chariot had more similarities to the Egyptian than to the Syrian or Mesopotamian vehicle, but

---

tions are keen, they too often serve impossible arguments. At pages 718–19, for example, he argues that upon their return from Egypt, the Greek soldiers of fortune began making chariots for themselves, but (having imperfectly observed the vehicles they saw in Egypt) maladroitly put four wheels on some of them. Schachermeyr draws this amazing conclusion from the fact that on one of the shaft-grave reliefs the artist has depicted a chariot in profile, but has also depicted two wheels. Adding to these the two wheels that he imagines on the far side of the chariot, Schachermeyr comes up with his four-wheeled chariot. The more normal explanation, of course, would be that the shaft-grave artist had trouble with profiles: just as his warriors are shown in profile, but have both shoulders turned toward us, so when attempting to depict a two-wheeled chariot he supposed it necessary to depict two wheels. At any rate, having "established" that some of the shaft-grave chariots had four wheels, Schachermeyr went on to argue that such inefficiency ruled out the possibility that the chariots could have been brought in by invaders: no invaders would have been able to prevail with such cumbersome vehicles (cf. p. 719: "Dieser Befund der Schachtgräber ist insofern von höchstger Bedeutung, als er die Einführung des Streitwagens durch zuwandernde Streitwagenritter ausschliesst. Diese hätten aus ihrer früheren Heimat den Streitwagen doch zweifellos bereits in seiner fertigen Form mitgebracht und würden nimmermehr zuerst mit einem vierrädigen Typus experimentiert haben").

47. Stubbings, *CAH* II, 1: 633–40. As support for an "Egyptian connection," Stubbings cites the Danaus myth, and concludes (p. 637) that "in tune with the tradition, we may postulate the conquest of the Argolid by some of the displaced Hyksos leaders from Egypt in the early sixteenth century B.C."

Crouwel's more exhaustive study concludes that an Egyptian origin "is not very likely" (among other small differences, the Aegean chariot—like those shown in Syrian art—has a rectangular box, whereas the Egyptian chariot had a rounded box).[48]

Crouwel's own explanation for the arrival of chariots in Greece is rather different from Schachermeyr's. Like Schachermeyr, however, Crouwel accounts for the chariots without postulating an invasion of the Argolid ca. 1600 B.C. and supposes that the shaft-grave charioteers were native Greeks (both scholars assumed that by 1600 B.C. the Greeks had been in Greece for several centuries). Since Crouwel's book is and will long remain the definitive study of Mycenaean chariots, his reconstruction of the way in which the shaft-grave chariots came to Greece deserves careful scrutiny:

> It has sometimes been suggested that they were introduced, and to Mycenae in particular, by foreign immigrants, possibly invaders (both Hyksos expelled from Egypt and Indo-European Greeks have been put forward) and that the people of the Shaft Graves were no other than these same intruders. I believe this is unlikely. As O. Dickinson has recently argued, the Shaft Graves of Mycenae probably represent the rise of vigorous local chieftain families. The growth of an indigenous ruling class, which can also be observed at this time in other parts of mainland Greece, notably Messenia, marks the transition from the Middle Helladic period to Mycenaean civilization. Striking, if not yet fully understood, features of this process are the massed wealth of the early Mycenaeans and their close ties with the Cyclades and especially with Crete. These rulers had a great interest in weaponry, fighting and hunting, and the chariot would have fitted in

48. Crouwel, *Chariots*, 148.

very well with their life style, becoming a symbol
of their aristocratic standing.[49]

This explanation appears vulnerable on several counts. One
must first of all observe that to explain the shaft graves as the
result of the growth of an indigenous ruling class is circular:
the only evidence for the growth of such a class are the shaft
graves. Secondly, the theory posits a remarkable coincidence:
the local chieftain families of Mycenae made their rocketlike
ascent to the requisite level of opulence and sophistication at
precisely the time when somewhere in the Near East (all of
which was at that time suffering through a calamitous dark
age) chariots were first being made available for export to foreign buyers. This touches on an even greater difficulty. There
is good reason to believe that when an Hattusilis or an ambitious amurru prince acquired chariotry for himself, he did not
simply purchase vehicles. He also acquired teams of trained
chariot horses; but even good horses and good chariots would
by themselves have been useless. The most important ingredi-
ent would have been the men who knew how to repair the vehicles, to care for the horses, to drive them in battle, and to
fight from a fast-moving chariot. One cannot imagine wealthy
natives of Mycenae ordering from a foreign manufacturer war
chariots that they themselves planned to drive and to fight
from.

Nor, by way of escape, can one interpret the chariots of the
shaft-grave lords as sportsmen's hobbies, or as status symbols.
As Crouwel himself well demonstrated, the stelai reliefs portray scenes of combat and not, as was once thought, of chariot
racing. In addition, interpretation of the shaft-grave chariots
as status symbols seems to reverse the relationship of the chariots (and the weaponry) to the wealth that accompanied them.
If one interprets the chariots and the weapons as the playthings
with which these extraordinarily wealthy men chose to amuse
themselves, one is left with the considerable problem of ex-

49. Ibid.

plaining how these men became so rich in the first place. Surely it is more reasonable and economical to explain the wealth as a result of military dominance, of which the weapons and the chariots are an expression. It may very well be that in Middle Helladic Lerna or Malthi a wealthy or eccentric individual occasionally acquired a horse and hitched it to a "chariot" for sport or display, as did Shamshi-Adad and Zimri-Lim in Mesopotamia ca. 1800 B.C. But chariots as instruments of war, arrayed against an infantry of the old style, were another matter. Unlike such peaceful arts as alphabetic writing or ivory carving, chariot warfare was not peacefully transmitted. Wherever we encounter chariot warfare in the middle of the second millennium, it has been violently introduced: in the Levant and in Egypt, in Mesopotamia and in India, we first catch sight of it when the light begins to dawn after a disastrous dark age.

Finally, Crouwel's reconstruction does not confront the argument from language. That argument indicates that the Greek language and the chariot arrived in Greece at the same time, which is to say that the chariot was brought to Greece by Indo-European invaders. More conservatively stated, as Wyatt does in his meticulous and concise article, the argument holds that "the Greeks" could not have come to Greece *before* they made an acquaintance with the chariot. The argument is based on a linguistic generalization: if a language includes an inherited word with its original meaning, then the object denoted by that word must have been "constantly and continuously known" to the speakers of that language.[50] If, then, we find the early Greeks using Indo-European (or "Greek") terms for a new contraption that arrived in Greece ca. 1600 B.C., we may conclude either that the Indo-Europeans (or "Greeks") arrived at the same time as the contraption, or that they arrived at a later date (having in the meantime become acquainted elsewhere with the chariot). At any rate, "the Greeks" cannot have been living in Greece before the innovation occurred.[51]

50. Wyatt, "The Indo-Europeanization of Greece," 99.
51. More elegantly stated by Wyatt, "The Indo-Europeanization of

The argument that the Shaft Grave Dynasty was indigenous to the Argolid, and that Middle Helladic Greece evolved into Late Helladic Greece without interruption or invasion, depends entirely on pottery: the absence of an invader's ware and the persistence of local wares. Much is made of the fact that from the clay pots found in the two grave circles a continuum can be traced from Middle to Late Helladic shapes and motifs. This is, of course, true (although the progress from the drab Middle Helladic wares to the striking, Minoanized pottery of the Late Helladic period is more revolutionary than evolutionary), but ceramic continuity says nothing about the provenance of the shaft-grave dynasts. Pottery was one of the least significant artifacts in the shaft-grave corredo. In Grave IV, as we have seen, there were only eight pots, but there were forty-three vases of faience, alabaster, silver, and gold. To focus one's attention on the pots, and to ignore the foreign materials and motifs, the weaponry, the chariot stelai, and the gold (more gold than has been found in any excavation before or since) is to espy the gnat and overlook the camel.

The dynasts were charioteers and not potters, and it is hardly surprising that their pottery, like other humble necessities of daily life, should have been supplied to them by the subject population (even here, however, it is evident that the charioteers encouraged the Argolid potters to make more interesting pots than was their custom). Linguistic evidence in fact almost requires us to assume that the first Greek speakers in the land secured their pottery from pre-Greek potters. The Greek words for potter's clay (*keramos*), for a potter's kiln (*keramion*), and for a range of ceramic vessels (*kantharos, aryballos, lekythos, depas, phiale*) did not come from the Proto-Indo-European vocabulary.[52] The fact of ceramic continuity from the

---

Greece": "If we can attach a Greek (IE) name to a cultural innovation on Greek soil, either the IE invaders came at the same time as that innovation, or they found it already there when they arrived, and themselves possessed the object before they arrived. They cannot have preceded it" (p. 99).

52. On this linguistic point, see Grumach, "The Coming of the Greeks," 85–86.

Middle to the Late Helladic period does not at all contradict our thesis about "the coming of the Greeks."

The shaft-grave princes belonged to an international elite. The same was true of the charioteers who took over lands in the Fertile Crescent. The Indo-European and Hurrian princes in the Levant maintained surprisingly close connections with each other over distances of hundreds of miles, exchanging not only lavish gifts but also daughters and sisters in marriage. Similarly, the Kassite aristocracy of southern Mesopotamia, held together by gifts, correspondence, and an interest in chariotry, was also assiduous in cultivating personal and diplomatic relations with the rulers of lands as far away as Egypt. The *hyksos* rulers in Egypt, at the beginning of the sixteenth century B.C., seem to have been in touch with Crete as well as with Mesopotamia and, of course, the Levant. (In contrast, Mesopotamian and Egyptian kings in the eighteenth century B.C . were relatively parochial: in the voluminous documentation for Mesopotamia in the Age of Hammurabi there is no mention of Egypt.) The rulers of Mitanni and the imperial kings of Hatti likewise had close personal and diplomatic ties with their peers in other lands. James Breasted fittingly named the Late Bronze Age "The First International Civilization."

In utter contrast with the provincialism of Middle Helladic Greece, the shaft-grave dynasts delighted in the foreign and the exotic. In Emily Vermeule's catalog, we find "ostrich eggs from Nubia sent through Egypt and Crete, lapiz lazuli from Mesopotamia, alabaster and faience from Crete, raw ivory from Syria, silver from Anatolia, amber from Prussia brought down the Adriatic or out of Odessa across the north Aegean."[53] The trading partners of the dynasty at Mycenae were obviously a varied lot. Minoan artifacts and motifs are plentiful enough to have convinced Sir Arthur Evans that the people buried in the shaft graves were his Minoans. Several scholars have cited the Egyptian material in the shaft graves as evidence that the shaft-grave charioteers had fought in Egypt. The theories of Persson,

---

53. Vermeule, *Greece in the Bronze Age*, 89–90.

Schachermeyr, and Stubbings have been summarized above. Jan Best's explanation is even more radical. Rejecting—as one must—the theory that the Greeks came to Greece in 1900 B.C. or earlier, Best reasonably associated their arrival in Greece with the Mycenaean shaft graves. Less reasonably, Best concluded that "the earliest Greeks must have been identical to the Hyksos."[54] Although that position is untenable, it is conceded all round that in the sixteenth century B.C. the rulers of Mycenae had productive connections with Egypt. Alongside the Egyptianizing and Minoanizing artifacts, the shaft graves gave evidence of connections with eastern Anatolia and Mesopotamia. Several gold diadems, from both Circle A and Circle B, are paralleled most closely by diadems found in a grave at Assur that dates from the first half of the second millennium. The decoration of another diadem recalls immediately a sixteenth-century Kassite ring, and still other artifacts are paralleled at Kültepe and other Anatolian sites.[55]

In addition to the influences and imports from Crete, Egypt, Anatolia, and the Fertile Crescent, there is the gold. There are no gold mines in the Argolid, and the gold buried in the shaft graves necessarily came from far away, undoubtedly exchanged for more utilitarian commodities that the dynasts had squeezed from the subject population of the Argolid. The tastes of the new rulers at Mycenae have with reason been characterized as vulgar and barbarous, but they were indisputably cosmopolitan.

Ironically, the international character of the shaft-grave ar-

54, Best, *The Arrival of the Greeks*, 29. Best's thesis depended in part on the Egyptian parallels in the shaft graves, but also on what he calls "literary accounts of the origin of the Greeks from the Near East," especially Diodorus's account (40.3.2) of Danaus's and Cadmus's migration from Egypt to Greece. Unfortunately, neither Diodorus nor his source—Hecataeus of Abdera—was in any position to tell us anything about second-millennium history. To Best's thesis, linguists would undoubtedly object that the Greek language shows no sign of an Egyptian substrate.

55. For details and references see Hooker, *Mycenaean Greece*, 47–48.

tifacts has from time to time been used as an argument that the people buried in the shaft graves could *not* have been the first Greek speakers to come to Greece. Thus George Mylonas, in his response to L. R. Palmer's *Mycenaeans and Minoans*:

> Professor Palmer brings the "Greeks" into the Mainland of Greece ca. 1600 BC. If we actually assume their arrival on that date, we shall have to account for the fact that on their establishment, or even before that, they were able to amass so much gold, certainly introduced from the outside and possibly from Egypt, that they were able to absorb at once the Minoan artistic ways, that they were capable of establishing overseas connections with Egypt or the Eastern Mediterranean territories indicated by objects such as ostrich eggs, the inlaid daggers, the embalmed body found in Grave v, etc. This I believe would prove a most difficult if not impossible task.[56]

A most difficult task it certainly would be, if one imagines "the coming of the Greeks" as a massive migration of nomads or pastoralists, perhaps evicted from their original homeland and therefore forced to seek new lands in which to make an honest living. In such a picture, the Greeks arrive by an overland route, driving their herds and flocks in front of them, and several centuries are required before the Greek yeomen work up their nerve to go to sea.

If "the coming of the Greeks" was a takeover of Greece by a charioteering community who came from the lands south of the Caucasus, the invaders would most likely have come by sea,

---

56. G. Mylonas, "The Luvian Invasions of Greece," *Hesperia* 31 (1962): 300. Perhaps it should be pointed out that the "embalmed body" of Grave v may owe a great deal to the vivid imagination of Heinrich Schliemann, although according to Hooker (*Mycenaean Greece*, 52–53), "Mylonas promises a closer investigation of a lump of earth that may contain remains of this 'mummy.' "

from the coasts of Pontus. The notion that anyone could have shipped horses ca. 1600 B.C. may initially seem preposterous, but the thing was obviously done. At a later time, Homer's audience apparently had no difficulty imagining the Achaean heroes transporting their horses to Troy. We need not rely, however, on Iron Age traditions about the Bronze Age, for we have contemporary evidence that in the Late Bronze Age, chariots were used on the islands of the Mediterranean. There were horses and chariots in Cyprus at this time, the chariots (like those of the Hittite kings) apparently carrying three-man crews.[57] On the island of Paros, two horse skeletons from the LH IIIB period were recently discovered.[58] And the Greeks brought the horse and chariot to Crete no later than ca. 1450 B.C. Unknown in Crete in the MM period, the horse appears frequently in LM art.[59] As it happens, among the earliest of the Late Minoan artistic representations is an LM II seal impression of a horse standing in a ship.[60] There is no reason to think that the seal represents a mythical horse in a mythical ship. The Chariot Tablets from the Linear B archive found at Knossos (and dating, on Evans's chronology, to ca. 1400 B.C.) show how much the Greek overlords depended on chariots for the defense of their regime on the island.

That PIE speakers from Armenia could have been capable of going anywhere by sea is again a surprise, but I think that the proposition is not only not out of the question, but almost certain. Let us consider the invasion of India. It has usually been assumed (there is even less evidence for "the coming of the Aryans" than for "the coming of the Greeks") that the Aryans came overland, somehow, to India, taking either a northern route through Afghanistan and across the Hindu Kush to the Punjab, or possibly a dreadfully arid southern route, through Baluchistan, across the Kirthar range, and into the

57. Schachermeyr, "Streitwagen," 726.
58. Crouwel, *Chariots*, 35.
59. Schachermeyr, "Streitwagen," 722–24.
60. Ibid., 723.

lower Indus Valley (the one ancient army known to have traveled this route was Alexander's, which barely made it through).[61] However, if the Aryans started on their journey from Armenia, an infinitely easier route for them to have taken to the Indus Delta would have been through Mesopotamia to the Persian Gulf, and then through the gulf to the Indian Ocean. The sea route through the gulf and along the coast of the Indian Ocean had been used, in the early second millennium, by Mesopotamian merchants in their occasional traffic with the cities of India.[62]

Linguistic evidence in fact suggests rather strongly that the Aryans who came to India came by way of Mesopotamia. One must note, first of all, Kammenhuber's conclusions about the Aryan glosses in the Kikkuli text: the words came from a developmental stage of Aryan *earlier* than the bifurcation of Indian and Iranian, and they came from the dialect ancestral to Sanskrit (rather than the Proto-Avestan dialect). Now, if the language of the Aryan speakers of Mitanni was ancestral to the language of the conquerors of northwest India, it is difficult to escape the conclusion that the Aryan speakers who went to India went by way of Mesopotamia. Also relevant here are conclusions reached by a distinguished linguist and Indo-Europeanist, Oswald Szemerenyi. Noting that there now is general agreement among Indo-Europeanists that Proto-Indo-European phonology was built on a five-vowel system, Szemerenyi investigated the exceptions to that rule, and specifically the

61. Fairservis, *The Roots of Ancient India*, 352–77, presents the archaeological evidence that might conceivably be relevant to the two hypotheses. Cf. the caution of A. B. Keith, *Cambridge History of India*, 1: 78–79: "It is easy to frame and support by plausible evidence various hypotheses, to which the only effective objection is that other hypotheses are equally legitimate, and that the facts are too imperfect to allow of conclusions being drawn. It is, however, certain that the Rigveda offers no assistance in determining the mode in which the Vedic Indians entered India."

62. A. L. Oppenheim, "Seafaring Merchants of Ur," *JAOS* 74 (1954): 6–17.

three-vowel system employed in Aryan (both Sanskrit and Avestan). This feature of Aryan, he concluded, seems to have been adopted from the Semitic languages of Mesopotamia.[63] The linguistic arguments are here more useful than the archaeological and supply at least a fragile basis for reconstructing the Aryan route to India. With Mitanni and southern Mesopotamia taken over soon after 1600 B.C., the next most attractive target may have been the rich Indus Valley far to the east. Those Aryans who were too slow off the mark to carve out a domain closer to home may very well have embarked their horses and chariots and sailed to India.[64]

A sea-borne invasion of Greece ca. 1600 B.C. is suggested by the four sites known to have been destroyed at that time: Argos, Eleusis, Pylos, and Kirrha are all on the sea (Kirrha, on Phocis's Corinthian Gulf coast, was apparently a thriving little town before its destruction at the end of the Middle Helladic period). By the fifteenth century, the Greeks were evidently able to land a fleet on Crete, which by that time must have lost whatever "thalassocracy" it may once have had. And it is quite clear that even in the sixteenth century the Mycenaean Greeks were quite dependent on the sea, for the wealth and the imports found in the shaft graves require the conclusion that the Mycenaeans engaged rather seriously in overseas trade.

Although the shaft graves of Mycenae give us by far our best

63. O. Szemerényi, "Structuralism and Substratum—Indo-Europeans and Semites in the Ancient Near East," *Lingua* 13 (1964): 1–29. Cf. his summary statement on page 19: "If we want to save continuity, both geographical and chronological, we must assume that part at least of the later Indians also lived for a time in, or on the fringes of, Mesopotamia."

64. On linguistic grounds, Gamkrelidze and Ivanov, "Migrations," 75–76, observed that "we must also consider the possibility that the Indo-Europeans migrated by water. . . . The Indo-European lexicon of terms concerning navigation (cf. the words *erH-/reH- 'to navigate in a boat or a ship with oars,' *naHu- 'vessel, boat,' *p/h/leu- 'to navigate') indicates a familiarity on the part of the speakers of these dialects with means of transport over large bodies of water." Proto-Indo-European *mari- became the Latin *mare*, the English "mere," and German *Meer*.

evidence for a sixteenth-century takeover, the Argolid was apparently not the only part of Greece taken over in "the coming of the Greeks." The argument here depends especially upon the sudden appearance of momumental tombs, quite unprecedented in Middle Helladic Greece. Nothing quite so spectacular as the shaft graves has been found elsewhere, but tumuli and tholos tombs—the circular and corbeled "beehive" tombs that were to culminate in the "Treasury of Atreus" and the "Tomb of Clytemnestra"—suggest that five or six other plains were subjugated in the sixteenth century B.C.[65] In Lacedaemonia, first of all, the Eurotas valley must have been under the domination of the Vaphio princes well before 1500 B.C., the date of the Vaphio Tomb. This Laconian tholos, one of the earlier tholos tombs thus far discovered, held a splendid array of grave goods. Although dwarfed by the shaft graves' corredo, in quality the Vaphio treasure compares rather well. Here, too, we find expertly crafted weapons, ornaments, and other gifts, and a cosmopolitan taste. The two Vaphio Cups, made of gold and showing strong Minoan influence, are among the most famous of all Late Helladic artifacts. No palace has yet been found, but it is likely that the Vaphio princes ruled Lacedae-

65. The funerary innovations at the end of the Middle Helladic and the beginning of the Late Helladic period can hardly be explained without some foreign derivation. The tholos tomb itself seems to have developed rather quickly from the tumulus burial and the grave circle, perhaps under the influence of the built tombs of Crete and Egypt. However, there has been considerable controversy about the origins of the grave circle, with its deep shaft graves, and the tumulus burial. It has been held that the Mycenaean shaft graves developed from the cist graves of the MH period, but that view is increasingly difficult to maintain. For arguments against the evolution from MH tombs, defended especially by Mylonas, see M. J. Mellink, "The Royal Tombs at Alaca Huyuk and the Aegean World," in *The Aegean and the Near East: Studies Presented to Hetty Goldman*, ed. Saul S. Weinberg (Locust Valley, N.Y.: Augustin, 1956), 55–56. That both the tumuli and the grave circles of the LH I period have a "kurgan" origin is maintained in the massive study by O. Pelon, *Tholoi, tumuli et cercles funéraires. Recherches sur les monuments funéraires de plan circulaire dans l'Égée de l'âge du bronze* (Athens: École Française d'Athènes, 1976).

mon from Therapne, on the left bank of the Eurotas and a few miles downstream from the later site of Sparta. As already mentioned, a cylinder seal from the Vaphio tomb portrays a chariot carrying a driver and a fighter.[66]

On the western coast of the Peloponnese, three tholos tombs were excavated by Spyridon Marinatos at a tiny place called Peristeria (near Kyparissia, about twenty kilometers north of Pylos). The pottery from these tholoi dated from the first half of the sixteenth century B.C. and was of "that same mixture of Middle Helladic and Late Helladic which characterizes the Mycenaean Shaft Graves."[67] In one of the tholoi, Marinatos found grave goods that had escaped the notice of tomb robbers, and these turned out to be extraordinary and also informative. Gold ornaments, gold cups, and a gold diadem at Peristeria not only have parallels at Mycenae, "but even, in some cases, are apparently the products of the same school of craftsmen whose works are preserved in the Shaft Graves."[68] A tholos found at Koryphasion, near Pylos, also seems to date from the very beginning of the Late Helladic I period.[69] Remains from the LH I and II periods have also been found at Kakovatos, a further thirty kilometers to the north. All of these Messenian sites are on the sea, and in small sea plains.

Altogether, it appears that the Messenian coast was especially affected by a sixteenth-century takeover. Sinclair Hood, writing before the Peristeria material was published, postulated a surge of Minoan influence: "in Messenia, the southwest tip of the Peloponnese, Cretan influence seems to have been strong from the very beginning of the Late Bronze Age c. 1600 B.C. Tholos tombs are more numerous, and appear to have been built there earlier than in any other part of the Greek

66. Crouwel, *Chariots*, 123 (with plate 11).
67. Stubbings, *CAH* II, 1: 641.
68. Hooker, *Mycenaean Greece*, 56. Hooker sets out the parallels between the Peristeria offerings and those of the shaft graves in his Table 3 (233–34).
69. Stubbings, *CAH* II, 1: 641.

mainland."[70] Hood, of course, thought of Minoans rather than Greeks because he supposed that the Greeks did not enter Greece until the end of the Bronze Age. But the Peristeria tholoi rule out the thesis that Minoans were responsible for what happened in Messenia in the LH I period, for these tholoi yielded very little Minoan or Minoanizing material. Not until the second half of the sixteenth century did the lords of Messenia, like their contemporaries in the Argolid, begin to develop a taste for Cretan things. A more natural explanation than Hood's would be that a ruling elite established itself in Messenia early in the sixteenth century B.C., and that the intruders spoke the form of Proto-Indo-European that was to evolve into Greek.

In central Greece, the spacious Boeotian plain was dominated by establishments at Thebes and Orchomenos (and in the thirteenth century B.C. at Gla). The recent discovery of a palace at Orchomenos was mentioned above. What has thus far been recovered at the site seems to belong, according to first reports, to a palace of the LH IIIA period.[71] The Orchomenos tholos is also relatively late: it has been dated no earlier than the LH II period, and as late as ca. 1300 B.C. At Thebes, however, a dynasty had established itself well before the end of the sixteenth century, since a palace was apparently standing there by 1500 B.C.[72]

The evidence from Attica is of extraordinary interest. Until recently, the known Mycenaean remains in Attica were neither very early nor very significant; but recent excavations have changed the situation dramatically. Tholoi assigned to the fifteenth century have been found at Thorikos and Marathon (the slaughtered team of horses in the dromos of the Marathon tomb

70. Hood, *Home of the Heroes*, 76.

71. Catling, *AR 1984–85*, 31.

72. H. Reusch, *Die zeichnerische Rekonstruktion des Frauenfrieses im böotischen Theben* (Berlin: Akademie-Verlag, 1956), concluded that the fragments of a frieze from the Kadmeion at Thebes show it to have been one of the earliest "Mycenaean" frescoes yet discovered.

have already been mentioned). Adjacent to the tholoi at these two sites were graves of a "tumulus" type that recall both the shaft graves at Mycenae and the kurgans of the Caucasus. At Thorikos, on a great hill that overlooks a bay on Attica's eastern coast, a group of three tombs seems to bridge two centuries.[73] A rather conventional tholos here, looted long before its excavation, dates to the fifteenth century B.C. A second tholos is architecturally unusual: it has a short dromos and an oblong chamber. It appears to have been built in the LH I period (its excavators date its construction shortly before 1500 B.C.). Although it too was robbed, a fair number of objects—including some in gold—escaped the robbers' notice. The grave goods seem to parallel those from Graves III and IV of Grave Circle A at Mycenae. Still earlier, and lying only five meters from the Oblong Tholos, was a tumulus surrounded by a *peribolos*. The burials under this tumulus, which was a grave circle of sorts, were not distinguished by costly grave goods. So laborious must have been its construction, however (the tumulus, even without the peribolos, must have been the work of a great many men), that the Belgian archaeologists who excavated it have not hesitated to describe it as "royal."[74] The pottery dates the tumulus to the same period as the earliest graves of Mycenae's Grave Circle B. The Thorikos tumulus yielded a great deal of Gray Minyan Ware and seems to date from the very end of the Middle Helladic or the very beginning of the Late Helladic period. The excavators concluded that the three Thorikos tombs represent a single dynastic family.

Four tumuli have also been found at Vrana, at the edge of the Marathon plain.[75] The latest of these dates from the LH IIIB

73. J. Servais and B. Servais-Soyez, "La tholos 'oblongue' (tombe IV) et le tumulus (tombe V) sur le Vélatouri," *Thorikos 1972/1976* (Ghent: Comité des fouilles belges en Grèce, 1984; vol. 8 of the *Thorikos* reports), 60ff.

74. Ibid., 64.

75. On these, see S. Marinatos, "Further News from Marathon," *AAA* 3 (1970): 155–63, and the same author's "Anaskaphai Marathonos,"

period, but one seems to have been constructed in the sixteenth century, and still another (Tumulus I) can be dated to the end of the Middle Helladic period. Each of the four tumuli was surrounded by a ring of slender stone slabs, just as were the grave circles at Mycenae.[76] Tumulus I at Vrana and the tumulus at Thorikos are the earliest tumulus burials thus far discovered in Greece. They do not appear to have been simple elaborations of Middle Helladic cist graves, but instead seem to belong to a tradition of tumuli and of grave circles that is best attested in eastern Anatolia and the Caucasus region. Parallels are known from the Kurgan Culture above the Caucasus and from Alaca Huyuk in Anatolia.[77]

Especially interesting for our purposes is the skeleton of a horse found in one of the eight graves under Tumulus I at Vrana. Marinatos concluded that the tomb was meant for the horse and noted that the small size of the horse fit quite well with skeletal remains of other horses from the second millennium.[78] Petros Themelis, however, accutely observed that underneath the horse's skeleton the excavators had found what could only have been part of the slab that had once covered the grave,[79] and Themelis rightly concluded that the grave could not have been intended for the horse. In Themelis's reconstruction of events, the grave at some point collapsed (possibly after it had been robbed of not only its grave goods but also its human skeleton). After the collapse, and possibly as late as the Byzantine or the Turkish period, either a horse fell into the grave and was killed, or the body of a dead horse was thrown into the collapsed grave. This solution, however, is not entirely

---

Praktika 1970, 9–18. Marinatos described the tumuli in more cursory fashion in "Prehellenic and Protohellenic Discoveries at Marathon," *Acta of the Second Int. Colloquium*, 184–90.

76. Pelon, *Tholoi*, 82–85. Pelon is persuaded that Grave Circles A and B at Mycenae were likewise once covered by tumuli.

77. Ibid., 450–51.

78. Marinatos, "Anaskaphai Marathonos," 11, and plate 15B.

79. P. Themelis, in *AD* 29 (1974): 242–44.

persuasive, since in such a sequence of events, one should have found more than a meter of soil—the soil of the tumulus—between the slab lid and the skeleton. A better solution, I believe, is provided by the analogous kurgans of southern Russia and the "royal tombs" at Alaca Huyuk. At the Anatolian site, "bones of sacrificed animals were found in situ on the roofs of the graves."[80] In the Timber Graves north of the Caspian, archaeologists have frequently found "horses buried above the roof in the covering barrow."[81] Although perhaps common in various societies within the horse-breeding koine, the dispatch of a horse to accompany a warrior in the afterlife was certainly a primitive Indo-European practice. At the funerals of Germanic warriors, Tacitus tells us, horses were sometimes slaughtered, and a tumulus was heaped over the remains of both warrior and horse.[82] So far as the Mycenaean world is concerned, our evidence is not limited to Homer's description of Patroclus's funeral pyre, with the bones of slaughtered men and horses lying *epimix* around its periphery. That in their funerary rites the lords of the Marathon plain at least occasionally sacrificed horses is shown by the slaughtered team in the fifteenth-century tholos (the tholos lies only a kilometer east of the Vrana tumuli). It may very well be, then, as James Muhly has suggested,[83] that after the deceased human was interred in Grave 3 of Tumulus I at Vrana, a horse was slaughtered over the lid of the grave, and the tumulus was then heaped over the grave and the horse. However the horse skeleton is to be explained, the tumuli at Vrana and at Thorikos indicate that Attica was taken over no later than the Argolid and Messenia.

The evidence for Thessaly is less clear.[84] In part this may be the result of Thessaly's peculiarities. The region is essentially a

80. Mellink, "Royal Tombs," 55.

81. Piggott, *Earliest Wheeled Transport*, 91.

82. Tacitus, *Germania* 27.

83. Muhly, "On the Shaft Graves," 312.

84. For Mycenaean Thessaly, see now B. Feuer, *The Northern Mycenaean Border in Thessaly* (B.A.R. International Series, no. 176) (Oxford: B.A.R., 1983).

vast basin drained by a single river system—the Peneios—and is rimmed by mountain walls. Stone is readily available near the mountain rims, but that is seldom the case in the interior of the basin. Most building here was done in mud brick, which tends to disintegrate in the moist soil. The Thessalian plain is exceptionally fertile (although the severe winters discourage the growth of olive trees and other flora common to much of the Mediterranean) and seems to have supported a large population all through the neolithic period and the Bronze Age. Like the Egyptian Delta, however, it has not been archaeologically productive.

It is not entirely surprising, therefore, that there is rather little material evidence for a takeover of Thessaly at the beginning of the Late Helladic period. Although in historical times Thessaly was renowned for its horses, we have no material record for chariots in this region in the middle of the second millennium. In a tholos tomb at Mega Monastirion, twenty kilometers northwest of Volos, a painted toy chariot with yoked horses was found, but this terracotta figurine is assigned a LH IIIB date.[85] Funerary architecture, however, does seem to indicate an early takeover. Tholos tombs apparently of LH II date have been found near the Gulf of Volos. The tombs themselves (in which gold ornaments were found)[86] can hardly be dated before the fifteenth century B.C., although it may be noteworthy that the Iolkos region has yielded a considerable quantity of LH I pottery.[87] More significant, although problematic, is a large tholos found far in the interior, more than a hundred kilometers west of Iolkos and in fact almost at the Pindus rim of the Thessalian plain: at Kouphia Rachi, five kilometers southwest of Kardhitsa, Dimitrios Theochares excavated a tholos that purportedly contained pottery from the LH I and even the

85. R. Hope Simpson, *Mycenaean Greece* (Park Ridge, N.J.: Noyes, 1981), 165; for illustration of the figurine, see Crouwel, *Chariots*, plate 41.

86. Hooker, *Mycenaean Greece*, 64–65.

87. Feuer, *Thessaly*, 49.

very end of the MH period.[88] If this tholos was in fact constructed ca. 1600 B.C., it would suggest very strongly that at
that date virtually the whole of the Thessalian plain had been
taken over by PIE speakers. In general, "Mycenaean" pottery
has been found at some seventy sites in Thessaly, but few sites
have produced "Mycenaean" architecture. At Iolkos, a Late
Helladic building designated as a palace by its excavator has
not yet been precisely dated. Most puzzling of all is the site of
Petra, on the western edge of what was once Lake Boibe. Here
a circuit wall, of "Cyclopean" construction that in some
stretches reached a thickness of five meters, ran for more than
four kilometers. If the wall is indeed Mycenaean in date, the
1,000,000 square meters that it encloses would be the largest
fortified site of the period.[89]

Archaeology thus provides only occasional and ambiguous
evidence that "the Greeks" took over the Thessalian basin at a
very early date. An argument can nevertheless be made that
the PIE speakers came first to Thessaly, and from there went on
to take over central and southern Greece. The argument is
based on linguistics and on the Greek myths. The latter make
Thessaly something of an Hellenic cradle. Here the original
Hellas was located, and it was here that Prometheus begat
Deucalion, Deucalion begat Hellen, and Hellen begat Aeolus,
Dorus, and Xuthus. Despite Nilsson's arguments to the contrary,[90] it is evident that a great many myths have Thessalian
connections, and that some must have originated in Thessaly

88. D. R. Theochares, "Thessalian Antiquities and Monuments,"
AD 16 (1960): 168–86. Hope Simpson, *Mycenaean Greece*, 173–74, ex-
pressed reservations about the date of the pottery, conceding only that "the
time of the construction of the tomb must surely lie within the Mycenaean
period, to judge from its size and quality." Cf. also Feuer, *Thessaly*, 44.

89. Feuer, *Thessaly*, 44.

90. M. Nilsson, *The Mycenaean Origin of Greek Mythology* (Berkeley:
Univ. of California Press, 1932), argued vigorously that most of Greek mythology originated near the "Mycenaean" palace centers in central Greece
and the Peloponnese. Thessaly, he proposed (p. 232), was much too poor a
place, and too far from the Greek mainstream, to have played any significant role in the creation of the stories.

(for example, the Titanomachy, the battle between the Lapiths and the Centaurs, the expedition of the Argonauts).[91] It is from Thessaly that many of the heroic genealogies proceed, and, of course, it was Thessaly's Mt. Olympus that the Greeks regarded as the home of the gods.

Linguistic considerations are also pertinent. The differentiation of North Greek from the South Greek dialect of the Linear B tablets shows clearly enough that by 1200 B.C., Greek had for several centuries been spoken in the lands north of the "Mycenaean" zone.[92] Perhaps one can go further. A detailed analysis of the dialectal evidence led Wyatt to the conclusion that Thessaly was linguistically the most conservative area of Greece, a residual area from which rather than to which Greek speakers moved. He therefore assumed "that the PG [Proto-Greek] world was restricted to Thessaly, though it may not have embraced all of Thessaly," and he suggested that South Greek arose when some of the Proto-Greek speakers "moved away from Thessaly and established colonies elsewhere in the south of Greece."[93]

There is, then, some reason to believe that the great Thessalian plain (far and away the largest plain in all of Greece) was the initial destination of the PIE speakers who came to the Greek mainland, and that from Thessaly the PIE speakers went on to subjugate the plains further to the south. If Thessaly was the original "home of the heroes," we would expect to find that during the Mycenaean Age there was a greater concentration of Greek speakers in Thessaly than elsewhere. Unusually good evidence to that effect comes from what is widely regarded as the earliest extant piece of Greek literature: the Catalog of the

91. In "Argos and Argives in the *Iliad*," *CP* 74 (1979): 111–35, I have argued that the Trojan saga (and the story of the Seven against Thebes) originated in Thessaly, the Pelasgic Argos.

92. See especially García-Ramón, *Les Origines postmycéniennes*, 40–59 (García-Ramón uses the terms "grec oriental" and "grec occidental" for what I—following Risch's terminology—have called South Greek and North Greek).

93. Wyatt, "The Prehistory of the Greek Dialects," 628 and 629.

Ships, in the second book of the *Iliad*. In the catalog, which seems to have been composed when the geography of Mycenaean Greece was still a living memory, almost one-quarter of the Achaeans' ships (280 of 1,186) come from Thessaly (in contrast, only 50 come from Attica, 40 from Euboea, 80 from Boeotia, 80 from all of Crete). We may say with some confidence that early in the Dark Age the Greeks recalled that during the Age of the Heroes, more warriors had lived in Thessaly than anywhere else.

In summary, it appears that "the coming of the Greeks" was to the best lands of the Greek mainland: the plains, which not only were fertile and thickly settled, but also were unusually vulnerable to charioteering invaders. By 1450 B.C., the newcomers had also invaded Crete and are assumed to have taken over at least the region around Knossos and possibly much of eastern Crete. The takeover in Crete was evidently secondary—launched from the Greek mainland rather than from the homeland of the PIE speakers. Several of the takeovers on the Greek mainland may have been primary, although it is more likely that Thessaly served—however briefly—as a staging area for most of the takeovers further to the south. At any rate, it is probable that ca. 1600 B.C., speakers of a form of Proto-Indo-European came to Greece in considerable numbers, breaking up into smaller groups soon after their arrival in the Aegean, and taking over choice plains all round the mainland and eventually on Crete. Wherever they went, certainly the invaders would have for several generations maintained close contact with each other (and especially, I think, with their Thessalian "base"). It would have been during this time that their form of Proto-Indo-European, much affected by the pre-Indo-European language(s) of the Aegean, significantly differentiated itself from other forms of Proto-Indo-European and evolved into the language that we may call Common Greek or Proto-Greek.[94]

94. If the Linear B tablets found at Knossos were indeed inscribed

In this scenario for "the coming of the Greeks" we are dealing certainly with thousands of people, very likely with tens of
thousands, but not with hundreds of thousands. The forces
upon which the *hyksos* depended in Egypt, or upon which the
Kassite kings depended in southern Mesopotamia, could not
have been more than a tiny fraction of the indigenous population of Egypt or Mesopotamia, too small a number to be archaeologically detectible. In the Levant and in Mitanni a mi-
nuscule Aryan minority took control over Semitic-speaking
and Hurrian-speaking majorities, but, of course, in the Levant
and in Mitanni the Aryan language was ultimately submerged.
Those PIE speakers who—as suggested here—crossed the seas
to take over Greece and northwest India, and whose language
ultimately was adopted by the people they conquered, may
have constituted a considerably larger fraction of the total population in the lands they took over. Nevertheless, we may still
suppose that when PIE speakers took over the best parts of the
Greek mainland—a land that seems to have had almost no po-
litical organization, and a populace that seems to have set little
store by military prowess—they controlled an alien population
perhaps ten times as large as their own. Such was the ratio of
helots to Spartiates at a much later time, and even the Greeks
who took over a relatively well-organized Knossos ca. 1450
B.C. may not have numbered over a tenth of their Minoan subjects. One can only guess at the numbers involved in "the com-

---

ca. 1400 B.C., as Sir Arthur Evans asserted, Proto-Greek must have evolved
very quickly, and the dialect of the Linear B tablets must have immediately
thereafter branched off from Proto-Greek and reached its "classical" Mycenaean form (which it must then have retained, virtually unchanged, for the
next two centuries). Many specialists, however, now believe that the Linear
B tablets from Knossos, like those from Pylos, date from ca. 1200 B.C. The
argument met with considerable resistance when put forward by Leonard
Palmer in his *Minoans and Mycenaeans*, but since then has steadily won adherents. An unusually vigorous assault on Evans's position has recently been
made by F.C.D. Hentschel, "The Basis for the Standard Chronology of the
Late Bronze Age at Knossos" (Ph.D. diss., Yale University, 1982 [Univer-
sity Microfilms: Ann Arbor, 1982]).

ing of the Greeks," and I shall hazard mine: if at the beginning of the sixteenth century B.C. the population of the Thessalian plain, the Argolid, the Eurotas Valley, Messenia, Boeotia, and Attica was approximately three-quarters of a million men, women, and children, the PIE-speaking conquerors may have numbered no more than about 75,000 men, women, and children.

CONCLUSION

The history of the ancient world in the second millennium B.C. is a patchwork of light and darkness. For a few major topics we have reasonable documentation, but on other topics of equal importance we have virtually no evidence at all. Although "the coming of the Indo-Europeans" falls (not coincidentally) in one of the darkest squares, this historic episode is slightly illuminated by adjacent topics. Since the episode itself will perhaps always remain undocumented, it must be reconstructed so as to accommodate what few and slender clues we have, and that is what I have tried to do in this essay.

Some dubious assumptions about the PIE speakers are interlocked and of long standing. One of these assumptions is that when poised on the threshold of history, the PIE speakers were a numerous people, making up a fair portion of the world's population. For such a multitude, a spacious home must be imagined, and a second assumption is that the Indo-European homeland was a vast territory, perhaps covering much of eastern Europe or the Eurasian steppe. From this homeland, the Indo-Europeans are supposed to have set out, in prehistoric times, in a series of massive Völkerwanderungen; eventually, they came to rest in the lands in which during historical times the Indo-European languages were spoken. The beginnings of these mass migrations are placed between ca. 4500 and ca. 2000 B.C., and the reasons for the migrations are seldom stated.

An alternative picture is more likely. At the end of the third millennium, the PIE-speaking community was no larger than the Hurrian, the Sumerian, the Hattic, or the Proto-Anatolian

197

and was only a fraction the size of the Semitic. The PIE-speaking community remained intact, playing no significant historical role, until the second quarter of the second millennium. In the late seventeenth or early sixteenth century, individuals and then whole communities of PIE speakers began leaving their native lands (probably in the lake district of eastern Anatolia). None of these movements of PIE speakers involved a population much larger than that of one Mesopotamian city of the first rank. Nor were the movements *Wanderungen* at all. The relocations—some of them apparently by sea—were well planned and organized, and their leaders knew where they were going and what they would do when they got there. The PIE speakers' object in leaving their native lands was to take control of societies that were vulnerable and that could be profitably exploited.

Takeovers rather than Völkerwanderungen are what seem to have plagued the ancient world in the second millennium B.C. The Indo-European takeovers appear to have been analogous to the *hyksos* takeover of Egypt, and to the Kassite and Hurrian takeovers of various communities in the Fertile Crescent (the Kassites and the Hurrians may have been neighbors of the PIE speakers before they set out on their adventures). For all of these intruders, chariotry was essential: it was their mastery of chariot warfare that made it possible for the intruders to conquer and then to dominate lands from Egypt and Greece to India. The takeovers were motivated, it need hardly be said, by the desire for power and wealth.

Our alternative framework has been constructed on the basis of evidence from the civilized and semicivilized world, but it also has implications for those lands for which we have no written records at all. On the present thesis, the *terminus post quem* for the arrival of PIE speakers in Italy and central Europe would be ca. 1600 B.C. If evidence from either Italy or the Carpathian Basin should indicate the practice of chariot warfare in the middle of the second millennium, one could then begin to make a case that the area in question had by then been taken over by PIE speakers. For Italy, it must be noted, there seems to be no evidence for chariotry at so early a date. Antler bits once associated with Terramara settlements of the Middle Bronze period seem in fact to be no earlier than the Late Bronze period, which in Italy is conventionally assigned a commencement in the thirteenth century B.C.[1] It is possible that the first PIE speakers to settle in Italy came by sea in the last quarter of the second millennium.[2] In the Carpathian Basin, as we have seen, the chariot is attested as early as 1500 B.C., but whether it was anything other than a prestige vehicle is not known. In general, it is a corollary of the thesis here presented that Europe was Indo-Europeanized much later than has usually been supposed.

The thesis of this book has been occasioned by a few relatively solid conclusions and one provocative hypothesis. The first of the conclusions pertains to "the coming of the Greeks." This event, usually imagined as a massive ethnic transformation of the Greek mainland, has conventionally been dated ca. 1900 B.C. The archaeological support for this date has now disappeared, and linguistic considerations suggest a considerably later date for the dissemination of Proto-Greek in Greece. Furthermore, circumstantial evidence (including evidence on the end of the Aegean Bronze Age) and sixteenth-century parallels indicate that "the coming of the Greeks" did not ethnically transform the land; instead, it seems to have superimposed upon the indigenous population of Greece a small

1. Heavy disk wheels of the Middle Bronze period have been found, but the antler bits, which may be evidence for draft horses, are apparently no earlier than the last quarter of the second millennium. See, for example, G. Säflund, *Le Terremare delle provincie di Modena, Reggio Emilia, Parma, Piacenza* (Lund: Gleerup, 1939), 223: "quanto al cavallo non credo che sia stato allevato nella zona terramaricola prima della fase II B." Säflund's II B covers the years from 1250 to 750 B.C.

2. The Urnfielders are obvious suspects. Like other warrior societies late in the second millennium, the Urnfielders may have relied primarily on spear-throwing infantry.

minority of PIE speakers. In this respect, as in its date, the Hellenization of Greece thus seems to parallel the Aryanization of northwest India. The material record of the event is preserved in the shaft graves of Mycenae and in the tholoi and tumuli found in the plains of the Peloponnese, central Greece, and Thessaly.

A second conclusion on which our alternative picture of "the Indo-European invasions" is based has to do with the so-called Hittites. There was once a consensus among historians that a Hittite nation had invaded central Anatolia by the beginning of the second millennium. This Hittite nation, historians supposed, was the first in a series of Indo-European nations to have left its distant homeland and to have arrived in the more-or-less civilized world. Indo-Europeanists, however, have long known that the relationship of Hittite (or Proto-Anatolian) to the other Indo-European languages is unclear: although possibly a sibling to Greek, Sanskrit, Latin, and the other daughter languages of Proto-Indo-European, it is increasingly more likely that Proto-Anatolian was an "aunt" rather than a sister of the Indo-European languages. In a clear light not only the Hittite invasion but even the Hittite nation disappears: its existence depended not upon any evidence, literary or archaeological, but upon a cluster of presuppositions (the most important being that a Greek nation had come to the other side of the Aegean by 1900 B.C.).

A third conclusion indispensable for our new picture has to do with the time and place effective chariot warfare began. Specialized studies now permit us to be rather precise about the chronology of this development: although "chariots" were first made in the nineteenth century B.C., and although they may have occasionally appeared on Anatolian battlefields as early as ca. 1800 B.C., effective chariot warfare (dependent upon the bit, and perhaps upon the composite bow) seems not to have begun before the middle of the seventeenth century B.C. So far as the locale is concerned, specialists have for some time suggested that eastern Anatolia played the leading role in the development of the "chariot," which is to say a light, spoked-wheel cart. It is certain that the inhabitants of the forested areas of Armenia very early became accomplished woodworkers, and it now appears that in the second millennium they produced spoked-wheel vehicles that served as models as far away as China. And we have long known that from the second millennium onward, Armenia was important for the breeding of horses. It is thus not surprising to find that what clues we have suggest that chariot warfare was pioneered in eastern Anatolia.

Finally, our picture of what the PIE speakers did, and when, owes much to the recently proposed hypothesis that the homeland of the PIE speakers was Armenia. Although this identification is problematic, there is much to be said for it. The present essay departs rather widely from the chronological and historical assumptions within which Gamkrelidze and Ivanov constructed their hypothesis, but I believe that in so doing, it provides a more reasonable picture of how, when, and why the PIE speakers made their entry into history.

Appendix One

THE END OF
THE BRONZE AGE IN GREECE

Consideration of an apparently unrelated topic, the Dorian Invasion, supports the construction here presented of "the coming of the Greeks" and the Indo-European conquests in the middle of the second millennium. The problematical Dorian Invasion has from time to time been held responsible for the destruction of the Mycenaean world, or for the creation of historical Greece, or for both. Conversely, some scholars have denied that a Dorian Invasion ever took place. The polarity of the solutions to the problem reflects what appear to be irreconcilable contradictions in the evidence, each solution emphasizing one part of the evidence and discounting another.[1] The contradictions tend to disappear, however, if the evidence is seen against the background suggested in Chapter Eight.

In the Classical Period of the fifth and fourth centuries, various dialects conventionally called "Doric" were spoken in much of the Peloponnese, in Crete, in some of the small islands of the southern Aegean, in Rhodes, and along the southwestern coast of Asia Minor. For this linguistic fact the Classical Greeks had an ethnic explanation: the Dorian *ethnos* had early on appropriated these lands from other Greek nations. Herodotus told the story in some detail (1.56), and being Herodotus he started at the beginning. The Dorian nation inhabited Phthio-

1. A colloquium on the Dorians was held in Rome in April 1983 and brought together a variety of viewpoints from historians, linguists, Mycenologists, and archaeologists. The papers have been critically summarized by C. Brillante, "L'invasione dorica oggi," *Quaderni Urbinati di Cultura Classica* n.s. 16 (1984): 173–85.

tis (a Thessalian district on the Malian Gulf) during the reign of Deucalion, but under Dorus moved to the lands just below Olympus, and from there was driven to the Pindus. The Dorians worked their way back, however, to Dryopis (this place, later called Doris, was on the southern coast of the Malian Gulf, and so not far from where the Dorians had started off on their perigrinations). It was from Dryopis that they came to the Peloponnese.

Throughout most of classical antiquity, this rather colorless and impersonal story was overshadowed by a more interesting tale: the story of the Return of the Heraclidae. According to this story, the progeny of Heracles were expelled from the Peloponnese by Eurystheus. Hyllus attempted to lead them back, but the attempt ended in the Heraclids' defeat and Hyllus's death. Thereupon the Heraclidae settled down in central Greece until Delphic Apollo informed them that the time had come for their return to their ancestral lands. Brigaded in three divisions, the Heraclidae conquered most of the Peloponnese: Messenia fell to Cresphontes, Laconia to Aristodemus, and the Argolid to Temenos. The story was an old one, and Herodotus accepted at least parts of it.

Thucydides saw the two stories as facets of the same event. In the eightieth year after the Trojan War, he said (1.12.3), the Dorians "together with the Heraclidae" took over the Peloponnese. Taking their cue from Thucydides, chronographers fixed the date to the eightieth year after the Trojan War, being the 329th year before the First Olympiad (1104 B.C.).

In the first half of the nineteenth century, critical history disengaged the two stories and threw out the story of the Return of the Heraclidae as so much fiction. Herodotus's pedestrian story of the migration, on the other hand, seemed worthy of respect. George Grote accepted the tradition of a Dorian migration from Doris. The migration was by sea and came to the Argolid. From there, the Dorians eventually expanded to Laconia and Messenia. But although Grote accepted Herodotus's account, he did not assign a great deal of importance to the migration. Nor, with a few exceptions, did other historians of the early nineteenth century.

Schliemann's excavations put things in a very different light. None of the ancient writers had suggested that the Dorian migration, or the Return of the Heraclidae, was an especially destructive affair, and Thucydides had in fact presented it as not unlike the return of exiles to cities in his own day. But Schliemann found that the splendid centers of Mycenaean Greece had been suddenly and terribly destroyed, surely by human hands. The logical culprits were, of course, the Dorians. Thus the Dorian migration became, at the end of the nineteenth century, the Dorian Invasion. The invasion was a disaster of vast proportions and was the watershed between the Mycenaean Age and historical Greece. Its date was synchronized with the fall of Mycenae, somewhere between the end of the thirteenth and the end of the twelfth centuries.

The most compelling and comprehensive picture was published by Eduard Meyer in 1893.[2] Meyer imagined the end of the Bronze Age in Greece and the rest of the eastern Mediterranean world to have been rather like the Fall of Rome. The Dorian Invasion he saw as part of a general movement of barbarians into the civilized world in the decades before and after 1200 B.C., a movement most clearly seen in Egyptian records of the Sea Peoples' assault on the Delta. After the Dorian Invasion of Greece, as after the Germanic invasion of the Roman Empire, came a dark age during which primitive tribesmen appropriated the ruins of a once-sophisticated civilization. And just as the foundations of modern Europe were laid early in the European Middle Ages, so the institutions and ideals of Classical Greece took root in the *Mittelalter* that began with the fall of the Mycenaean world. Thus the Dorians were both the destroyers of one world and the creators of another.

Although the overall picture was a valuable contribution,

2. E. Meyer, *Geschichte des Alterthums* (Stuttgart: Cotta, 1893), 2: 249–532.

parts of it turned out to be wrong. By paralleling the Dorians with the Germanic invaders of the Roman Empire, for example, Meyer ushered historians down a lengthy cul-de-sac. Just as the Germanic peoples, on racist presuppositions, were endowed with virile and martial qualities that were indispensable for the European triumph over the rest of the world, so the Dorians represented a younger and more vigorous Hellenic strain than the somewhat effete "Achaeans" and Ionians. Dorianism reached the height of its popularity in the 1930s, but rapidly subsided after World War II.[3]

By the 1960s the creative side of the Dorian Invasion was seldom celebrated. The invasion was still understood, however, as responsible for the fall of the Mycenaean world. Yet even the destructive side of the invasion was difficult to substantiate. That catastrophe had overwhelmed Greece at the end of the Bronze Age was beyond question: archaeologists had found dozens of sites that were either destroyed or abandoned at the end of the LH IIIB or during the LH IIIC period. The difficulty was that the destruction did not seem to have been wrought by newcomers, or by invaders who came to stay. The destructions, first of all, occurred over a fairly long period, from about 1225 B.C. to the end of the twelfth century, and according to no geographic pattern that hinted at invasion. More disturbing was the fact that no intrusive artifacts—whether pottery, ornaments, tools, or weapons—had been found above the destruction levels.

The lack of "Dorian" material at particular sites, and even on regional levels, had for some time been observed by archaeologists. The first systematic survey of the end of the Greek Bronze Age, however, was presented by Vincent Desborough in 1964.[4] In magisterial fashion Desborough traced the de-

3. The ideological basis of Dorianism was most thoroughly exposed by E. Will, *Doriens et Ioniens* (Paris: Les Belles Lettres, 1956). See also C. Starr, *The Origins of Greek Civilization* (New York: Knopf, 1961), 70–74.

4. V. Desborough, *The Last Mycenaeans and their Successors. An Ar-*

struction of Mycenaean Greece and showed that a Dorian Invasion could not have caused it. Not only was there no positive evidence for a new population in the twelfth-century Peloponnese, but there was good reason to think that many parts of the Peloponnese and Central Greece had almost no population at all at the end of the second millennium. The term "Dark Age" had frequently been applied to the period 1200–800 B.C., but Desborough's *Last Mycenaeans* showed how dreadfully dark and desolate at least the first half of that period had been. Desborough found no evidence of Dorian intruders until ca. 1075–1050 B.C. At that time, well after the Mycenaean world had been ruined, innovations in burial practice (specifically, the frequent use of cist-grave burials) suggested the arrival of newcomers. The "Dorian Invasion," Desborough concluded, could only have been an infiltration into a half-empty land. In other words, the Dorians came not as destroyers and conquerors but as squatters.[5]

The thoroughness of Desborough's survey made his conclusions authoritative for a time, but in 1971 they were broadly challenged by Anthony Snodgrass.[6] Snodgrass pointed out that the eleventh-century cist graves not only seemed to have indigenous precursors, but also did not correspond geographically with any conceivably Doric movement: cist graves appeared in Attica, for instance, and not in Messenia, Crete, or Thera. Snodgrass concluded that if one was looking for new customs or intrusive artifacts, the evidence for a Dorian migration into the Peloponnese was no better for the eleventh century than it

chaeological Survey ca. 1200 B.C.–1000 B.C. (Oxford: Oxford Univ. Press, 1964).

5. Desborough reviewed the question of the Dorians once more in *The Greek Dark Ages* (New York: St. Martin's, 1972) and reached rather different conclusions. In this study Desborough dated the arrival of the Dorians *ca.* 1125 B.C., and credited them with introducing the Submycenaean culture into central Greece and the northern Peloponnese.

6. A. Snodgrass, *The Dark Age of Greece* (Edinburgh: Edinburgh Univ. Press, 1971), 296–317.

was for the twelfth. The salient fact, Snodgrass urged, was the destruction of Mycenaean Greece: that was the most visible sign of intruders, and it indicated that the Dorians came to the Peloponnese and other parts of mainstream Greece ca. 1200 B.C. The absence of anything novel in the material record for the LH IIIC period, Snodgrass suggested, showed only that the Dorians had come from a nearby province, and that their material way of life was virtually identical to that of their Mycenaean victims.

Yet another solution to the problem of the Dorian Invasion was formulated and advanced in the light of Desborough's survey of the end of the Greek Bronze Age. In 1976 John Chadwick proposed that the Dorians did not enter the Peloponnese at the end of the Bronze Age, either as conquerors ca. 1200 B.C. or as infiltrators in the eleventh century: they had been in the Peloponnese all along, as a lower class.[7] Like most other students of the Greek dialects, Chadwick sees Doric as a very conservative descendant of Common Greek, the language of all the Greeks before innovations began to produce South Greek. But Chadwick's theory is eccentric in explaining how South Greek differentiated itself from this Common Greek that Doric so faithfully preserved: what made the difference was not geography, but class. According to Chadwick's theory, the new South Greek dialect arose when the royal administration—the palace officials—came under the influence of Minoan scribes. But while the speech of this narrow aristocracy was Minoanized into South Greek, the great bulk of the populace in the palace states continued to speak Common Greek. What happened at the end of the thirteenth and throughout the twelfth centuries,

7. J. Chadwick, "Who were the Dorians?" *Parola del Passato* 31 (1976): 103–17. The thesis has been defended by J. T. Hooker, "New Reflexions on the Dorian Invasion," *Klio* 61 (1979): 353–60; see also Hooker's *Mycenaean Greece*, 163–80. In the 1950s Chadwick held the more traditional view that during the LH period the ancestors of the Dorians lived in northern Greece; cf. Chadwick, "The Greek Dialects and Greek Pre-History," 38–50.

then, was that in much of the Peloponnese and in certain other areas the palace class was displaced—mostly, perhaps, by attacks from abroad, but in part also by revolution from below. The commoners and their Common Greek dialect—Doric—remained.

This thesis is based on the fact, noted by Ernst Risch in 1966, that the Linear B tablets give evidence (in the form of certain scribal variants) that alongside what Risch called a "normal" Mycenaean dialect there was also a "special" dialect spoken at Knossos and Pylos.[8] Specifically, Risch called attention to three features (for example, in third declension nouns a dative ending in -*i* instead of -*e*) in which "special Mycenaean" occasionally manifested itself in the tablets. To the three features noted by Risch, Gregory Nagy added a fourth: unassibilated *ti*, as opposed to the "normal Mycenaean" *si*.[9] Unassibilated *ti* was in later times a North Greek characteristic, and Chadwick proposed that the "special" dialect of several Mycenaean scribes was in fact Common Greek, or what in historical times would be called North Greek. Now, it is not unlikely that Chadwick is correct in seeing the scribal variants as survivals of Common Greek, and it may be that among the Mycenaean scribes a few retained some Common Greek usages that distinguished their speech from the more "advanced" speech of their fellows. But that is about as far as one can go. It is one thing to say that on four points a few scribes in the Peloponnese and Crete continued to adhere to Common Greek usage while most of the scribes consistently used the more innovative South Greek; it is quite another thing to say that through Mycenaean times most people in the Peloponnese and Crete spoke Com-

8. Risch, "Les différences dialectales dans le mycénien," in *Proceedings of the Cambridge Colloquium on Mycenaean Studies*, ed. L. R. Palmer and J. Chadwick (Cambridge: Cambridge Univ. Press, 1966), 150–57.

9. G. Nagy, "On Dialectal Anomalies in Pylian Texts," *Atti e memorie del primo Congresso Internazionale di Micenologie* 2 (Rome: Consiglio nazionale delle Ricerche, 1968), 667–76.

mon (or Doric) Greek and that South Greek was the dialect of a "narrow aristocracy."

The argument appears to have run into considerable opposition among Mycenologists.[10] Several do not agree, first of all, that the four scribal variants are to be explained as manifestations of a "special" dialect.[11] Among Mycenologists who do concede that point, not all are inclined to identify that dialect with Common Greek.[12] Most importantly, even those scholars who do see the variants as manifestations of Common Greek (or of North Greek) are not agreed that the sporadic appearance of four Common Greek forms in an otherwise South Greek dialect attests to the survival—to say nothing of the preponderance—of a Common Greek dialect in southern Greece during the LH period.[13]

The thesis has formidable difficulties that even a nonspecialist can appreciate. For instance, Chadwick explains the Doric dialect of Crete as the survival of the Common Greek that was brought to the island when the Greeks first conquered Crete, ca. 1450 B.C. The aristocrats who engineered the conquest "were accompanied by large numbers of the lower classes; they would have served as soldiers for the invasion, but thereafter been rewarded with grants of land in Crete, so that within two generations there would be a substantial Doric-speaking population entrenched in all the main centres."[14] Here one must

10. Brillante, "L'invasione dorica oggi," 176, reports that when Chadwick repeated his analysis at the Rome colloquium, "riserve sono state espresse da Soesbergen, Crossland, De Simone."

11. P. G. van Soesbergen, "The Coming of the Dorians," *Kadmos* 20 (1981): 38–51, holds that none of the variants reflect a "special" or substandard dialect.

12. E. Risch, the discoverer of "special" Mycenaean, sees nothing diagnostic in the special forms and continues to hold that Doric was a conservative descendant of the dialect spoken in northern Greece in LH times; cf. his "Die griechischen Dialekte im 2. vorchristlichen Jahrtausend," *Studi Micenei ed Egeo-Anatolici* 20 (1979): 102.

13. See, most recently, R. D. Woodard, "Dialectal Differences at Knossos," *Kadmos* 25 (1986): 49–50 and 73–74.

14. "Who were the Dorians?" 114.

object that if any Greek speakers' dialect was Minoanized, it should have been the dialect of these soldiers who kept the peace in Crete; but in Chadwick's thesis, the Doric-speaking soldiers in LH Crete retain their dialect without Minoan contamination.[15]

A second major objection to the thesis is that there were a great many South Greek speakers in the Dark Age—enough to hellenize all of Arcadia, much of Cyprus, and all the lands and islands where in historical times the Ionic dialect was spoken. If all of these South Greek speakers were the survivors of the Mycenaean palace administration (among whom, surely, casualties in the raids of ca. 1200 B.C. must have been quite high), one would need to conclude that the palace class in Mycenaean Greece was enormous (and this class, in Chadwick's thesis, does not include the soldiers).

The difficulties do not stop here. The thesis proposes that in Attica the commoners' speech was so much affected by the Minoanizing South Greek of the upper class that a new dialect—Ionic—arose, and that in Thessaly the interaction resulted in Aeolic. Yet in the Peloponnese (where Minoan influences were apparently greater than they were in Attica, and far greater than they were in Thessaly), the speech of the commoners was entirely unaffected by the Minoanizing dialect of their superiors.

In addition to these paradoxes, the thesis must completely ignore the Greeks' traditions on the matter—the story of the Dorian migration and the Return of the Heraclidae. In fact,

15. A potential difficulty with Chadwick's theory is that if one accepts Evans's date for the Knossos Linear B tablets (as Chadwick does), one would have to conclude that neither the upper-class dialect, nor the lower-class dialect, nor their relationship to each other changed between 1400 and 1200 B.C. It is difficult enough to explain how a single dialect could have remained unchanged for two hundred years, and one would be hard pressed indeed to explain how two dialects, supposedly in daily contact with each other, could have remained unchanged over such a period. However, since Evans's date for the tablets is increasingly suspect, this objection is of little import.

the thesis seems to have resulted from a misunderstanding of these traditions. Chadwick denied the possibility of an "invasion" primarily because he saw no place from which the invaders could have come. After disqualifying the other areas of the Greek mainland, he concluded that the invaders could only have come from northwest Greece—the mountainous country north and west of Aetolia—that was never densely settled. "Where in north-western Greece," he asked, "was there room enough for the tens of thousands of migrants" who must be imagined as participating in the invasion?[16] It is true that one can hardly imagine invaders pouring out of northwest Greece, but there should be little difficulty in picturing them coming from Thessaly, where North Greek speakers seem to have been thickly settled. Despite Chadwick's surprising claim that Greek traditions did not associate the Dorians with Thessaly,[17] it was precisely in Thessaly that Herodotus (1.56) said the Dorians had lived before they came to the Peloponnese. The tradition about a Dorian migration into the Peloponnese is an oral tradition, and not a fact, but a migration tradition can not be easily dismissed. At the least, before dismissing it, one would need to explain why the Dorians told this story, and the story of the Return of the Heraclidae, if they could in fact have made the same claims to "autochthony" made by the Arcadians and Athenians.

Finally, Chadwick's explanation for the destruction of the Mycenaean centers is anachronistic: the lower-class Dorians turned on their South Greek masters because they "had for so long lived under the heel of the Mycenaean aristocracy"[18] (in an identical upheaval, according to Chadwick, the South Greeks of Knossos had been overthrown by the Doric-speaking lower classes ca. 1400 B.C.). Such a class revolution is unat-

16. "Who were the Dorians?" 109.

17. In ibid., Chadwick argues that the Dorians could not have come from Thessaly, since that area "shared the uniform Mycenaean culture; nor are there traditions linking the Dorians with Thessaly" (p. 108).

18. Ibid., 115.

tested anywhere in the ancient world in the Bronze Age, and one can hardly posit such an event for LH III Greece without some very good evidence to that effect. The only evidence thus far advanced is an allegorization of the legend that Heracles, "the Dorian hero par excellence," was once in servitude to Eurystheus, king of Tiryns.[19] The legend can hardly make credible the thesis that the armed forces—including over a thousand charioteers—of the Mycenaean palace states could have been "under the heel" of an administrative class and its Minoan clerks. Altogether, Chadwick's thesis has very little to be said in its favor, and much against it.

The thesis presented by Desborough in 1964 is initially attractive, but has disabling weaknesses. An infiltration of Dorians into the Peloponnese in the eleventh century might possibly be reconcilable with the story of a Dorian migration. It does not, however, explain the story of the Return of the Heraclidae, which assumes a more organized and violent entry into the land. Three arguments tell powerfully against Desborough's thesis. The first is Snodgrass's point that the cist graves (and there is virtually no other archaeological evidence for a population movement ca. 1075–1050 B.C.) do not match the geography of Doric Greece. A second argument is linguistic: in order for the Doric dialect to have been transplanted into the Peloponnese without suffering considerable modifications from South Greek, something other than an infiltration would have been required. On Desborough's thesis, a core of South Greek speakers (numerous enough to account for the continuity in pottery and other artifacts) must have continued to occupy the Argolid, Laconia, Messenia, and other Doric destinations all through the eleventh century. The absence of South Greek ele-

---

19. Ibid., 117: "Can we not see how historical truth has here been slightly warped to present the Dorian people in the guise of their hero compelled to serve alien masters? He does eventually launch attacks on several Mycenaean kingdoms: Eurystheus himself is killed in Attica, and Elis and Pylos suffer under Herakles' assaults. Here we have a reflexion of later Dorian successes in replacing their erstwhile masters."

ments in Peloponnesian Doric indicates that the Dorian immigrants were not infiltrators into a predominantly South Greek population.

The third argument focuses on the distribution of the Dorians, across a wide area from the Corinthian Isthmus to Rhodes. If the Dorians came to these lands as infiltrators and squatters, one wonders why and how they went so far. Most of the Peloponnese, as Desborough so convincingly showed, was sharply underpopulated in the eleventh century, even after the supposed arrival of the cist-grave Dorians. Surely, if all that the Dorians wanted was a bit of land for farming and grazing, all of them could have been accommodated in a small part of the Greek mainland. And if we can find a reason why some of the Dorians would have chosen to cross the seas in search of land when plenty of land was available nearby, we shall next need to imagine how an island could have been Doricized by infiltrators. If the Dorians came only a few at a time to Thera, for example, surely the straggle would have been continually swallowed up by the indigenous majority, and the island would never have been Doricized. On the other hand, if the Dorians came en masse, and slaughtered or expelled the indigenous population, their arrival should have been detectable in the material record. The infiltration theory does not work.

Let us look then at Snodgrass's theory—that the Dorians were the destroyers of the Mycenaean world in the late thirteenth and twelfth centuries, and that they settled down in its ruins. As it stands, the theory attributes contradictory behavior to the Dorians. Aggressors who intend to take over a region do not destroy the established settlements and towns of the region, unless the aggressors are so primitive that they would prefer life among the ruins to life in a town. That proviso, however, can not be used here, for an indispensable element in Snodgrass's theory is that the Dorians' life style was indistinguishable from that of the Mycenaean Greeks. And even if we grant, for the sake of the argument, that the Dorians had good reason to destroy the Mycenaean settlements that they intended to occupy, the theory runs into a second obstacle. Very reasonably, given the material evidence, Snodgrass concludes that there was considerable continuity of population in the conquered areas. As it now stands, Snodgrass's theory suggests that the South Greek population was not exterminated, but that a fair number of South Greek speakers survived to live side by side with the newcomers. Here one faces the same dilemma encountered with the theses of Desborough and Chadwick: how could the North Greek essence of Peloponnesian Doric have been so faithfully maintained if in the Peloponnese the North Greeks merged with a South Greek population?

In order to get around this dilemma, we must make two adjustments. Instead of imagining the Dorians moving into lands occupied by speakers of South Greek, let us imagine them taking over lands from which the South Greeks had already departed, and in which the people who remained did not speak Greek at all. In other words, let us suppose that the Greek speakers of the LH Argolid, for example, had not survived the destruction wrought in the late thirteenth and the twelfth centuries, and that what remained toward the end of the twelfth century was the village and rural population, few of whom spoke Greek. And then let us imagine that some time elapsed between the destructions and the second coming of Greek speakers to the Argolid—the arrival of Dorian conquerors from northern Greece. Such a reconstruction would account both for the continuity (however steep the decline) from the Bronze Age to the Dark Age in pottery, artifacts, and the entire material record, and for the remarkably clean discontinuity between a South Greek and a North Greek dialect. On this view, Doric speakers did not come to the Argolid as destroyers, nor did they come as squatters and infiltrators. They "took over" the Argolid and its population just as the shaft-grave dynasts had taken it over in the sixteenth century.

The date of the proposed Dorian takeover may have been not far removed from the Apollodoran date of 1104 B.C. A considerably later date, varyingly placed in the first or the second half of the tenth century, has been defended on the basis of what little can be pieced together from archaeological evidence and from dialectology (Doric influence is what differentiated Attic from Ionic; therefore one can suppose that Doric speakers did not begin to influence speech patterns on the borders of Attica until after the Ionian migration). Both the archaeological and the linguistic evidence is equivocal, however,[20] and it is not impossible that the Dorian takeover occurred at the end of the twelfth century (the legends presented the Return of the Heraclidae as the close of the Heroic Age, and as the reason for the cessation of the old royal lines). Our thesis would at any rate separate the "Dorian Takeover" from the destruction of the Mycenaean world. That destruction had been effected by ca. 1125 B.C., and the destruction had almost certainly been perpetrated, as we shall see, by raiders and city-sackers of the sort familiar to us from the *Iliad*.

The reconstruction proposed here fits the evidence—historical, archaeological, and linguistic—that we have on the end of the Bronze Age in the Aegean. There is, to begin with, good reason to think that the South Greek speakers vacated the lands that would one day be Doric. Destruction of the richest settlements on the periphery of the Peloponnese, and on Crete, began shortly before 1200 B.C. (and not long after the sack of

20. It is conceivable, for example, that Doric speakers were already in contact with western Attica before a migration from Attica to Ionia, but that the presence of Doric speakers had not yet begun to alter speech patterns in Attica. It is also possible that the Ionian Migration departed chiefly from Achaea, and in that case no relative chronology could be established for the Ionian Migration and the Doric contamination of the South Greek dialect of Attica.

Although in *Last Mycenaeans* Desborough had proposed that the Dorians migrated *ca.* 1050 B.C., in *Greek Dark Ages*, 64–79, he presents an archaeological argument for their incursion into Boeotia, western Attica and the northern Peloponnese *ca.* 1125 B.C. P. Cartledge, *Sparta and Lakonia: A Regional History 1300–362 B.C.* (London: Routledge & Kegan Paul, 1979), 79–92, argues that the Dorians came to Laconia in the later tenth century when Laconian Protogeometric ware came into use.

Thebes and of Troy) and continued into the twelfth century.[21] Undoubtedly many of the Greek speakers in these lands were killed when the palaces and towns were destroyed, but many survived. The survivors, however, seem to have gone off to safer places. Although several LH IIIC sites in the pertinent lands were destroyed, many were simply abandoned. The evidence of dialects shows that some Mycenaean Greeks sailed off to Cyprus, and that others withdrew into the Arcadian interior of the Peloponnese. Archaeological evidence suggests that still other Mycenaean Greeks banded together in Achaea, the northern rim of the Peloponnese, along the Corinthian Gulf: during the twelfth century, as settlements in the Argolid and the southern Peloponnese were abandoned, new settlements with strong LH IIIC characteristics appeared in Achaea, as well as in Cyprus. One must suppose that what brought about the collapse of Mycenaean civilization was not so much the actual destruction of its towns and palaces, and the slaughter of their inhabitants, but the *fear* of these things—a fear sufficient to motivate migration into less attractive but more secure lands. The sanctuary of Achaea, as it turned out, was temporary. In the eleventh century the South Greek speakers seem to have left their asylum on the Corinthian Gulf, possibly going initially to Attica but eventually to the coast of Asia Minor.

Although there was an exodus from the Argolid, Messenia,

---

21. The details are available in Desborough's *The Last Mycenaeans*. For a tabular summary of the destruction and abandonment of sites, see Vermeule, *Greece in the Bronze Age*, 323–25. In his detailed presentation of the subject, Hooker, *Mycenaean Greece*, 140–52, emphasizes the fact that there was no single, once-for-all destruction ca. 1200 B.C., and that the destructions continued sporadically for almost a century. The evidence on destruction of Cretan sites (especially the palace at Khania, ancient Kydonia) at the end of the LM IIIB period is most comprehensively presented by A. Kanta, *The Late Minoan III Period in Crete: A Survey of Sites, Pottery and their Distribution (Stud. in Medit. Archaeol.* LVIII) (Göteborg: Paul Åströms Förlag, 1980), 324ff.; it was most recently presented by L. Godard at the 1983 colloquium in Rome (for a summary of Godard's paper, see Brillante, "L'invasione dorica oggi," 179–80).

and other rich Mycenaean regions, very obviously not everyone emigrated. The evolution of LH IIIC pottery into Submycenaean and Protogeometric is paralleled by continuity and decline in all aspects of the material culture.[22] The continuity, I would suggest, was provided by a lower class, mostly rural, among whom Greek was seldom spoken, and then only as a second language. After the death or departure of the town and palace population, whose first language was certainly South Greek, the Greek language may have almost disappeared from what was once Mycenaean Greece.

That there were people in the palace states who spoke something other than Greek, even at the end of the Late Helladic period, is suggested by the Linear B tablets. Almost a third of the people who show up in the Pylos texts do not have Greek names, and it is a reasonable inference that for them Greek was at best a second language. In the Linear B tablets from Knossos, almost half of the names seem to be non-Greek. Where in society the individuals with non-Greek names were concentrated is not clear, but many of them certainly were at the lower levels.[23]

22. On this continuity, see Desborough, *The Last Mycenaeans*, 225–30, and Snodgrass, *The Dark Age of Greece*, 28ff. and 296ff.

23. The entire question is unusually obscure. M. Ventris and J. Chadwick, *Documents in Mycenaean Greek* (Cambridge: Cambridge Univ. Press, 1956), 93, noted the presence of non-Greek names in the tablets but attributed no significance to them: "certainly the names cannot be used to support a theory that any language other than Greek was in actual use in the Mycenaean kingdoms" (whether this statement was intended to apply to fifteenth-century Crete is not clear). According to S. Hiller, "Personennamen," in *Die frühgriechischen Texte aus mykenischer Zeit*, ed. S. Hiller and O. Panagl, (Darmstadt: Wissenschaftliche Buchgesellschaft, 1976) of the almost two thousand names studied "insgesamt ca. 60% zufriedenstellend gedeutet werden" (p. 246), which seems to imply (if an "intelligible" name is synonymous with a Greek name) that ca. 60 percent of the names are Greek (Hiller observes that the "deutbaren Personennamen" are 68 percent of the total for Pylos, and 56 percent of the total for Knossos). Where the people with non-Greek names were located in society is a question not addressed in M. Lindgren's *The People of Pylos. Prosopographical and Methodologi-*

In addition, it is not irrelevant that in historical times many people in the Doric areas of the Peloponnese and Crete considered themselves as belonging to an *ethnos* other than (and frequently "older" than) the Dorian.[24] On Crete, inscriptions found at three sites, the most productive of which is Praisos, show that as late as the third century B.C., speakers of a non-Greek language survived in the eastern part of the island.[25] No such non-Greek inscriptions have been discovered in the Peloponnese, but circumstantial evidence suggests that at the beginning of the Dorian occupation a non-Greek population must have been present. In Archaic and Classical Laconia the bulk of the population consisted of helots. These people were apparently quite distinct from their Dorian superiors, yet in the fifth century they seem to have spoken the Doric dialect. That so large a population could have exchanged one Greek dialect for another without substantially diluting the new dialect is unlikely. A population can exchange one language for another, but dialects do not survive such a borrowing.[26] It is

---

cal Studies in the Pylos Archives (Stockholm: Almqvist & Wiksell, 1973). Some of them were bronzeworkers. M. Lejeune, "Les forgerons de Pylos," *Historia* 10 (1961): 426, observed that the total of 270 smiths mentioned in the Pylos tablets "comprend un assez grand nombre de noms prehelleniques," but that it also included "un nombre appreciable" of Greek names. Apparently many of the slaves mentioned in the tablets also have non-Greek names: see Lejeune, "Textes mycéniens relatifs aux esclaves," *Historia* 8 (1959): 129–44.

24. Herodotus 8.73 declared that "seven *ethne* inhabit the Peloponnese" and enumerated them: Arcadians, Kynourians, Achaeans, Dorians, Aetolians, Dryopes, and Lemnians. The poet of the *Odyssey* (19.172–79) has Odysseus speak of five peoples as inhabiting Crete, each with its own tongue: Achaeans, Eteocretans, Kydonians, Dorians, and Pelasgians.

25. On the inscriptions and the language, see R. F. Willetts, *The Civilization of Ancient Crete* (Berkeley: Univ. of California Press, 1977), 154.

26. It is now appreciated, as it was not a hundred years ago, that dialects in preliterate societies are quite unstable: when two dialects are in contact, they influence each other profoundly, in effect producing a third dialect (it was in this way, it now appears, that the historical Greek dialects were formed). The coexistence of two languages, on the other hand, does

therefore far more likely that before the Dorians' arrival the helots spoke a non-Greek language, that after the Dorian conquest they became bilingual, and that after a generation or two they abandoned their non-Greek language and spoke only Doric Greek.[27]

In Messenia the same situation seems to have obtained, for here, too, the helots of the fifth century were apparently Doric speakers. For the Argolid the question is thornier. Herodotus (8.73) says that the Kynourians, whom he equates with Orneatai or *perioikoi*, "were doricized over time, and because they were ruled by the people of Argos." There also were traditions that in certain cities—Hermione, Asine, and Sicyon being the most important—there had once been a substantial non-Dorian population. But in the Classical Period (and very likely even in the Archaic Period) all of the inhabitants of the Argolid spoke Doric Greek. Altogether, it seems to me, the evidence would support a thesis that the Dorians "took over" a population whose first language was something other than Greek, and whose ancestors had been at the lower levels of Mycenaean society.

The legend of the Return of the Heraclidae may therefore have a basis in fact. As a charter myth, it bestowed legitimacy

not produce a third language. Cf. the remarks of W. Hallo, *The Ancient Near East* (New York: Harcourt, Brace, Jovanavich, 1971; coauthored with W. Simpson): "The symbiosis of two population groups differing in both race and language may produce a new stock that is mixed physically but not linguistically: the resulting generation may be wholly bilingual, that is, speaking both languages equally well, or wholly unilingual, that is opt for one language in preference to the other. Rarely does a truly mixed language result" (p. 21).

27. It is unlikely that Doric and a non-Greek language coexisted for several centuries in Laconia or anywhere else in the regions where Doric was spoken in historical times. Had such coexistence occurred, Doric would surely have been modified in the same way that Proto-Greek had been in the LH period. Perhaps under the Dorians the structure of society was more conducive to the hellenization of the helots than it had been under the palace regimes.

on those who told it: the Dorians are the descendants of Heracles, whose sons were wrongfully expelled from the Peloponnese. This legitimizing element in the legend is as fictitious as Heracles himself. However, the story that the newcomers in three divisions established three regimes in the Peloponnese—one in Laconia, one in Messenia, and one in the Argolid—can not be explained as a charter myth. The Dorians did establish themselves in these places, they did so by force (there is, as we have seen, no persuasive alternative), and they may have come to all three regions at about the same time.

As has recently been pointed out, the legend of the return does not depict the Dorians as destroyers, nor as founders of a new way of life, but as conquerors[28] (who, for example, merely displaced the ruling house in Messenia and coexisted with the rest of the Messenian population).[29] If we imagine smallish companies of Dorians taking over the most profitable parts of the Peloponnese, we shall have no difficulty at all in explaining why other small companies went as far as Crete and even Rhodes: they went not in search of land that they themselves could cultivate, but in hopes of taking over an agricultural population inured to service. Whatever communities had in Mycenaean times been productive and profitable, the Dorians saw as attractive. The legend of the Return of the Heraclidae can tell no more than a partial story. While some Doric speakers were taking over the best parts of the Peloponnese, others must have been carving out domains in Crete and the other islands where in historical times the people spoke Doric. A memory of the Dorians' conquest of Rhodes may appear at *Iliad* 2.653–57: here the descendants of Heracles, once again bri-

28. D. Musti's paper, "Continuità e discontinuità tra Achei e Dori nelle tradizione storiche," delivered at the Rome colloquium, is summarized by Brillante, "L'invasione dorica oggi," 180–81. In the legends, the Dorians "appaiono piuttosto come conquisatori e organizzatori di forme di rapporto nuove con i vinti."

29. For the tradition see Pausanias 4.3.6–7.

gaded in three divisions, take over Lindos, Ialysos, and Ka-
meiros.

The Herodotean story that the Dorians came to the Peloponnese from Doris (or Dryopis), on the Malian Gulf, may indicate their point of embarcation. A slightly later story said
that the Dorian invaders of Crete came from the same place.[30]
As has been suggested above, it is probable that "the coming
of the Greeks" in 1600 B.C. had been first of all to Thessaly,
and that it was immediately from Thessaly that the PIE speakers had come to Mycenae, Pylos, Vrana, and other sites of central and southern Greece. If that reconstruction is correct, it is
not surprising that in the twelfth or eleventh century B.C.,
Doric-speaking Greeks in Thessaly were numerous enough to
conquer a considerable area.

Linguistic analysis also points in the direction of Thessaly.
During most of the LH III period, North Greek seems to have
been spoken in the areas of the mainland to the north of the
Mycenaean world. Toward the end of the Bronze Age, some of
the speakers of North Greek began to differentiate themselves
from the rest of their linguistic community, and the innovation
is called the Aeolic dialect. This innovating group of North
Greeks seems to have lived on the Thessalian coast. Doric—
the more conservative branch of North Greek—ceased to have
contact with Aeolic speakers at about the same time that they
came into contact with the Attic variety of South Greek, and
that suggests that the Dorians' ancestors had been neighbors of
the coastal Thessalians. It is perhaps relevant to remember in
this connection that in the Peloponnese in historical times
there were a great many place names that seem to have been
transferred from Thessaly, including an Ithome, a Peneios

30. Strabo 10.4.6 tells us that according to Andron of Halicarnas-
sus (*FGrHist* no. 10, fr. 16), an antiquarian writer who lived in the fourth
century B.C., the Dorians who established themselves in Crete "came from
that part of Thessaly that was earlier called Doris but is now called Hes-
tiaeotis."

River, and Mts. Ossa and Olympus (along with the nearby
Olympia).[31]

Although our thesis proposes an interlude between the collapse of the Mycenaean world and the Dorian conquest, it is
not at all unlikely that the culprits in the collapse had also been
North Greeks. I have argued elsewhere that the men who
sacked Troy and Thebes came from the Thessalian coast, and
that it was among the ancestors of the Aeolic speakers that
"sacker of cities" was a proud epithet in the thirteenth and
twelfth centuries.[32] Most of the richest Mycenaean sites destroyed at this time lay on or near the sea—Tiryns, Pylos, Kydonia in Crete—and I think it is not impossible that the raiders
who pillaged and destroyed these places came from the Thessalian coast. It seems that by the twelfth century, North Greek
had bifurcated into an Aeolic and a Doric-Northwest Greek
branch, Aeolic having come about because of an admixture of
South Greek to the North Greek base. Although there are
other explanations for the admixture, one comes to mind rather
quickly: Thessalian raiders who sacked South Greek towns may
have carried back with them the women of these towns.
Women, after all, ranked ahead of horses, cattle, and gold as
prizes for the pillagers.[33] Perhaps it is not out of the question

31. On the high incidence of Thessalian names in the Peloponnese,
see Grumach, "The Coming of the Greeks," 402–403.

32. Drews, "Argos and Argives in the *Iliad*."

33. Perhaps the most vivid reconstruction of the raiders' ethos was
offered by G. Murray in his *The Rise of the Greek Epic*, 4th ed. (Oxford: Oxford Univ. Press, 1934), 54–55. Murray imagined himself among raiders
who at the end of the Bronze Age descended upon an island in the Aegean:
"After due fighting it is ours. The men who held it yesterday are slain.
Some few have got away in boats, and may some day come back to worry
us; but not just yet, not for a good long time. There is water to drink; there
is bread and curded milk and onions. There is flesh of sheep or goats. There
is wine, or, at the worst, some coarser liquor of honey or grain, which will
at least intoxicate. One needs that, after such a day. . . . No more thirst,
no more hunger, no more of the cramped galley benches, no more terror of
the changes of wind and sea. The dead men are lying all about us. We will

to suppose that Aeolic arose from the cohabitation of North Greek raiders with South Greek wives, concubines, and slaves.

The above scenario for the end of the Bronze Age in the Aegean implies that all through the LH III period, from the fourteenth century to the twelfth, there were many Greek speakers in Thessaly. Although more concentrated, they were not necessarily more numerous than the South Greek speakers. The raiders' success, ca. 1200 B.C., in terrorizing and ultimately dislodging the South Greek speakers was more likely a simple result of the advantage that sea-borne aggressors, all of them adept as spear-throwing infantrymen, had over defenders. A band of raiders could select a prey on which to pounce and assemble enough ships to guarantee success. The chosen place, no matter how well defended, would eventually have succumbed. As we have seen, the palace at Pylos counted on at least two hundred chariots; several thousand spear-throwing marauders, arriving suddenly in sixty or eighty ships, would have been a force sufficient to overwhelm whatever forces the palace could muster.

The raids seem to have continued for as long as there were places worth raiding. By the late twelfth century, however, raiding no longer was worth the effort, and the pattern of exploitation changed. The Dorians, I would suggest, were North Greek latecomers who, *faute de mieux*, had to content themselves with settling down in the despoiled land and with exploiting the helots who worked it.

The reconstruction here presented of the end of the Greek Bronze Age has as its prerequisite the thesis that at the end of the Late Helladic period, many—perhaps between a third and a half—of the people in the best parts of central and southern

---

fling them into the sea to-morrow. The women are suitably tied up and guarded. The old one who kept shrieking curses has been spiked with a lance and tossed over a cliff. The wailing and sobbing of the rest will stop in a day or two: if it torments you, you can easily move a few paces away out of the sound. If it still rings in your ears, drink two more cups and you will not mind it."

Greece still did not speak Greek. Stated another way, a necessary link between this essay's reconstruction of events ca. 1600 B.C. and ca. 1200 B.C. is the persistence in the palace states (at least of the Argolid, Laconia, Messenia, and Crete) of a non-Greek-speaking population, most likely in the villages and rural areas. The percentage of people in Mycenaean Greece who spoke a non-Indo-European language would, one may reasonably assume, have shrunk rather than grown during the Late Helladic period, and one can therefore infer that ca. 1600 B.C. far less than half the population was PIE speaking. Thus in a roundabout way the apparently conflicting evidence about the end of the Greek Bronze Age strengthens the case that I have tried to make in this book: the "coming of the Greeks," like the other Indo-European movements for which we have some documentation, occurred no earlier than ca. 1600 B.C. And it was essentially a takeover of a relatively large alien population by a relatively small group of PIE speakers, whose advantage lay in their chariotry.

Appendix Two

THE UMMAN MANDA
AND THE PIE SPEAKERS

Cuneiform records of the second and first millennia from time to time refer to *umman manda*, a term that has been understood by some scholars as referring to Indo-Europeans. For Emil Forrer, the term was nothing other than the Akkadian name for "the Indo-Europeans,"[1] but this interpretation has its difficulties. The Akkadian *ummanu(m)* means "horde" or "troops,"[2] but the meaning of *manda* is unclear. Benno Landsberger suggested that the word was a variant of *minde*, an adverbial particle signifying uncertainty.[3] On that interpretation, the two words together would initially have meant "horde (or people) of uncertain origin," and only later became a proper name. The more likely possibility is that "manda" was itself a proper name. Most translators render the two words as "Manda horde" and believe that the term was all along a particular ethnic designation.

In cuneiform sources most names for peoples came from the lands they occupied, and so it is likely that Manda began as a vague term for an area somewhere beyond the perimeter of Mesopotamia: just as Hurrians were "the people of Hurri" and

1. E. Forrer, 8000 *Jahre Menschheitsgeschichte im Alten Orient nach den letzten Ausgrabungen und den neuesten Erkenntnissen* (Zurich, 1947; privately printed; vol. 4 of Forrer's *Forschungen*), 21.

2. The Meissner-Von Soden *Akkadisches Handwörterbuch* translates *ummanu(m)* as "Menschenmenge, Heer, Arbeitstruppe."

3. B. Landsberger and Th. Bauer, "Zu neuveröffentlichten Geschichtsquellen der Zeit von Asarhaddon bis Nabonid," *ZA* 37 (1927): 80. The Chicago *Assyrian Dictionary* offers the following, s.v. *minde*: "adv.; perhaps; possibly; who knows? who can say?"

Hittites were "the people of Hatti," so one would assume that the *Umman Manda* were the "horde from Manda." It has been suggested that Manda was a conventionalized corruption and combination of the actual place names—Mana and Madai—of two lands that lay side by side, some three hundred miles north of Babylon.[4] Mana, whose inhabitants were called Mannai, was located around and to the south of Lake Urmia. Madai, next door, lay southeast of Lake Urmia and southwest of the Caspian. The "Medes" of Assyrian scribes were not yet a nation, as they have been in histories from Herodotus's time to our own, but simply the inhabitants of Madai (the name first appears in texts of the late ninth century). In the seventh and sixth centuries the old term "Umman Manda" was sometimes used by Babylonian scribes as a synonym for our "Medes." This slightly strengthens the possibility that originally Manda was for the Babylonians a vague designation for faraway lands to the north and northeast, across the Zagros Mountains. If the term *Umman Manda* does mean the "horde from Manda," it was evidently not a synonym for "PIE speakers." The latter term defines a people linguistically rather than territorially.

It is possible, however, that in the middle of the second millennium the people living in Manda, wherever that was, were PIE speakers. The one leader of Umman Manda who is mentioned in texts of the period (the Hittite "Zukrashi Text") has the name Za-a-lu-ti, which has been given an Indo-Iranian etymology.[5] Za-a-lu-ti rendered his military services to the prince of Aleppo in the second half of the seventeenth century

---

4. In ibid., 83n. 1, the authors suggest that such a corruption or combination might account for the place name "Manda" in the annals of Sargon II.

5. Albright, "Further Observations," 31, passes on P. E. Dumont's interpretation of the name (with Sanskrit parallel). Za-a-lu-ti was one of the generals employed by the prince of Aleppo against the Hittite great king late in the seventeenth century B.C. Albright suggested that this Za-a-lu-ti may have been not only an Aryan, but the same man as the "Salitis" who founded the *hyksos* Fifteenth Dynasty.

B.C., and that is one of the two earliest references we have to Umman Manda outside their natural habitat. The other reference appears in the astronomical observations made in the reign of Ammisaduqa of Babylon: in his sixteenth or seventeenth year (1631 or 1630 B.C.), Ammisaduqa defeated the Umman Manda.[6] Ammisaduqa was not a predator, and it is improbable that he had the wherewithall to march three hundred miles across the Zagros into the homeland of the Umman Manda. The more likely alternative is that a force that Babylonian scribes chose to call Umman Manda was on the move, and that ca. 1630 B.C. it joined battle with Ammisaduqa somewhere on Babylon's eastern frontier.

The name "Manda" appears as a place name in Section 54 of the Hittite Laws, where it describes one group of military men upon whom the Hittite kings of the Old Kingdom[7] depended: "Hitherto the Manda warriors, the Sala warriors, the warriors of the town of Tamalkiya, the warriors of the town of Hatra, the warriors of the town of Zalpa, the warriors of the town of Tashiniya, the warriors of the town of Himuwa, the archers, the carpenters, the pages and the . . . did not render feudal dues and did not perform feudal duties."[8] The five place names identified as towns in the translation all are prefixed by the ideogram URU ("town") in the original text, whereas the ideogram is not prefixed to "Manda" and "Sala." Although Manda was probably not a town, it very likely was (like all the other proper names in Section 54) the name of a place several hundred miles to the east or southeast of Hattusas. Julius Lewy localized the homeland of the Umman Manda as the "östlich

6. Ibid., 31.

7. J. Friedrich, *Die hethitischen Gesetze* (Leiden: Brill, 1959), in his commentary on Section 54 notes that the places named in this section played an important role "vor allem in Alten Chattireich." Billie Jean Collins, "§54 of the Hittite Laws and the Old Kingdom Periphery," *Orientalia* 56 (1987): 136–41, locates the places on the Upper Euphrates.

8. Translation from Neufeld, *The Hittite Laws.*

des Halys gelegenen Teil Kleinasiens, insbesondere auch Kappadokien."[9]

As Houwink ten Cate has pointed out,[10] the various warriors mentioned at Section 54 of the code were very likely charioteers. The phrase, "the archers, the carpenters, the LU.MESH.ISH,"[11] seems to be in apposition to the roster, and the three specialties could only have been found together in a corps of charioteers. In the chariot forces from Nuzi, there is a similar association of carpenters, archers, and drivers.

For our purposes, the most tantalizing reference to the Umman Manda appears in a text known as "The Kuthaean Legend of Naram-Sin." Here we are told of a great and devastating sweep made by the Umman Manda, beginning in eastern Anatolia and proceeding all the way to "Dilmun, Magan, Meluhha, and all the countries in the midst of the sea."[12] Sumerologists and Assyriologists customarily identify these place names with lands along the Persian Gulf and with India. The Legend of Naram-Sin was a constantly changing (and growing) piece of folk history, and so it is not clear at what time this particular episode was attached to it. The text here cited dates from the seventh century B.C. A thousand years earlier, in the Old Babylonian period, the legend had a very different shape and is not known to have mentioned the Umman Manda or the devastating sweep to India.[13] It is thus barely possible that at

9. J. Lewy, *Forschungen zur alten Geschichte Vorderasiens* (Leipzig: Hinrichs, 1925), 3.

10. "The History of Warfare according to Hittite Sources," 56.

11. The Sumerogram is translated by Neufeld as "pages," by Houwink ten Cate as "squires," and by Friedrich as "Wagenlenker."

12. O. Gurney, "The Sultantepe Tablets, IV. The Cuthaean Legend of Naram-Sin," *AS* 5 (1955): 101 (line 60 of the text).

13. For the fragmentary text of the legend in Old Babylonian times, see J. J. Finkelstein, "The So-Called 'Old Babylonian Kutha Legend,'" *JCS* 11 (1957): 83–88. The thirteenth-century text at Hattusas mentioned the Umman Manda, but seems to have contained no reference to Dilmun, Magan, and Meluhha; for the Hittite "epische Erzählung von Naramsin," see Güterbock, "Die historische Tradition bei Babyloniern und

some time, perhaps toward the end of the Late Bronze Age, two oral traditions were fused: the one told of the wreckage wrought by the Manda hordes on their way to India, and the other was the melancholy tale of Naram-Sin, who in legend (although not in fact) was the last king of Akkad, and the victim of all of the evils that the gods could devise for Mesopotamia.

Hethitern," 50–59, and for the reference to Umman Manda, see line 20 of that text.

BIBLIOGRAPHY

Acta of the Second International Colloquium on Aegean Prehistory: The First Arrival of Indo-European Elements in Greece. Athens: Ministry of Culture and Science, 1972.

Adrados, Francisco. "The Archaic Structure of Hittite: The Crux of the Problem." *JIES* 10 (1982): 1–35.

Albright, Wm. F. "Further Observations on the Chronology of Alalakh." *BASOR* 146 (1957): 26–34.

———. "New Light on the History of Western Asia in the Second Millennium BC." *BASOR* 77 (1940): 20–32, and 78 (1940): 23–31.

Aldred, Cyril. *Akhenaten and Nefertiti.* New York: Brooklyn Museum and Viking Press, 1973.

Anderson, J. K. "Greek Chariot-Borne and Mounted Infantry." *AJA* 79 (1975): 175–87.

———. "Homeric, British and Cyrenaic Chariots." *AJA* 69 (1965): 349–52.

Anthony, David W. "The 'Kurgan Culture,' Indo-European Origins, and the Domestication of the Horse: A Reconsideration." *Current Anthropology* 27 (1986): 291–304.

Avila, Robert. *Bronze Lanzen- und Pfeilspitzen der griechischen Spätbronzezeit.* Munich: Beck, 1983.

Baldi, Philip. *An Introduction to the Indo-European Languages.* Carbondale, Ill.: Southern Illinois Univ. Press, 1983.

Balkan, Kemal. *Kassitenstudien I: Die Sprache der Kassiten* (American Oriental Series, no. 37). New Haven: American Oriental Society, 1954.

Bartoněk, Antonín. "The Place of the Dorians in the Late Helladic World." In *Bronze Age Migrations*, ed. Crossland and Birchall, 305–11.

Bibliography

Bauer, Th. See Landsberger, B.

Beloch, K. J. *Griechische Geschichte*. 2d ed. Vol. 1. Berlin and Leipzig: De Gruyter, 1924.

Benton, Sylvia. Review of Snodgrass's *Early Greek Armour*. *Antiquity* 42 (1968): 69.

Berger, R. See Protsch, R.

Best, Jan, and Yigael Yadin. *The Arrival of the Greeks*. Amsterdam: Hakkert, 1973.

Bietak, Manfred. "Problems of Middle Bronze Age Chronology: New Evidence from Egypt." *AJA* 88 (1984): 471–85.

Bilgiç Emin. "Die Ortsnamen der 'kappadokischen' Urkunden im Rahmen der alten Sprachen Anatoliens." *Archiv für Orientforschung* 15 (1945–1951): 1–37.

Birchall, Ann. See Crossland, R. A.

Blegen, Carl, John Caskey, and Marion Rawson. *Troy: Excavations Conducted by the University of Cincinnati, 1932–1938*. Vol. 3, *The Sixth Settlement*. Princeton: Princeton Univ. Press, 1953.

Blegen, Carl. See Haley, J. B.

Blegen, Carl. See Wace, Alan.

Bökönyi, Sandor. "The Earliest Waves of Domesticated Horses in East Europe." *JIES* 6 (1978): 17–76.

Bosch-Gimpera, Pedro. *Les Indo-européens: problèmes archéologiques*. Paris: Payot, 1961.

Breasted, James. *Ancient Times: A History of the Early World*. Boston: Ginn and Co., 1916.

Brillante, C. "L'invasione dorica oggi." *Quaderni Urbinati di Cultura Classica* n.s. 16 (1984): 173–85.

Buchanan, Briggs. *Ancient Near Eastern Seals in the Ashmolean Museum*. Oxford: Oxford Univ. Press, 1966.

Buchholz, H. G. "Der Pfeilglätter aus dem VI. Schachtgrab von Mykene und die helladischen Pfeilspitzen." *Jahrbuch des Deutschen Archäologischen Instituts* 77 (1962): 1–58.

Burney, Charles, and David M. Lang. *The Peoples of the Hills: Ancient Ararat and Caucasus*. London: Weidenfeld and Nicolson, 1971.

Cardona, G., H. M. Hoenigswald, and A. Senn, eds. *Indo-European and Indo-Europeans. Papers Presented at the Third Indo-European*

Conference at the University of Pennsylvania. Philadelphia: Univ. of Pennsylvania Press, 1970.

Cartledge, Paul. *Sparta and Lakonia: A Regional History 1300–362 BC.* London: Routledge & Kegan Paul, 1979.

Caskey, John. "Greece and the Aegean Islands in the Middle Bronze Age." *CAH* II, 1: 117–40.

———. "Greece, Crete, and the Aegean Islands in the Early Bronze Age." *CAH* I, 2: 771–807.

———. See Blegen, Carl.

Catling, H. W. "Archaeology in Greece, 1984–1985." *AR 1984–85,* 3–69.

Cavaignac, Eugene. *Les Hittites.* Paris: Maisonneuve, 1950.

Cazelles, H. "The Hebrews." In *Peoples of Old Testament Times,* ed. Wiseman, 1–28.

Chadwick, John. "Aegean History 1500–1200 BC." *Studii Classice* 11 (1969): 7–18.

———. "The Greek Dialects and Greek Pre-History." *Greece and Rome* n.s. 3 (1956): 38–50.

———. "The Organization of the Mycenaean Archives." In *Studia Mycenaea. Proceedings of the Mycenaean Symposium, Brno, April 1966,* ed. A. Bartoněk, 11–21. Brno: Universitas Purkyniana Brunensis, 1968.

———. "Who were the Dorians?" *Parola del Passato* 31 (1976): 103–17.

———. See Ventris, Michael.

Childe, V. Gordon. *The Aryans.* New York: Knopf, 1926.

Chubinishvili, T. N. *Ancient Culture of the Twin Rivers Kura and Araxes* (in Georgian, with Russian summary). Tbilisi: Sabchota sakartvelo, 1965.

Civil, M. "Notes on Sumerian Lexicography." *JCS* 20 (1966): 119–24.

Clutton-Brock, Juliet. "The Buhen Horse." *Journal of Archaeological Science* 1 (1974): 89–100.

Collins, Billie Jean. "§54 of the Hittite Laws and the Old Kingdom Periphery." *Orientalia* 56 (1987): 136–41.

Collon, Dominique. "Hunting and Shooting." *AS* 33 (1983): 51–56.

Crossland, R. A. "Immigrants from the North." *CAH* I, 2: 824–76.

———. "Retrospect and Prospects." In *Bronze Age Migrations*, ed. Crossland and Birchall, 329–47.

———, and Ann Birchall, eds. *Bronze Age Migrations in the Aegean: Archaeological and Linguistic Problems*. Park Ridge, N.J.: Noyes Press, 1974.

Crouwel, Joost H. *Chariots and Other Means of Land Transport in Bronze Age Greece*. Amsterdam: Allard Pierson Museum, 1981.

Crouwel, Joost H. See Littauer, Mary.

Curtius, Ernst. *The History of Greece*. Vol. 1. New York: Scribner, Armstrong and Co., 1876.

Davies, Norman de Garis. *The Tomb of Ken-Amun at Thebes*. New York: n.p., 1930.

Delaporte, Louis. *Les Hittites*. Paris: La Renaissance du Livre, 1936.

Delebecque, Edouard. *Le Cheval dans l'Iliade*. Paris: Klincksieck, 1951.

Dent, A. A. *The Horse through Fifty Centuries of Civilization*. New York: Phaidon, 1974.

Desborough, Vincent. *The Greek Dark Ages*. New York: St. Martin's, 1972.

———. *The Last Mycenaeans and their Successors. An Archaeological Survey ca. 1200–1000 B.C.* Oxford: Oxford Univ. Press, 1964.

Devoto, Giacomo. *Origini Indoeuropee*. Florence: Sansoni, 1962.

Diakonoff, I. M. "Die Arier im Vorderen Orient: Ende eines Mythos." *Orientalia* 41 (1972): 91–120.

Diakonoff, I. M. "Media." In *Cambridge History of Iran*. Vol. 2, 36–148. Cambridge: Cambridge Univ.Press, 1985.

D'iakonov, I. M. (see also Diakonoff). "On the Original Home of the Speakers of Indo-European." *JIES* 13 (1985): 92–174.

Dickinson, O.T.P.K. *The Origins of Mycenaean Civilisation* (Studies in Mediterranean Archaeology, vol. 49). Göteborg: Paul Aströms Förlag, 1977.

———. Review of Mylonas' *Grave Circle B. JHS* 96 (1976): 236–37.

————. "The Shaft Graves and Mycenaean Origins." *BICS* 19 (1972–1973): 146–47.

Dittmann, K. H. "Die Herkunft des altägyptischen Streitwagens in Florenz." *Germania* 18 (1934): 249–52.

Drews, Robert. "Argos and Argives in the *Iliad*." *CP* 74 (1979): 111–35.

————. *Basileus. The Evidence for Kingship in Geometric Greece.* New Haven: Yale Univ. Press, 1983.

Drower, Margaret S. "Syria c. 1550-1400 B.C." *CAH* II 1: 417–525.

Dumezil, G. *Archaic Roman Religion.* Chicago: Univ. of Chicago Press, 1970.

Dumont, P. E. *L'Asvamedha.* Paris: Geuthner, 1927.

Dumont, P. E. "Indo-Iranian Names from Mitanni, Nuzi and Syrian Documents." *JAOS* 67 (1947): 251–53.

Ernout, A., and A. Meillet. *Dictionnaire étymologique de la langue latine.* Paris: Klincksieck, 1939.

Evans, Sir Arthur. *The Palace of Minos.* Vol. 4, pt. 2. London: Macmillan, 1935.

Fairservis, Walter A., Jr. *The Roots of Ancient India.* New York: Macmillan, 1971.

Falkenstein, Adam. "Sumerische religiöse Texte, 2. Ein Shulgi-Lied." *ZA* 50 (1952): 61–91.

Faulkner, R. O. "Egyptian Military Organization." *JEA* 39 (1953): 32–47.

Feuer, Bryan. *The Northern Border in Thessaly* (B.A.R. International Series, no. 176). Oxford: British Archaeological Reports, 1983.

Fick, August. *Vorgriechische Ortsnamen als Quelle für die Vorgeschichte Griechenlands.* Göttingen: Vandenhoeck & Ruprecht, 1905.

Figulla, H. H. *Cuneiform Texts from Babylonian Tablets in the British Museum XLVII.* London: British Museum, 1967.

Finkelstein, A. J. "The So-Called 'Old Babylonian Kutha Legend,' " *JCS* 11 (1957): 83–88.

Finley, M. I. *Early Greece: The Bronze and Archaic Ages*, 2d ed. New York: Norton, 1981.

Bibliography

Forrer, Emil. *8000 Jahre Menschheitsgeschichte im Alten Orient nach den letzten Ausgrabungen und den neuesten Erkenntnissen.* Zurich: privately printed, 1947.

Fowler, W. Warde. *The Roman Festivals of the Period of the Republic.* London: Macmillan, 1916.

Friedrich, Johannes. "Arier in Syrien und Mesopotamien." In *Reallexikon der Assyriologie* 1 (1932): 144–48.

———. *Die hethitischen Gesetze.* Leiden: Brill, 1959.

Gadd, C. J. "Tablets from Chagar Bazar and Tall Brak, 1937–38." *Iraq* 7 (1940): 22–66.

Gamkrelidze, T. V., and V. V. Ivanov. "The Ancient Near East and the Indo-European Question: Temporal and Territorial Characteristics of Proto-Indo-European based on Linguistic and Historico-Cultural Data." *JIES* 13 (1985): 3–48.

———. *Indoevropejskij jazyk i indoevropejcy.* 2 vols. Tbilisi: Tbilisi University, 1985.

———. "The Migrations of Tribes Speaking Indo-European Dialects from their Original Homeland in the Near East to their Historical Habitations in Eurasia." *JIES* 13 (1985): 49–91.

———. "The Problem of the Original Homeland of the Speakers of Indo-European Languages in Response to I. M. Diakonoff's Article." *JIES* 13 (1985): 175–84.

García-Ramón, José L. *Les Origines postmycéniennes du groupe dialectal éolien (Minos* Supplement, no. 6). Salamanca: Universidad de Salamanca, 1975.

Gejvall, N.-J. *Lerna I. The Fauna.* Princeton: American School of Classical Studies in Athens, 1969.

Gelb, Ignace F. *Hurrians and Subarians.* Chicago: Univ. of Chicago Press, 1944.

Gimbutas, Marija. "The First Wave of Eurasian Steppe Pastoralists into Copper Age Europe." *JIES* 5 (1977): 277–338.

———. "Old Europe in the Fifth Millennium B.C.: The European Situation on the Arrival of Indo-Europeans." In *The Indo-Europeans in the Fourth and Third Millennia,* ed. Polomé, 1–60.

———. "Primary and Secondary Homeland of the Indo-Europeans: Comments on the Gamkrelidze-Ivanov Articles." *JIES* 13 (1985): 185–202.

————. "Proto-Indo-European Culture: The Kurgan Culture during the Fifth, Fourth and Third Millennia B.C." In *Indo-European and Indo-Europeans*, ed. Cardona et al., 815–36.

————. "The Three Waves of the Kurgan People into Old Europe, 4500–2500 B.C." *Arch. suisses d'anthropol. gen.* 43 (1979 [1981]): 113–37.

————. " 'Timber-Graves' in Southern Russia." *Expedition* 3 (1961): 14–20.

Goetze, Albrecht. "State and Society of the Hittites." In *Neuere Hethiterforschung (Historia Einzelschrift* 7), ed. G. Walser, 23–33. Wiesbaden: Steiner, 1964.

————. "Warfare in Asia Minor." *Iraq* 25 (1963): 124–30.

Greenhalgh, P.A.L. *Early Greek Warfare: Horsemen and Chariots in the Homeric and Archaic Ages.* Cambridge: Cambridge Univ. Press, 1973.

Greppin, John. Review of Gamkrelidze and Ivanov, *Indoevropejskij jazyk. Times Literary Supplement*, March 14, 1986, 278.

Grottanelli, Christiano. "Yoked Horses, Twins, and the Powerful Lady: India, Greece, Ireland and Elsewhere." *JIES* 14 (1986): 125–52.

Grumach, E. "The Coming of the Greeks." *BRL* 51 (1968–1969): 73–103 and 399–430.

Gurney, Oliver. *The Hittites.* Harmondsworth: Penguin, 1961.

————. "The Sultantepe Tablets, IV. The Cuthaean Legend of Naram-Sin." *AS* 5 (1955): 93–113.

Güterbock, H. "Die historische Tradition und ihre literarische Gestaltung bei Babyloniern und Hethitern bis 1200, II (Hethiter)," *ZA* 44 (1938): 45–149.

Haley, J. B., and Carl Blegen. "The Coming of the Greeks." *AJA* 32 (1928): 141–54.

Hallo, William, and Wm. Simpson. *The Ancient Near East.* New York: Harcourt, Brace, Jovanavich, 1971.

Hampl, F. "Die Chronologie der Einwanderung der griechischen Stämme und das Problem der Nationalität der Träger der mykenischen Kultur." *MH* 17 (1960): 57–86.

Hançar, Franz. *Das Pferd in prähistorischer und früher historischer Zeit*

(Wiener Beiträge zur Kulturgeschichte und Linguistik 11). Vienna: Herold, 1956.

Häusler, Alexander. "Neue Belege zur Geschichte von Rad und Wagen im nordpontischen Raum." *Ethnogr.-Archäolog. Zeitschrift* 25 (1984): 629–92.

Hehn, Victor. *Culturpflanzen und Hausthiere in ihrem Übergang aus Asien nach Griechenland und Italien, sowie in das übrige Europa: Historisch-linguistische Skizzen.* Berlin: Borntraeger, 1870. English translation of 1885 titled *Cultivated Plants and Domesticated Animals in their Migration from Asia to Europe: Historico-Linguistic Studies,* reprinted as *Amsterdam Classics in Linguistics,* vol. 7, E.F.K. Koerner, general editor. Amsterdam: John Benjamins, 1976.

Helck, Wolfgang. *Die Beziehungen Aegyptens zu Vorderasien im 3. und 2. Jahrtausend v. Chr.* Wiesbaden: Harrassowitz, 1962.

Hentschel, Faith C. D. "The Basis for a Standard Chronology of the Late Bronze Age at Knossos." Ph.D. diss., Yale University, 1982 (Ann Arbor, Mich.: University Microfilms, 1982).

Hermes, Gertrud. "Das gezähmte Pferd im alten Orient." *Anthropos* 31 (1936): 364–94.

———. "Das gezähmte Pferd im neolithischen und frühbronzezeitlichen Europa?" *Anthropos* 30 (1935): 803–23.

———. "Der Zug des gezähmten Pferdes durch Europa." *Anthropos* 32 (1937): 105–46.

Heurtley, W. A. *Prehistoric Macedonia.* Cambridge: Cambridge Univ. Press, 1939.

Hiller, Stefan. "Personennamen." In *Die frühgriechischen Texte aus mykenischer Zeit,* ed. S. Hiller and O. Panagl, 245–56. Darmstadt: Wissenschaftliche Buchgesellschaft, 1976.

Hirt, Hermann. *Die Indogermanen. Ihre Verbreitung, ihre Uhreimat und ihre Kultur.* 2 vols. Strasburg: Trübner, 1905.

Hoenigswald, H. M. See Cardona, G.

Hoffmann, O. *De mixtis graecae linguae dialectis.* Göttingen: Vandenhoeck, 1882.

Hoffner, H. A. "The Hittites and Hurrians." In *Peoples of Old Testament Times,* ed. D. J. Wiseman, 197–228.

Hood, Sinclair. *The Home of the Heroes: The Aegean before the Greeks.*

London: Thames and Hudson, 1967.

Hooker, J. T. *Mycenaean Greece*. London: Routledge & Kegan Paul, 1976.

———. "New Reflexions on the Dorian Invasion." *Klio* 61 (1979): 353–60.

Hope Simpson, Richard. *Mycenaean Greece*. Park Ridge, N.J.: Noyes Press, 1981.

Houwink ten Cate, P.H.J. "The History of Warfare according to Hittite Sources: The Annals of Hattusilis I." *Anatolica* 11 (1984): 47–83.

Howell, R. J. "The Origins of the Middle Helladic Culture." In *Bronze Age Migrations*, ed. Crossland and Birchall, 73–99.

Hrozny, Bedrich. "L'entrainement des chevaux chez les anciens Indo-Européens au 14e siècle av. J. C." *Archiv Orientalni* 3 (1931): 431–61.

Ivanov, V. V. See Gamkrelidze, T. V.

Kammenhuber, Annelies. *Die Arier im vorderen Orient*. Heidelberg: Carl Winter Universitätsverlag, 1968.

———. *Hippologia Hethitica*. Wiesbaden: Harrassowitz, 1961.

———. "Philologische Untersuchungen zu den 'Pferdetexten' aus dem Keilschriftarchiv von Boghazköy." *Münchener Studien zur Sprachwissenschaft* 2 (1952): 47–120.

———. "Zu den hethitischen Pferdetexten." *Forschungen und Fortschritt* 28 (1954): 119–24.

Kanta, A. *The Late Minoan III Period in Crete: A Survey of Sites, Pottery and their Distribution* (Studies in Mediterranean Archaeology 58). Göteborg: Paul Åströms Förlag, 1980.

Karo, Georg. *Die Schachtgräber von Mykenai*. 2 vols. Munich: Bruckmann, 1930 and 1933.

Keith, A. Berriedale. "The Age of the Rigveda." *Cambridge History of India*. Vol. 1, 77–113. Cambridge: Cambridge Univ. Press, 1922.

Kendall, Timothy. "The Helmets of the Warriors at Nuzi." In *Studies on the Civilization and Culture of Nuzi and the Hurrians in Honor of Ernest R. Lacheman*, ed. M. A. Morrison and D. I. Owen, 201–31. Winona Lake, Ind.: Eisenbrauns, 1981.

Bibliography

Knudtzon, J. A. *Die El-Amarna Tafeln.* Leipzig: Hinrichs, 1915.

Korfmann, M. "Demircihüyük, 1977." *AS* 28 (1978): 16–18.

Kossinna, Gustaf. "Die indogermanische Frage archäologisch beantwortet." *Zeitschrift für Ethnologie* 34 (1902): 161–222.

Kretschmer, Paul. *Einleitung in die Geschichte der griechischen Sprache.* Göttingen: Vandenhoeck & Ruprecht, 1896.

———. "Zur Geschichte der griechischen Dialekte." *Glotta* 1 (1909): 1–59.

Kühn, Herbert. "Herkunft und Heimat der Indogermanen." *Proceedings of the First International Congress of Prehistoric and Protohistoric Sciences,* 237–42. London: Oxford Univ. Press, 1932.

Kuz'mina, E. E. "Stages in the Development of Wheeled Transport in Central Asia during the Aeneolithic and Bronze Age (On the Problem of the Migration of Indo-Iranian Tribes)." *Soviet Studies in History* 22 (1983): 96–142.

Landsberger, Benno, and Th. Bauer. "Zu neuveröffentlichten Geschichtsquellen der Zeit von Asarhaddon bis Nabonid." *ZA* 37 (1927): 61-98.

Lejeune, Michel. "La civilization mycénienne et la guerre." In *Problèmes de la guerre en Grèce ancienne,* ed. J.-P. Vernant, 31–51. Paris: Mouton, 1968.

———. "Les forgerons de Pylos." *Historia* 10 (1961): 409–34.

———. "Textes mycéniens relatifs aux esclaves." *Historia* 8 (1959): 129–44.

Leskov, A. M. "The Earliest Antler Psalia from Trakhtemirova." *Sov. Arkh.* (1964, 1): 299–303 (in Russian).

Lewy, Hildegard. "Anatolia in the Old Assyrian Period." *CAH* 1, 2: 707–28.

Lewy, Julius. *Forschungen zur alten Geschichte Vorderasiens.* Leipzig: Hinrichs, 1925.

Lindgren, M. *The People of Pylos. Prosopographical and Methodological Studies in the Pylos Archives.* Stockholm: Almqvist & Wiksell, 1973.

Littauer, Mary. "The Military Use of Chariots in the Aegean in the Late Bronze Age." *AJA* 76 (1972): 145–57.

————. "Rock Carvings of Chariots in Transcaucasia, Central Asia and Outer Mongolia." *PPS* 43 (1977): 243–62.

————, and J. H. Crouwel. "Evidence for Horse Bits from Shaft Grave IV at Mycenae?" *Praehistorische Zeitschrift* 48 (1973): 207–13.

————. *Wheeled Vehicles and Ridden Animals in the Ancient Near East.* Leiden: Brill, 1979.

Lorimer, H. L. *Homer and the Monuments.* London: Macmillan, 1950.

Luckenbill, D. D. *Ancient Records of Assyria and Babylonia.* 2 vols. Chicago: Univ. of Chicago Press, 1927.

Mallory, J. P. Response to D. Anthony's "The 'Kurgan Culture.' " *Current Anthropology* 27 (1986): 308.

————. "The Ritual Treatment of the Horse in Early Kurgan Tradition." *JIES* 9 (1981): 205–26.

————. "A Short History of the Indo-European Problem." *JIES* 1 (1973): 21–65.

————. "Victor Hehn: A Bio-bibliographical Sketch." In 1976 reprint of Hehn, *Cultivated Plants*, ix–xvi.

Manatt, J. I. See Tsountas, Chr.

Marinatos, Sp. "Anaskaphai Marathonos." *Praktika* 1970, 5–28.

————. "The First Mycenaeans in Greece." In *Bronze Age Migrations*, ed. Crossland and Birchall, 107–13.

————. "Further News from Marathon." *AAA* 3 (1970): 153–66 and 349–66.

————. "Prehellenic and Protohellenic Discoveries at Marathon." *Acta of the Second International Colloquium on Aegean Prehistory*, 184–90.

Maringer, Johannes. "The Horse in Art and Ideology of Indo-European Peoples." *JIES* 9 (1981): 177–204.

Mayrhofer, Manfred. *Die Arier im Vorderen Orient—ein Mythos?* (*Oesterreichische Akademie der Wissenschaften, Philosophisch-historische Sitzungsberichte*, Bd. 294, Abhandlung 3). Vienna, 1974.

————. *Die Indo-Arier im Alten Vorderasien.* Wiesbaden: Harrassowitz, 1966.

————. "Zur kritischen Sichtung vorderasiatisch-arischer Personennamen." *IF* 70 (1965): 146–63.

McLeod, Wallace. "An Unpublished Egyptian Composite Bow in the Brooklyn Museum." *AJA* 62 (1958): 397–401.

———. "The Bow in Ancient Greece, with Particular Reference to the Homeric Poems." Ph.D. diss., Harvard University, 1966 (summary in *Harvard Studies in Classical Philology* 71 [1966]: 329–31).

———. "The Range of the Ancient Bow." *Phoenix* 19 (1965): 1–14.

Meid, Wolfgang. See Neu, Erich.

Meillet, A. See Ernout, A.

Mellaart, James B. "Anatolia and the Indo-Europeans." *JIES* 9 (1981): 135–49.

———. "Anatolia *c.* 4000–2300 B.C." *CAH* I, 2: 363–410.

———. "Anatolia *c.* 2300–1750 B.C." *CAH* I, 2: 681–703.

———. "The End of the Early Bronze Age in Anatolia and the Aegean." *AJA* 62 (1958): 1–31.

Mellink, Machteld J. "The Royal Tombs at Alaca Huyuk and the Aegean World." In *The Aegean and the Near East: Studies Presented to Hetty Goldman*, ed. Saul S. Weinberg, 39–58. Locust Valley, N.Y.: Augustin, 1956.

Meyer, Eduard. *Geschichte des Alterthums*. 1st ed. Vol. 2. Stuttgart: Cotta, 1893.

———. *Geschichte des Altertums*. 2d ed. Vol. 2, pt. 2. Stuttgart and Berlin: Cotta, 1926.

———. *Geschichte des Altertums*. 3d ed. Vol. 1, pt. 2. Stuttgart and Berlin: Cotta, 1913.

Miroschedji, Pierre de. "La fin du royaume d'Anšan et de Suse et la naissance de l'Empire perse." *ZA* 75 (1985): 265–306.

Moorey, P.R.S. "The Earliest Near Eastern Spoked Wheels and their Chronology." *PPS* 34 (1968): 430–32.

———. "The Emergence of the Light, Horse-Drawn Chariot in the Near East c. 2000–1500 B.C." *World Archaeology* 18 (1986): 196–215.

———. "Pictorial Evidence for the History of Horse-riding in Iraq before the Kassite Period." *Iraq* 32 (1970): 36–50.

Muhly, James. "On the Shaft Graves at Mycenae." In *Studies in Honor of Tom. B. Jones (Alter Orient und Altes Testament*, Bd. 203), ed.

M. A. Powell, Jr., and Ronald H. Sack, 311–23. Neukirchen-Vluyn: Neukirchener Verlag, 1979.

Muhly, James. Review of *Acta of the Second International Colloquium on Aegean Prehistory*. *AJA* 79 (1975): 289–91.

Murray, Gilbert. *The Rise of the Greek Epic*, 4th ed. Oxford: Oxford Univ. Press, 1934.

Mylonas, George. "The Figured Mycenaean Stelai." *AJA* 55 (1951): 134–47.

―――. *Grave Circle B at Mycenae* (in Greek). Athens: Greek Archaeological Service, 1973.

―――. "The Luvian Invasions of Greece." *Hesperia* 31 (1962): 284–309.

―――. *Mycenae and the Mycenaean Age*. Princeton: Princeton Univ. Press, 1966.

Nagy, Gregory. "On Dialectal Anomalies in Pylian Texts." *Atti e memorie del primo Congresso Internazionale di Micenologie* 2, 667–76. Rome, 1968.

Neu, Erich. *Der Anitta-Text (Studien zu den Bogazköy-Texten*, Heft 18). Wiesbaden: Harrassowitz, 1974.

―――, and Wolfgang Meid, eds. *Hethitisch und Indogermanisch: Vergleichende Studien zur historischen Grammatik und zur dialektgeographischen Stellung der indogermanische Sprachgruppe Kleinasiens*. Innsbruck: Innsbruck Institut für Sprachwissenschaft der Universität, 1979.

Neufeld, E. *The Hittite Laws*. London: Luzac & Co., 1951.

Nilsson, Martin. *Homer and Mycenae*. London: Methuen, 1933.

―――. *Minoan-Mycenaean Religion and its Survival in Greek Religion*. Lund: Gleerup, 1927.

―――. *The Mycenaean Origin of Greek Mythology*. Berkeley: Univ. of California Press, 1932.

Noëttes, Commandant Lefebvre des. *La force motrice animale à travers les âges*. Nancy: Berger-Levrault, 1924.

O'Brien, S. "Dioscuric Elements in Celtic and Germanic Mythology." *JIES* 10 (1982): 117–36.

O'Callaghan, R. T. *Aram Naharaim. A Contribution to the History of*

Upper Mesopotamia in the Second Millennium B.C. Rome: Pontificium Institutum Biblicum, 1948.

——. "New Light on the *maryannu* as Chariot-Warriors." *Jahrbuch für kleinasiatische Forschung* 1 (1950): 309–24.

Oettinger, Norbert. *Die militärische Eid der Hethiter*. Wiesbaden: Harrassowitz, 1976.

Oppenheim, A. L. "Seafaring Merchants of Ur." *JAOS* 74 (1954): 6–17.

Otten, Heinrich. "Das Hethiterreich." In *Kulturgeschichte des Alten Orients*, ed. Hartmut Schmökel, 313–446. Stuttgart: Kröner, 1961.

——. "Harsumna." *Reallexikon der Assyriologie*. Vol. 4, 126.

——. "Zwei althethitische Belege zu den Hapiru (SA.GAZ)." *ZA* 52 (1957): 216–23.

Page, Denys. *History and the Homeric Iliad*. Berkeley: Univ. of California Press, 1959.

Palmer, L. R. *Minoans and Mycenaeans*. London: Faber and Faber, 1961.

Pelon, Olivier. *Tholoi, tumuli et cercles funéraires. Recherches sur les monuments funéraires de plan circulaire dans l'Égée de l'âge du Bronze*. Athens: École Française d'Athènes, 1976.

Perrot, Georges. "Les fouilles de Schliemann à Mycènes." *Journal des Savants* (1892): 442–50.

Persson, A. W. *New Tombs at Dendra near Midea*. Lund: Gleerup, 1942.

Piggott, Stuart. *Ancient Europe*. Chicago: Aldine, 1965.

——. "Bronze Age Chariot Burials in the Urals." *Antiquity* 49 (1975): 289–90.

——. "Chariots in the Caucasus and in China." *Antiquity* 48 (1974): 16–24.

——. "Chinese Chariotry: An Outsider's View." In *The Arts of the Eurasian Steppelands* (Colloquies on Art and Archaeology in Asia, no. 7), ed. P. Denwood, 32–51. London: 1978.

——. *The Earliest Wheeled Transport: From the Atlantic to the Caspian Sea*. Ithaca, N.Y.: Cornell Univ. Press, 1983.

————. "The Earliest Wheeled Vehicles and the Caucasian Evidence." *PPS* 34 (1968): 266–318.

————. *Prehistoric India*. Harmondsworth: Penguin, 1950.

Poesche, Th. *Die Arier: Ein Beitrag zur historischen Anthropologie*. Jena: H. Costenoble, 1878.

Polomé, Edgar. "Indo-European Culture, with Special Attention to Religion." In *The Indo-Europeans in the Fourth and Third Millennia*, ed. Polomé, 156–72.

————. ed. *The Indo-Europeans in the Fourth and Third Millennia*. Ann Arbor, Mich.: Karoma Publishers, 1982.

Porada, Edith. Review of Buchanan's *Ancient Near Eastern Seals*. *Bibliotheca Orientalis* 27 (1970): 13.

Porzig, Walter. "Sprachgeographische Untersuchungen zu den griechischen Dialekten." *IF* 61 (1954): 147–69.

Potratz, H. A. *Das Pferd in der Frühzeit*. Rostock: Hinstorff, 1938.

————. *Die Pferdetrensen des Alten Orient*. Rome: Pontificium Institutum Studi Orientalis, 1966.

Protsch, R., and R. Berger. "Earliest Radiocarbon Dates for Domesticated Animals." *Science* 179 (1973): 235–39.

Puhvel, Jan. "Dialectal Aspects of the Anatolian Branch of Indo-European." In *Ancient Indo-European Dialects*, ed. H. Birnbaum and J. Puhvel, 235–47. Berkeley: Univ. of California Press, 1966.

Rainey, A. F. "The Military Personnel of Ugarit." *JNES* 24 (1965): 17–27.

Rawson, Marion. See Blegen, Carl.

Renfrew, Colin. "Problems in the General Correlation of Archaeological and Linguistic Strata in Prehistoric Greece: the Model of Autochthonous Origin." In *Bronze Age Migrations*, ed. Crossland and Birchall, 263–75.

Reusch, H. *Die zeichnerische Rekonstruktion des Frauenfrieses im böotischen Theben*. Berlin: Akademie-Verlag, 1956.

Risch, Ernst. "Altgriechische Dialektgeographie?" *MH* 6 (1949): 19–28.

————. "Die Gliederung der griechischen Dialekte in neuer Sicht." *MH* 12 (1955): 61–75.

Risch, Ernst. "Die griechischen Dialekte im 2. vorchristlichen Jahr-tausend." *Studi micenei ed egeo-anatolici* 20 (1979): 91–111.

——. "Les différences dialectales dans le mycénien." In *Proceedings of the Cambridge Colloquium on Mycenaean Studies*, ed. L. R. Palmer and John Chadwick, 150–57. Cambridge: Cambridge Univ. Press, 1966.

Royen, R. A. van, and B. H. Isaac. *The Arrival of the Greeks: The Evidence from the Settlements*. Amsterdam: Grüner, 1979.

Rutter, Jeremy B. "Fine Gray-Burnished Pottery of the Early Helladic III Period: The Ancestry of Gray Minyan." *Hesperia* 52 (1983): 327–55.

Säflund, Gösta. *Le Terremare delle provincie di Modena, Reggio Emilia, Parma, Piacenza*. Lund: Gleerup, 1939.

Sakellariou, Agnes. "Un cratère d'argent avec scène de bataille provenant de la IVe tombe de l'acropole de Mycènes." *Antike Kunst* 17 (1974): 3–20.

Sakellariou, M. B. *Les Proto-grecs*. Athens: Ekdotikè Athenon, 1980.

Salonen, Armas. *Die Landfahrzeuge des alten Mesopotamien* (Annales Academiae Scientiarum Fennicae, vol. 72, fasc. 3). Helsinki, 1951.

——. *Hippologia Accadica*. Helsinki, 1956.

——. "Notes on Wagons and Chariots in Ancient Mesopotamia." *Studia Orientalia* 14, 2. Helsinki: Societas Orientalis Fennica, 1950, 1–8.

Schachermeyr, Fritz. "Streitwagen und Streitwagenbild im Alten Orient und bei den mykenischen Griechen." *Anthropos* 46 (1951): 705–53.

Schaefer, H. "Armenisches Holz in altägyptischen Wagnereien." *Sitzungsberichte der preussischen Akademie der Wissenschaften, Phil.-Hist. Klasse* 25 (1931): 730–38.

Scherer, Anton. "Das Problem der indogermanischen Urheimat." *Archiv für Kulturgeschichte* 33 (1950): 3–16.

——, ed. *Die Urheimat der Indogermanen* (Wege der Forschung 166). Darmstadt: Wissenschaftliche Buchgesellschaft, 1968.

Schmidt, Wilhelm. "Die Herkunft der Indogermanen und ihr erstes Auftreten in Europa." *Kosmos* 45 (1949): 116–18 and 159–60.

Reprinted in *Die Urheimat der Indogermanen*, ed. Scherer, 314–17.

———. *Rassen und Völker in Vorgeschichte und Geschichte des Abendlandes.* 2 vols. Lucerne: Stocker, 1946.

Schrader, Otto. *Sprachvergleichung und Urgeschichte. Linguistisch-historische Beiträge zur Erforschung des indogermanischen Altertums.* Jena: Costenoble, 1883.

Senn, A. See Cardona, G.

Servais, Jean, and Brigitte Servais-Soyez. "La tholos 'oblongue' (tombe IV) et le tumulus (tombe V) sur le Vélatouri." *Thorikos* 1972/1976, 15–71. Ghent: Comité des fouilles belges en Grèce, 1984.

Simpson, George G. *Horses: The Story of the Horse in the Modern World and through Sixty Million Years of History.* New York: Oxford Univ. Press, 1951.

Snodgrass, A. M. *The Dark Age of Greece.* Edinburgh: Edinburgh Univ. Press, 1971.

———. *Early Greek Armour and Weapons from the End of the Bronze Age to 600 BC.* Edinburgh: Edinburgh Univ. Press, 1964.

Soden, Wolfram von. "Das altbabylonische Briefarchiv von Mari." *Die Welt des Orients* 1 (1948): 187–204.

Soesbergen, Peter G. van. "The Coming of the Dorians." *Kadmos* 20 (1981): 38–51.

Sommer, Ferdinand. *Hethitisches.* 2 vols. (*Boghazköi Studien*, Heft 4 and 7). Leipzig: Hinrichs, 1920 and 1922.

Spengler, Oswald. "Dei Streitwagen und seine Bedeutung für den Gang der Geschichte." *Dei Welt als Geschichte* 3 (1937): 280–83.

Stagakis, G. J. "Homeric Warfare Practices." *Historia* 34 (1985): 129–52.

———. "Odysseus and Idomeneus: Did they have Charioteers in Troy?" *Historia* 27 (1978): 255–73.

Starr, Chester. *The Origins of Greek Civilization.* New York: Knopf, 1961.

Stubbings, Frank. "The Rise of Mycenaean Civilization." *CAH* II, 1: 627–58.

Sturtevant, E. H. "The Indo-Hittite Hypothesis." *Language* 38 (1962): 105–10.

———. "The Relationship of Hittite to Indo-European." *TAPA* 60 (1929): 25–37.

Szemerényi, Oswald. "Structuralism and Substratum—Indo-Europeans and Semites in the Ancient Near East." *Lingua* 13 (1964): 1–29.

Taylor, Isaac. *The Origin of the Aryans*. New York: The Humboldt Publishing Co., 1890.

Themelis, Petros. "Recent Archaeological Discoveries at Marathon." *AD* 29 (1974): 226–44 (in Greek).

Theochares, D. R. "Thessalian Antiquities and Monuments." *AD* 16 (1960): 168–86 (in Greek).

Thieme, Paul. "The 'Aryan' Gods of the Mitanni Treaties." *JAOS* 80 (1960): 301–17.

Thomas, Homer. "New Evidence for Dating the Indo-European Dispersal in Europe." In *Indo-European and Indo-Europeans*, ed. Cardona et al., 199–215.

Tölle-Kastenbein, Renata. *Pfeil und Bogen im alten Griechenland*. Bochum: Duris Verlag, 1980.

Tsountas, Chr., and J. I. Manatt. *The Mycenaean Age*. London: Macmillan, 1897.

Valmin, M. Natan. *The Swedish Messenia Expedition*. Lund: Gleerup, 1938.

Vaux, Roland de. "Hurrites de l'histoire et Horites de la Bible." *Revue Biblique* 74 (1967): 481–503.

Ventris, Michael, and John Chadwick. *Documents in Mycenaean Greek*. Cambridge: Cambridge Univ. Press, 1956.

Vermeule, Emily. *Greece in the Bronze Age*. Chicago: Univ. of Chicago Press, 1964.

Wace, Alan, and Carl Blegen. "The Pre-Mycenaean Pottery of the Mainland." *BSA* 22 (1916–1918): 175–89.

Ward, Donald J. "An Indo-European Mythological Theme in Germanic Tradition." In *Indo-European and Indo-Europeans*, ed. Cardona et al., 405–20.

————. *The Divine Twins: An Indo-European Myth in Germanic Tradition*. Berkeley: Univ. of California Press, 1968.

Weidner, Ernst. "Weisse Pferde im Alten Orient." *Bibliotheca Orientalis* 9 (1952): 157–59.

Wheeler, Mortimer. *The Indus Civilization*, 3d ed. Cambridge: Cambridge Univ. Press, 1968.

Wiesner, Joseph. "Fahren und Reiten in Alteuropa und im Alten Orient." *Der Alte Orient* 38 (1939), fascs. 2–4. Reprinted under separate cover by Olms (Hildesheim, 1971).

Will, Edouard. *Doriens et Ioniens*. Paris: Les Belles Lettres, 1956.

Willetts, R. F. *The Civilization of Ancient Crete*. Berkeley: Univ. of California Press, 1977.

Wiseman, D. J., ed. *Peoples of Old Testament Times*. Oxford: Oxford Univ. Press, 1973.

Woodard, Roger D. "Dialectal Differences at Knossos." *Kadmos* 25 (1986): 49–74.

Wyatt, Wm. F., Jr. "Greek Dialectology and Greek Prehistory." In *Acta of the Second International Colloquium on Aegean Prehistory*, pp. 18–22.

————. "The Indo-Europeanization of Greece." In *Indo-European and Indo-Europeans*, ed. Cardona et al., 89–111.

————. "The Prehistory of the Greek Dialects." *TAPA* 101 (1970): 557–632.

Yadin, Yigael. *The Art of Warfare in Biblical Lands in the Light of Archaeological Study*. 2 vols. New York: McGraw-Hill, n.d.

Yadin, Yigael. See Best, Jan.

Yeivin, S. "Canaanite and Hittite Strategy in the Second Half of the Second Millennium BC." *JNES* 9 (1950): 101–107.

Zeuner, Frederick E. *A History of Domesticated Animals*. New York: Harper and Row, 1963.

INDEX

"Achaean" (dialect), 8, 24
Aeolic (dialect), 8, 39–40, 222–24
Ahmose of Thebes, king, 57, 104n
aika vartanna, 141n, 145
Ajjul, Tell el (Gaza), 102
Alaca Huyuk, 189, 190
Alalakh, 56, 105
Albright, William, 137
Aleppo, 56, 227
Alexander the Great, 183
Amarna letters, 59
amber, 22, 171, 179
Amenhotep II, 89, 120
Ammisaduqa, 72, 228
Amorites (*amurru*), 47, 48, 57, 106, 153
Anatolia, eastern. *See* Armenia
Anittas: of Kushshara, 119; the text, 101–2
ANSHE.KUR, 83, 141n
Anthony, David, 31
Aplachanda of Carchemish, 99, 112, 113
Arabic, 37
Arcado-Cypriote (dialect), 8, 38, 39
Aristotle, 112
Armenia (eastern Anatolia), 32–34, 36, 107, 182–83, 229; decline during second millennium B.C., 157n; horses and chariots in, 107, 112–20, 125–26, 129, 139–40, 148–49, 201
"Armenian hypothesis," 32–35, 36, 54, 132, 139–40, 148–49
Armenian (language), 157n
Aryan: gods, 61, 142, 151–52, 155–56; language, 57, 58–59, 61, 62, 140–42, 151, 183–84; names, 58–59, 61, 62, 150, 227; "race," xiii, 5, 6, 7
Aryanism, 147

Aryans (Aryan speakers): in Egypt, 57, 227n; in India, 5n, 15, 62–63, 133, 200; in Levant, 58–60, 72, 73, 133, 139, 142, 150, 227; in Mitanni, 60–62, 72, 73, 139–46, 150, 154, 183; synonym for PIE speakers, xiii, 4, 5n
Ashur-uballit I, 61
Ashvamedha, 151
Ashvins. *See* Heavenly Twins
ashwash, 141, 145
ass, 74, 75, 81n
Attic (dialect), 216
Attica, 187–90, 211
Avaris, 57, 104n
*ayos, 35–36

Babylon, 56, 58, 72, 105, 228; date of Mursilis's sack, 15, 56, 136–37, 158
Beloch, K. J., 7, 9
Best, Jan G. P., 21, 180
bilingualism, 48, 52–53, 62, 66, 68, 219–20n
bit, 76, 93, 94–97, 102, 103, 106, 109, 114, 125, 133, 160–61, 163, 199
Blegen, Carl, 11–15, 42, 44, 164
Boghazköy, 63, 65, 66, 90, 113. *See also* Hattusas
Bopp, Franz, 4, 25
Bosch-Gimpera, Pedro, 28, 29
bow, composite, 86–87, 89, 100, 165, 167–70
Breasted, James, 10, 123–24, 179
Buhen horse, 103

Carchemish, 113
Carpathian Basin, 27, 28, 74, 108, 109, 110, 148, 198–99
"Carpathian hypothesis," 27, 31n, 63n, 130, 132, 148n

251

Index

Caskey, John, 18, 19, 20, 41, 43
Cavaignac, Eugene, 54
Chadwick, John, 16, 41, 164, 208–13
Chagar Bazar, 48, 97, 98–99, 101, 118
chariot: in Armenia, 115–20, 125–26,
129, 201; associated with *hyksos*,
102–3, 104n, 156; in Carpathian
Basin, 110, 199; construction and repair of, 84–86, 92, 111–12, 174–75;
earliest appearance, 93–94, 97–99,
106, 107–11, 115–17, 118–19,
124–25, 128–30, 200; earliest use in
hunting, 100; in Egypt, 86, 92,
102–3, 104n, 120, 137; in Eurasian
steppe, 96, 109–11, 118–19, 149; in
Fertile Crescent, 86–88, 97–99,
100–101, 105, 129–30; in Greece,
86, 92, 146, 153, 158–66, 169–70,
172–77; in Hatti, 86, 88, 89n, 93–
94, 101–2, 104–6; in India, 86, 92,
155–56; in Kassite Babylon, 154–55;
in Linear B tablets, 163–64; in Mitanni, 150, 154; in Museo Archeologico (Florence), 84, 120; place of invention, 107–11, 125; prestige
vehicle, 84, 93–94, 98–101, 108–
11, 116–17, 176–77; in scholarship
on PIE speakers, 26–27, 107–8, 121–
22, 124–25, 128–30, 134–35, 136–
48, 151–53
chariot warfare: earliest evidence for,
100–106, 118–20, 149, 158, 177,
200–201; in Greece, 164–70; in Hittite Old Kingdom, 89n, 104; nature
of, 86–89, 92; PIE speakers' association with, 122, 124–30, 135, 136–
57, 198–99, 200–201; varying assumptions about date of origins, 122,
124–26, 136–38, 143, 144–45, 147
Charsamna, 113
Childe, V. Gordon, 26, 124, 139
China, 116
chronology: of chariots and chariot warfare, 93–106, 109–10, 111, 115–16,
119, 136–37, 143, 144–45, 147,
156–67, 158, 200–201; of early-
Mesopotamian history, 15, 56, 136–
37, 138n, 153, 158; of Hittite Old
Kingdom, 15, 158; of Indus Valley
civilization, 15, 28, 62–63; of Knossos Linear B tablets, 194–95n, 211n;

of PIE speakers' arrival in Greece (*see*
"coming of the Greeks"); of PIE
speakers' dispersal (*see* Indo-European
dispersal)
"coming of the Greeks": Blegen's view,
11–15; dated 2800 B.C., 30, 45n;
dated 2100 B.C., 17–20, 42, 43–44,
45; dated 1900 B.C., 11–15, 29, 36–
37, 41–45, 136–37, 153, 172, 199;
dated 1600 B.C., 21–24, 41, 42, 45,
126, 137, 170, 181; dated 1200
B.C., 16–17; early opinions on date,
8–9; recent views on, 16–24
copper. See *ayos
corselet (*sharyan*; breastplate), 88, 166,
167n
Crete: destruction 1200 B.C., 217n; Dorians in, 203, 210–11, 221, 222;
horse and chariot in, 161, 163–64,
182, 184, 194; non-Greek population in, 218; Proto-Greek conquests
in, 182, 184, 194, 210–11
Crossland, R. A., 35
Crouwel, J. H., 108, 162, 172, 173,
175–77
Curtius, Ernst, 6–7
Cyprus, 182

Dark Age (17th–16th cent. B.C.), 55,
60, 66, 72–73, 177
de Coulanges, N. D. Fustel, 6
Delaporte, Louis, 54
Delebecque, Edouard, 63
Dendra: corselet, 166, 167n; horse skeletons, 82n, 162–63
Dereivka, 75n, 109
Desborough, Vincent: his 1964 views
on Dorian migration, 206–7, 213–
14, 215; his 1972 views, 207n, 216
des Noëttes, Commandant Lefebvre, 77
destruction levels (in Greece): ca. 2100
B.C., 18–20, 42, 43; ca. 1900 B.C.,
12, 18, 42n; ca. 1600 B.C., 42–43,
184; ca. 1200 B.C., 17, 205, 206–7,
216–17
Devoto, Giacomo, 27, 29
Diakonoff, I. M., 11, 27, 146–47
dialects, Greek: 25, 37–41; early theories on, 8–9, 24, 36–37. *See also*
"Achaean" (dialect); Aeolic (dialect);
Arcado-Cypriote; Attic (dialect);

Index

Doric (dialect); Ionic; North Greek;
   South Greek (East Greek)
Dioscuri. *See* Heavenly Twins
Dorian Invasion, 44, 203–25
Doric (dialect), 39, 40, 203, 208–14,
   216, 219–20
Doris (Dryopis), 204, 222
Drower, Margaret, 155

Early Trans Caucasian culture, 36, 114–
   15, 157n
*ekwos, 121
Elamite (language), 63n
Emery, W. B., 103
Eurasian steppe, 26, 29, 30, 74–75,
   76, 80–81, 96, 108, 109, 111–12,
   125
Evans, Sir Arthur, 11, 23, 169, 179;
   date for Knossos Linear B tablets,
   194–95n, 211n
Ezekiel, 113

Fick, August, 13
Finley, M. I., 19–20
Florence (Museo Archeologico), 84, 120
Forrer, Emil, 226

Gamkrelidze, T. V., and Ivanov, V. V.,
   32–35, 54, 131, 132, 148–49, 201
Gelb, Ignace, 48
Gimbutas, Marija, 27, 29–31, 33, 38,
   77, 131–32
GISH.GIGIR, 143
Goetze, Albrecht, 107, 124
gold, in LH Greece, 22, 171, 178, 180,
   181, 185, 186, 188, 191
Grave Circle A, 22–24, 159–61, 170–
   71; stelai, 159–60, 178, 180, 188
Grave Circle B, 22–24, 159–61, 180,
   188
Great King, 48, 56, 60, 62, 66, 70,
   71, 72, 73, 105
Greek. *See* Proto-Greek (Common
   Greek); North Greek; South Greek;
   the several dialects
Greenhalgh, P.A.L., 165–66
Grote, George, 3–4, 204
Gurney, Oliver, 49, 70, 71, 88

Haley, J. B., 13
Hammurabi, 47, 56, 72, 100, 136–37,
   138n4

Hançar, Franz, 107, 108, 114, 129–30,
   140
hapiru, 69, 70n
Hatti, 49, 52–53, 54–55, 64–65, 68–
   69
Hattic (language), 48, 49, 52, 55, 64–
   65, 67
Hattusas, 66–67, 86, 104; location,
   105
Hattusilis I, 56, 66–68, 70, 71, 104–6,
   119, 156, 158; Annals of, 66–67, 71
Häusler, Alexander, 30–31, 108
Heavenly Twins (Ashvins; Dioscuri),
   152
Hehn, Victor, 121–22
Hellen, 3, 192
helots, 195, 219–20, 224
Heracles, 204, 213, 221
Heraclidae, Return of, 8n, 204–5, 211,
   212, 213, 216, 220
Hermes, Gertrud, 26–27, 107, 125–
   27, 128–29, 136–37, 139, 147
Herodotus, 112, 128, 203–4, 220, 222
Heth, 64
"Hieroglyphic Hittite," 68
Hirt, Herman, 122–23
Hittite (language), 14–15, 50–51, 64–
   65, 66, 67, 90; relation to Indo-
   European family, 28, 49, 50–52, 200
Hittite Law Code, 69, 228–29
Hittites (Hittite speakers), xiv, 63–64;
   discovery of, 14–15, 124; early dates
   for, 136; "invasion" of, 14–15, 30,
   48–50, 53–54, 66, 72, 136–38, 200;
   name, 63–65; "race," 53–54; use of
   chariots, 86, 88–89, 90, 92, 104–5,
   165n, 228–29
Homer, xi, 36–37, 165, 167n, 168
Hood, Sinclair, 17, 186–87
horse: in Armenia, 80, 107, 112–16,
   118–19, 201; as draft animal, 77–78,
   82, 83–84, 88–89, 93, 96n, 99–
   100, 118, 122, 123, 124, 126, 127,
   133, 138; in Egypt, 102–3; in Europe, 27, 74, 75, 80; in Fertile Crescent, 78–80, 96–101; as food animal,
   74–75, 82, 122–23; in Greece, 22,
   78, 81–82, 162–63, 182, 189–90,
   191; in Hatti, 93–94, 101–2; natural
   habitat, 74, 90, 108–9, 112, 132; as
   pack animal, 75–76; as riding ani-

Index

horse (cont.)
mal, 76, 81n, 82–83, 94, 109, 119, 124, 128, 131, 165–66; as ritual animal, 130, 151, 190; in scholarship on PIE speakers ("Indo-Europeans"), 22, 26–27, 121–35, 151–52, 153; size in Bronze Age, 74–75, 77–78, 104n, 189; skeletal evidence for, 78, 82nn, 103, 104, 112, 162–63, 189–90; in southern Russia, 74–76, 80–81; speed, 84; training of (for chariots), 89–92, 142–45; at Troy, 81–82, 94

Houwink ten Cate, Philo H. J., 101–2, 104, 106, 229

Hrozny, Bedrich, 14, 53

Hurri, land of, 47–48, 105, 119

Hurrian (language), 48, 58–59, 88, 90

Hurrians (Hurrian speakers), 48, 57, 59, 61–62, 119, 125–26, 129–30, 142–46, 153, 155

Hyksos (hyksos), 57–58, 72, 102–3, 120, 153, 172, 173–74, 227n

Iliad, 216; Catalog of the Ships, 193–94, 221–22; horses in, 163, 164

India, Aryan conquest of, 6, 28, 62–63, 150, 182–84, 195, 229–30

Indo-European dispersal (in previous scholarship): date of, 9, 15, 28–31, 35–38, 63n, 123, 125–26, 127; reasons for, 63n, 138, 148n

Indo-European homeland: Armenia, 32–35, 54; Bactria, 5, 25–26; Carpathian Basin, 27; early attempts to locate, 4–5, 25–26; northern Europe, 5, 26–27; Pripet Marshes, 26; southern Russia 26–27

Indo-European language family, 4, 28, 33, 34, 49, 58, 148, 157n

Indo-European "race," 4–5, 6–7

Indo-Hittite, 51

Indo-Iranian. See Aryan: language

Indra, 155–56

Indus Valley civilization: destruction, 62–63; discovery and early dating of, 15, 28

infiltrations, 47–55

Iolkos, 192

Ionic, 24, 38, 39–41, 216

Iran, 4, 5n

Italy, 15, 198–99

Ivanov, V. V. See Gamkrelidze, T. V.

Japheth, 25

Jones, Sir William, 4

Kadesh, battle of, 92

Kammenhuber, Annelies, 129–30, 140–47, 183

Kamose, 103

Kassite (language), 48, 58, 154n

Kassites (Kassite speakers), 58, 72, 92, 154–55

Kikkuli, 90; Treatise of, 90–91, 124, 129–30, 140–41, 144–45, 154, 183

Knossos, 163–64, 194, 195, 209, 211n, 212, 218

Kossina, Gustav, 123

Kretschmer, Paul, 8, 13, 24, 26, 38

Kühn, Herbert, 31–32

Kültepe, 48, 52, 53, 64, 93, 94, 98, 113, 118

"Kurgan hypothesis," 29–30, 33, 131–32

kurgans, 24, 29, 185n, 188, 189–90

Kushshara, 66, 70, 71

Kuthaean Legend of Naram-Sin, 229–30

Labarnas. See Hattusilis I.

Lacedaemonia, 185–86

Landsberger, Benno, 226

Lchashen, 115–18, 161

Lerna, 18, 41, 43, 82

Lewy, Julius, 228

Linear B tablets, 38–39, 40, 163, 167, 169, 170, 209–11, 218

Littauer, Mary, 108, 172

Lorimer, Helen, 168

Luwian (language), 50, 66, 67–68

Luwians (Luwian speakers), 19, 20n, 49n

LU.ashshushshani, 90, 151

Mahabharata, 155

Maikop, 24

Malthi, 82

Manatt, J. I., 21

Manda, 226–27; Manda warriors (in Hittite Law Code), 69, 228–29

Index

Marathon: tholos, 162–63, 187–88, 190; Vrana tumuli, 188–90
Mari, 99, 101
Marinatos, Spyridon, 186, 189
maryannu, 59, 60, 142, 151, 155, 156
Medes, 227
Megiddo, battle of, 92, 106
Mellaart, James, 19, 131
Messenia, 82, 186–87, 220, 221
Meyer, Eduard, 9, 10, 54, 124, 136, 205–6
Middle Helladic, characterization of, 12, 18–19n, 23, 43
Minyans, 3
Minyan Ware, 12–13, 18, 28, 29, 41–42, 43, 44, 188
Mitanni, 120, 140–43, 145, 183–84; Great Kingdom of, 48, 60–61, 72, 73, 92, 150; location, 48
Muhly, James, 21, 24, 190
Müller, Max, 5n
Mursilis I, 56, 58, 72, 105–6, 153
Mycenae: in MH period, 171–72, 175–76; location, 172. *See also* Grave Circle A; Grave Circle B; shaft graves (Mycenae)
Mylonas, George, 160, 181
myths, Greek, 3–4, 9, 17, 163, 192–93, 204, 213, 220–21

Nagy, Gregory, 209
Naram-Sin, 229–30
narkabtu, 98, 105, 142–43
Nasatya Twins, 61, 152. *See also* Heavenly Twins
nationalism, 5–6, 53, 64, 65–66, 71; negligible factor in Bronze Age, 46–47, 48, 52–53, 55, 57, 62, 64–65, 66–69, 71, 72
"Nesaean" horses, 112
Neu, Erich, 102
Nichoria, 82
Nilsson, Martin, 21, 22
"northern European hypotheses," 5, 26, 123, 125, 127–28
North Greek, 39–41, 193, 209–10, 212, 215, 222–24
Nuzi, 86, 87–88, 150, 166n, 229

October Horse, 151
onager, 74, 75–76, 78

Orchomenos, 12, 162, 187
Osmankayasi, 104
Otten, Heinrich, 69
ox, 77, 78, 83, 84, 115, 116, 118, 143

Palaic, 50, 66
Palmer, L. R., 21, 181, 195n
pankus, 68–70, 71, 105
Paros, 182
Peristeria, 186–87
Perrot, Georges, 21
Persian (language), 63n
Persson, A. W., 173, 179
Petrie, Sir Flinders, 102
Phthiotis, 203–4
PIE speakers, 25, 27–28, 29, 33, 35, 58, 70, 193–96, 198–201; association with chariot warfare, 121, 124–28, 129–30, 134–35, 136–57, 159, 170, 177; definition of, xiii; specialty in making of wheeled vehicles, 121, 133–34, 170; travel by sea, 181–84, 195; Umman Manda and, 226–30
Piggott, Stuart, 30, 77, 108–9, 116, 134, 155, 156
place names, in Aegean, 5, 13, 20n
Porzig, Walter, 38
pottery: changes tied to Völkerwanderungen, 11–13, 43–45, 47, 126n; Greeks' "pre-Greek" words for, 178; and periodization, 11–12
Proto-Anatolian (language), 50–55, 66, 200
Proto-Indo-European (language), 4, 25, 50–51; definition, xii–xiii; relation to Proto-Anatolian, 50–52, 200; relation to Semitic and Kartvelian, 34
Proto-Greek (Common Greek), 25, 39, 40n, 193, 194, 195n, 199, 208–13
Proto-Minyan Ware, 41–43
Pylos, 162, 164, 186, 209, 218

racism, 5–7, 26, 53, 65, 147, 206
raids, 55–56, 67
reins, 96
Renfrew, Colin, 31
Rhodes, 203, 221–22
Rigveda, 5n, 15, 86, 121, 152, 155–56
Risch, Ernst, 38–39, 209, 210n
rock carvings, 118
Rutter, Jeremy, 42

255

Index

SA.GAZ (*hapiru*), 69, 155
Sakellariou, M. B., 20
Salatiwara, 101–2, 119
Sala warriors, 69, 228
Sanskrit, 4, 9, 28, 36–37, 52, 59, 61, 121, 183–84
Sargon of Akkad, 56
Sargon II, 113
Schachermeyr, Fritz, 107, 162, 165, 173, 174, 175, 180
Scherer, Anton, 27
Schliemann, Heinrich, 8, 12, 22–23, 158, 167, 205
Schmidt, Wilhelm, 128
Schmökel, Hartmut, 124
Schrader, Otto, 122, 123
Scythians, 128
sea, PIE speakers' travel by, 181–84, 195
Sea Peoples, 205
Sevan, Lake, 36, 115–18, 157n
Shaft-Grave Dynasty (Mycenae): 23, 158–61, 170–76, 178–80; foreign trade connections, 179–81; skeletal evidence, 158, 170–71
shaft graves (Mycenae): 22–23, 45, 171; chronology, 23n, 159n. *See also* Grave Circle A; Grave Circle B
Shamshi-Adad I, 56, 99, 112
Shulgi, 83, 106, 143, 145
Shuttarna I, 61
Sippar, 98
Smith, Sidney, 137
Snodgrass, Anthony, 207–8, 213, 214–15
Sommer, Ferdinand, 14–15, 53
South Greek (East Greek), 38–41, 193, 208–14, 215, 222–24
"south Russian hypothesis," 26–28, 123–24, 126, 130, 132
Sparta, 186, 195
Spengler, Oswald, 124
spoked wheel, 84–85, 97–98, 110, 118
Sprachgeographie, 38
Strabo, 112
Stubbings, Frank, 173–74, 180
Sturtevant, E. H., 51
Sumerians, 55, 143, 147; horses of, 83, 143, 145; wheeled vehicles of, 78–79, 111n, 134, 143, 147
Syunik, rock carvings of, 118

Szemerenyi, Oswald, 183–84

Taanach, 60
Table of Nations (Genesis 10), 64
Tacitus, 190
takeovers, 56–63, 72, 153–57, 172, 186, 192, 194–95, 198, 215–16, 220–21
Taylor, Isaac, 5n, 122
Telipinus, 70–71, 104
Tepe Hissar, 97n
Terramara sites, 199
Thebes (Boeotian), 187
Thebes (Egyptian), 57, 84
Themelis, Petros, 189
Theochares, Dimitrios, 191
Therapne, 186
Thessaly, 3, 29, 40, 190–94, 211–12, 222–24
Thirlwall, Connop, 3
tholoi, 162–63, 185–88, 190, 191, 200
Thomas, Homer, 28, 29, 131
Thorikos, 187–88, 189, 190
Thucydides, 204, 205
Thutmose III, 92
Tiglath-Pileser I, 113
Timber-Grave Culture, 81, 96n, 190
Tiryns, 162
Tocharians, 117
Togarmah (Til-Garimmu), 113
Trans Caucasia. *See* Armenia; Early Trans-Caucasian culture
Trialeti steppe, 115–16
Tripolye Culture, 75n, 80
Troy, 12, 81–82, 94
Tsountas, Christos, 21
Tudhaliyas II, 104
tumuli, 185, 187–90, 200
Tushratta, 150, 154

Umman Manda, 226–30
Ur, 55; horses at, 83; sea traffic from, 183n; Standard, 78
Urartian (language), 48, 157n
Urartu, 48, 113
Urshu: "Siege of Urshu," 105, 227

Vaphio, 161, 185
Vedas, 61
Ventris, Michael, 16, 169
Vermeule, Emily, 171, 179

Index

Völkerwanderungen: lack of evidence for, 46–47, 48, 55, 66, 72; in scholarship, 10–11, 14–15, 46–47, 49–50, 125, 137–38, 143, 197

Vrana, 188–90

Wace, Alan, 11–12, 45

Weidner, Ernst, 113, 137

wheeled vehicles (other than chariots): in Armenia, 115–20, 134; discovery and diffusion of, 30, 77–78, 111n, 133; disk wheeled, 77–78, 97; earliest evidence for, 30–31, 77, 131, 132n; not attested in Egypt and Greece before 17th cent. B.C., 133,

172–73; PIE speakers' specialty in, 121, 133–34, 170; Sumerian battle-wagons, 78. *See also* horse: as draft animal

Wiesner, Josef, 127–28, 137–39, 173

woodworking, 77, 84–86, 87, 97, 111, 117–18, 120, 133–34, 201

Woolley, Sir Leonard, 105

Wyatt, William, 21, 37–38, 41, 159, 170, 177

Yadin, Yigael, 21

Za-a-lu-ti, 227

Zimri-Lim, 56, 94n, 99, 112, 113